Daily Math Thinking Routines in Action

Bring math to life with routines that are academically rigorous, standards-based, and engaging! Go beyond circling ABCD on your *bell ringers* and *do nows*, and get your students reasoning, modeling, and communicating about math every day! In this new book from bestselling author and consultant Dr. Nicki Newton, you'll learn how to develop effective daily routines to improve students' thinking, reasoning, and questioning about math. The book provides a wide variety of rigorous, high-interest routines and explains how to rotate and implement them into your curriculum. Inside you'll find:

- Questioning techniques that encourage students to think beyond the "right versus wrong" continuum
- Tips for building a math-learning environment that is friendly and supportive of all students
- Math vocabulary exercises that are meaningful *and* fun
- An assortment of innovative daily activities, including "Fraction of the Day," "Truth or Fib," "Find and Fix the Error," "Guess My Number," "What Doesn't Belong?" and many, many more.

Each chapter offers examples, charts, and tools that you can use immediately. With these resources and the practical advice given throughout the book, you'll increase students' ability to understand math on a deeper level while keeping them engaged in their own learning processes.

Dr. Nicki Newton has been an educator for 30 years, working both nationally and internationally, with students of all ages. She has worked on developing Math Workshop and Guided Math Institutes around the country. She is also an avid blogger (www.guidedmath.wordpress.com), tweeter (@drnickimath), and Pinterest pinner (www.pinterest.com/drnicki7).

Daily Math Thinking Routines in Action

Distributed Practices Across the Year

Nicki Newton

Routledge
Taylor & Francis Group

NEW YORK AND LONDON

First published 2019
by Routledge
711 Third Avenue, New York, NY 10017

and by Routledge
2 Park Square, Milton Park, Abingdon, Oxon, OX14 4RN

Routledge is an imprint of the Taylor & Francis Group, an informa business

Library of Congress Cataloging-in-Publication Data
A catalog record for this book has been requested

ISBN: 978-0-8153-4962-4 (hbk)
ISBN: 978-0-8153-4963-1 (pbk)
ISBN: 978-1-351-16428-3 (ebk)

Typeset in Palatino
by Apex CoVantage, LLC

Printed and bound in the United States of America by Sheridan

Dedication

To Lin Goodwin: I am the teacher I am today because of you! You taught me more than you'll ever know.

Contents

Meet the Author

Dr. Nicki Newton has been an educator for 30 years, working both nationally and internationally, with students of all ages. Having spent the first part of her career as a literacy and social studies specialist, she built on those frameworks to inform her math work. She believes that math is intricately intertwined with reading, writing, listening and speaking. She has worked on developing Math Workshop and Guided Math Institutes around the country. Most recently, she has been helping districts and schools nationwide to integrate their State Standards for Mathematics and think deeply about how to teach these within a Math Workshop Model. Dr. Nicki works with teachers, coaches and administrators to make math come alive by considering the powerful impact of building a community of mathematicians who make meaning of real math together. When students do real math, they learn it. They own it, they understand it, and they can do it. Every one of them. Dr. Nicki is also an avid blogger (www.guidedmath.wordpress. com) and Pinterest pinner (https://www.pinterest. com/drnicki7/).

Acknowledgments

Thank you to my family and my friends. Thank you to all the teachers and students that I have ever worked with. Thank you to those of you (Alison and Ann Elise) who have given me feedback on my thoughts, pushed me to think more, and encouraged me in my work. Thank you to Ann Sabatini who allowed me to grow into the educator I am today. Thank you to Lin, who supported me throughout my entire doctorate and pushed me to finish. Thank you to Lauren who is always so supportive. Thank you to Terri Ruyter who has so graciously written the Foreword. Thank you everyone. I am honored to do the work I do and I hope it helps you to do the work you do a little bit better every day.

Foreword

When I first watched Nicki teach routines to students, I marveled at how she was able to bring forward the voices and thinking of all students. One child in particular – I'll call her Rosie – who was new to our school, had been a hesitant participant in most class lessons and activities. Her reluctance had made it difficult for teachers to assess her mathematical skills, and she was viewed, fairly or not, as a student who was not yet mathematically proficient. Nicki challenged all the students to try to come up with two ways to solve/explain a problem. She then partnered the students and challenged them to document four different solution paths. Each group rose to the challenge although some of the more "mathematically proficient" students had a harder time achieving this goal than others. They were used to quickly getting the "right answer" using a memorized procedure. When it came time for the students to share, "Rosie" had one of the most innovative solutions, that highlighted deep understanding of the mathematical concepts. I remember her being surprised by the respect her solution was given. She sat up a little straighter and became more eager to raise her hand.

The routine that Nicki used challenged students to go beyond answer-getting. She was striving to reveal their thinking. This approach was empowering to the students. It also provided rich data on student mathematical competencies – data that was useful in determining groups and partnerships and future lessons.

I read a draft of this book in August as the school year was gearing up. I am writing this forward one month into the school year. Teachers are teaching routines, they are looking at formal test data and results of early assessments, and they are planning for initial groupings in math class. And as a faculty, we are continuing to reflect on our teaching decisions and how these decisions foster committed attention to learning by the students.

"Perseverance," "strategic competence," "hard fun." These are some of the goals that Nicki Newton challenges us to achieve in math instruction. Drawing upon the visible thinking work of the researchers at Project Zero, Nicki offers up a range of accessible techniques and routines that build procedural fluency and conceptual understanding. By challenging them to draw upon mathematical practices and processes on their own and in small and whole groups, students describe their thinking, justify it, and challenge the thinking of others. This is the "hard fun" that students talk about in her math lessons.

I am excited for my teachers to get Nicki's book and study it together. I am eager for the students to have the opportunity for deep thinking combined with distributed practice as they go through their school year. I am confident that as they build numeracy and fluency, they will become more engaged in mathematics, more willing to take risks in solving problems and discussing math, and more confident, empowered learners.

Terri Ruyter, Principal
PS/IS 276, The Battery Park City School
New York NY

Introduction

Students grow into the intellectual life that surrounds them.

—(Vygotsky, 1978)

I walk into a second-grade classroom and an adorable little boy gets up, runs to me, squats, and points and yells to his classmates with a huge grin, "She's fun!" I walk into a third-grade classroom and the kids light up when they see me and they say, "She's fun!" and "I remember you from last year." I smile. I'm glad they think I'm fun. More importantly, I'm glad they think that math can be fun.

I remember a few years ago I was at a school in Colorado and the teacher said, "Dr. Nicki, I had been telling my students all day that the math lady was coming. And after you came and played all those games with them, one of my students came up to me and said, 'This is so fun. When is that math lady coming?'" We laughed because he just couldn't imagine that *I was that math lady*. Surely *that math lady* would not be playing games like this. Charlesworth (2010) wrote a book in which she describes some kids talking to each other about computer lab games – when the one asks how it was, the other replies, "It was hard fun."

RESEARCH NOTE

Routines must be "student-centered and student-friendly."

(Sanchez, 2010, p. 20)

Hard fun. I like the sound of that. See the games I play with students are challenging. They get stumped. They have to think really hard sometimes. It is cognitively demanding work. Students are willing to engage, though, because it's a game. They believe that they can do it. The context is free and easy. The math is rigorous. I require that they think, that they take risks, that they talk to each other, that they justify their own thinking, and that they challenge each other's thinking. I require that they stretch. I don't ask other students to help out when someone is stuck. I scaffold their thinking and refer them to their toolkits. I let them wrestle with a problem and persevere until they get it. This way I build not only mathematical knowledge but also self-efficacy and self-esteem. I make sure that they have tools to work with. We never give up; *in fact* we do Bonus Rounds!

RESEARCH NOTE

The Impact of Routines

Routines and ways of approaching knowledge and learning in a classroom impact student ideas about teaching and learning, their attitudes toward learning and knowledge, and their engagement in the teaching and learning process (Dahl, Bals, & Turi, 2005; Ritchhart, Church, & Morrison, 2011).

In all the consulting I do in schools, I always talk about the importance of daily math "thinking-rich" routines (Visible Thinking, n.d.). Routines promote numeracy throughout the year across grade levels and across math topics. Students look forward to them. They are challenged by them. They don't run away from the challenge; they move towards it. I worked in a school in New York City where the third graders were so intrigued by routines that they began making up their own. One day when I went back, they shared these fantastic twists to the routines I had done with them. They made sure that the math was there. See, students know when they are learning. They know when they are spending some meaningful time doing something. They know this is what school should be about. Moreover, Daily Math Thinking Routines "gain exponential power when implemented across a grade level or throughout the school" (Adkins, 2009, p. xxxi).

The Goals of this Book

The goals of this book are:

- to provide a collection of research-based daily math "thinking-rich" routines that can be used by classroom teachers, interventionists, Title I teachers, bilingual teachers, math coaches, special educators, teachers of English language learners (ELLs), and teachers seeking to improve the mathematical competency of all students;
- to provide teacher-friendly examples of the routines, which teachers can understand, adapt, and easily implement; and
- to talk about research that focuses on how students learn mathematics in a way that informs what we do in schools to improve achievement.

Who Needs this Book

I wrote this book because when I go into math classrooms and do the routines, teachers always ask, "Where can I find that?" I wrote this book so teachers would have a resource that was easy to read, easy to put into practice, and educational. More and more, standardized tests are driving the curriculum and students are getting left behind. So routines are a way to make sure everyone is on board with highly cognitively demanding mini-tasks that build competence over time.

Three Ways to Use this Book

Here are three ways to go about using this book:

- *Start.* Just start. Start small. Pick one routine and get really comfortable using it. All of the routines are research based, rigorous, and engaging. Students love routines. Just start and it will be OK. It will be more than OK. It will be amazing! So, just start.
- *Look at your data and zero in on something.* Pick a standard and then pick a routine to practice it. Maybe you want to work on place value so you start with *Number of the Day*. Maybe you want to work on fractions so you start with *Fraction of the Day*. Maybe you want to work on reasoning so you start with *True or False*. Remember, there is no one right way to start. Just start.
- *Integrate some of the routines into your small-group work or the workstations.* This is another way to start. With small groups, routines can be tailored. You can do different routines with different groups according to their specific needs.

Overview of the Contents

This book is divided into three parts. Part I provides the background information, such as the research, the structures, the setup for doing routines. Part II covers general routines across different mathematical topics. It is about routines that work specifically on fluency with whole numbers, fractions, and decimals. Part III is about action planning for routines.

Part I: Introduction

In Chapter 1 (Daily Math Thinking Routines in Action), I discuss the what, when, where, and how of doing Daily Math Thinking Routines. I discuss the difference between learning the math initially and practicing and owning the math over time. Chapter 2 (Planning Thinking Routines) takes a deeper dive into the theory that supports distributed practice across time. We know from research in neuroscience that practice does make much better, if not perfect. We also explore some of the different structures for working with error patterns. In Chapter 3 (Creating a Community of Public Mathematicians), we see that Daily Math Thinking Routines require students to think out loud, express themselves clearly, make mistakes, debate, and persevere. In Chapter 4 (The Art and Science of Questioning), I discuss the art and science of asking students questions that not only promote but also provoke their thinking. Questioning that scaffolds up through high levels of cognitive demand and invites students to come in and stay awhile. Questioning that grows their own thinking dispositions, building confidence, competence, and curiosity about the world they live in and how math is intricately connected to it.

Part II: Daily Math Thinking Routines

In Chapter 5 (Rotating Routines), I discuss the plethora of formats that can be used to build mathematical thinking across the year. I discuss how to use them in a variety of ways. Teachers can use the sections to look at differentiation across the grades and across the year. Chapter 6 (Number Flexes) covers number flex activities that you do every day. They build number sense. They develop flexible thinking. They require that students stretch their thinking. Based on data, they involve "clear and sequenced [and engaging] *lesson and unit structures* to advance student learning" (NYC Division of Teaching and Learning, n.d., emphasis in original). In Chapter 7 (Vocabulary Energizers), I look at whole-class math vocabulary routines which should be done at least once a week. Math is a language, and if students can't speak the words, then they won't ever fully understand the math. Vocabulary routines should have the students listening, speaking, reading, and writing the words. Chapter 8 (Problem Solving as a Daily Math Thinking Routine) considers problem solving as something that should happen every day. It should be engaging, interesting, and cognitively demanding. There should be various formats, but all should emphasize problem solving as a practice rather than an answer-getting activity.

Part III: Action Planning

In this final part, Chapter 9 (Action Planning) looks at implementation. Reading a good book and getting excited about it is only the start. But you do have to start! So this chapter is about the implementation. Where to start. How to start. How to build this into something that changes the very thinking of your students!

References

Adkins, E. (2009). *40 reading intervention strategies for K-6 students: Research-based support for RTI.* Bloomington, IN: Solution Tree Press.

Charlesworth, R. (2010). *Math and science for young children* (7th ed.). Belmont, CA: Cengage Learning.

Dahl, T.I., Bals, M., & Turi, A.L. (2005). Are students' beliefs about knowledge and learning associated with their reported use of learning strategies? *British Journal of Educational Psychology, 75*(2), 257–273.

NYC Division of Teaching and Learning. (n.d.). *1e: Designing coherent instruction next steps.* Retrieved December 11, 2016, from http://schools.nyc.gov/NR/rdonlyres/F8CD38CD-E097-492D-994F-0E722BD69E11/0/1eNextSteps.pdf

Ritchhart, R., Church, M., & Morrison, K. (2011). *Making thinking visible: How to promote engagement, understanding, and independence for all learners.* San Francisco, CA: Jossey-Bass.

Sánchez, F. (2010). *Interactive classroom strategies and structures for success: Focus on English learners.* Retrieved December 15, 2016, from https://www.csustan.edu/sites/default/files/SAIL/documents/InteractiveClassroomStrategiesandStructuresforSuccess-Dr.FranciscaSanchez.pdf

Visible Thinking. (n.d.) Introduction to thinking routines. Retrieved September 15, 2016, from www.visiblethinkingpz.org/VisibleThinking_html_files/03_ThinkingRoutines/03b_Introduction.html

Vygotsky, L. S. (1978). *Mind in society: The development of higher psychological processes.* Cambridge, MA: Harvard University Press.

Part I

Overview

1

Daily Math Thinking Routines in Action

There is no decision that teachers make that has a greater impact on students' opportunities to learn and on their perceptions about what mathematics is than the selection or creation of the tasks with which the teacher engages students in studying mathematics.

—(Lappan & Briars, 1995, p. 139)

Classroom Vignette

Mrs. Ching has been working with her fifth graders on fractions. She is doing a Do Not Solve *routine.*

Mrs. Ching: OK we are going to get started. Remember that you cannot use paper and pencil. You are going to visualize the fraction models in your head and reason about the size.

She presents the following task.

A. $\frac{1}{4} + \frac{1}{5}$
B. $\frac{4}{6} + \frac{4}{6}$
C. $\frac{1}{2} + \frac{3}{6}$
D. $\frac{6}{8} + \frac{6}{4}$

1. **Which expression is less than 1 whole?**
2. **Which expression is between 1 whole and $1\frac{1}{2}$?**
3. **Which expression is equal to 1 whole?**
4. **Which expression is between $1\frac{1}{2}$ and 2?**

Mrs. Ching: OK, first take some private think time. [*She gives them about 30 seconds.*] Now, turn and talk with your shoulder buddy. Discuss Problem 1. Be sure to explain your thinking. [*She waits for the children's discussion to end.*] OK who wants to share their thinking?
Tami: I think A is less than 1 whole. How I thought about it was that I know that $\frac{1}{4}$ is less than half and I know that $\frac{1}{5}$ is less than half, so the sum has to be less than 1 whole.
Dan: I thought about the decimals and I know that $\frac{1}{4}$ is .25 and $\frac{1}{5}$ is .2, so that is less than 1 whole.
Mrs. Ching: OK, how did you all think about Problem 2?
Kelly: I looked at the problems and I know that $\frac{4}{6}$ and $\frac{4}{6}$ is 1 whole and $\frac{2}{6}$, because I thought about the pattern blocks and $\frac{3}{6}$ is a half and then 1 more $\frac{1}{6}$ … so that is 1 whole and $\frac{2}{6}$ … so that is between 1 and $1\frac{1}{2}$.
Luke: Yeah that was what I did too.
Mrs. Ching: OK, what are your thoughts about Problem 3.
Jamal: That was easy because $\frac{3}{6}$ equals $\frac{1}{2}$, and $\frac{1}{2}$ and $\frac{1}{2}$ makes a whole.

The students continue the discussion. Mrs. Ching asks them to explain their thinking and, at times, the thinking of others. At the end of the routine, Mrs. Ching asks the students what was easy about the routine and what was tricky. The whole discussion takes about 7 minutes.

What are Daily Math Thinking Routines?

Quick energizers and routines help students to own the math they are doing. They are quick, intentional mini-tasks based on the topics that students are learning. They incorporate the use of concrete and digital manipulatives, drawings, diagrams, and actions. These types of engaging formats help students to get on friendly terms with numbers. Students get to practice and solidify their mathematical understandings. They are "quick tasks" with engaging, standards-based, rigorous brief activities that build mathematical muscle across time.

Daily math energizers and routines help to develop mathematically proficient students. Students build conceptual understanding by playing with ideas and talking about concepts over time. They build procedural fluency and mathematical confidence because they are asked to do a variety of procedures across different mathematical topics. Resnick, Lesgold, and Bill note that it is important for students to "develop trust in their own knowledge" (1990, p. 6). Routines allow students the chance to encounter sticky situations and stuff they must keep on going with – stuff that doesn't come immediately, stuff they have to work through – and to solve what may at times seem like daunting problems. Routines build strategic competence because they require students to think about a variety of ways to do something and to stick with it until it is accomplished. They require reasoning independently, with partners, and in groups. They build an "I can do that" mathematical disposition.

What is the Difference between an Energizer and a Routine?

An energizer is usually a short type of routine, lasting around 3 to 5 minutes. A regular routine is a bit longer – usually 5 to 10 minutes, sometimes 15. An energizer can be a routine if it is extended into one. The idea is that through distributed practice (doing something over a period of time), students gain the competency that they need. For example, the opening vignette of this chapter is a quick energizer with just a few problems put up on the board, but it could be extended with more problems being put up.

Importance of High-Level, Cognitively Demanding, Purposeful Practice

Daily Math Thinking Routines require that students take part in purposeful practice and become engaged in doing the math. They involve listening, looking, talking, discussing, agreeing, and disagreeing in meaningful ways. They are "thinking rich" mini-tasks and experiences (see below). Students look forward to doing them.

 RESEARCH NOTE

I agree with Ritchhart et al. that we must situate "thinking routines within the larger context of our enterprise to develop thoughtful classrooms and nurture students' thinking dispositions" (Ritchhart, Palmer, Church, & Tishman, 2006, p. 2). Thinking routines are part of a bigger picture about developing a thinking culture in a classroom and developing individual thinking mindsets.

Sometimes morning routines are somewhat mindless. Students are just filling in the answers because that is what they are supposed to do. The conversation is quick and superficial, meant to finish a certain amount of problems in a few minutes. Many times schools will use "bell ringer" programs, with students reviewing concepts throughout the year. Much of this work is "fill in the blank," "finish it and move on"-type of activities. They require a low level of cognitive demand and are "characterized as opportunities for students to demonstrate routine applications of known procedures or to work with a complex assembly of routine subtasks or non-mathematical activities" (Silver, 2010, p. 2).

Daily Math Thinking Routines are high-level, cognitively demanding mathematical structures "through which students collectively as well as individually initiate, explore, discuss, document, and manage their thinking in classrooms" (Ritchhart, 2002, p. 2). They provide "opportunities for students to explain, describe, justify, compare, or assess; to make decisions and choices; to plan and formulate questions; to exhibit creativity; and to work with more than one representation in a meaningful way" (Silver, 2010, p. 2).

Students engage in a variety of active learning experiences where they work in different formats: alone, with partners, in small groups, and with the whole group. Routines require students to focus their attention. Routines challenge student thinking. Routines require that students put their thoughts into words and express themselves publicly. Students are expected to share their thinking out loud and also write about it and share that writing. Students are expected to use the methods, practices, processes, and vocabulary of math (see below).

RESEARCH NOTE

I would like to expand on Richtner et al.'s criteria for a good "thinking-rich" routine:

- Has a specific math goal
- Is "math-rich"
- Is cognitively demanding
- Is repeatable
- Is engaging
- Is easy to teach
- Is easy to learn
- Makes it easy to "get in there" and scaffold the math learning
- Can be used across a variety of math topics
- Can be used with individuals, partners, in small groups, or with the whole group
- Can be done mentally or verbally

(Adapted from Visible Thinking, n.d.)

Practice Does Make Perfect

Teaching and learning in the 21st century affords us a research knowledge base that we have never had access to before. More and more work is being done with brain imaging technology. From this technology, we understand that the brain grows and changes "through a process called experience- or learning-dependent plasticity" (Society for Neuroscience, 2014).

Practice Gap

In schools today, most textbooks and pacing calendars race through the year. Students are presented with a topic, they get one or, if lucky, two days to learn something and then they are expected to move on to the next topic. However, we know that you don't learn how to add doubles or multiply fractions in a day. So Daily Math Thinking Routines allow students to own their knowledge. Through multiple exposure in engaging formats, students progress. Daily Math Thinking Routines help to fill the practice gap.

Massed Practice versus Distributed Practice

Massed practice is the practice that is done in a unit of study. It involves a concentrated time frame for teaching a specific topic. Distributed practice is practice that takes place across the year. So students are introduced to topics, they become familiar with ideas, and they are exposed to procedures during massed practice. They actually learn to do things over time. The more they work with the subject, the more they understand topics conceptually and gain procedural fluency. Daily Math Thinking Routines allow students the *opportunity to get the distributed practice that they need to become competent, confident, and creative thinking mathematicians.*

What Are the Topics of Routines?

Both routines and energizers talk about different mathematical topics such as:

- Operations
- Algebraic thinking
- Place value
- Fractions and decimals
- Measurement
- Geometry

Routines are to practice not only the content but also the processes or practices of mathematics. Students work on:

- Problem solving
- Reasoning
- Communicating thinking in written form and orally
- Modeling
- Using precise mathematical language
- Looking for structure
- Thinking about patterns

Mathematical routines help to develop number sense, which is a sense of numbers, a comfortableness with numbers, a rapport with numbers that says, "I know you. I can work with you."

Effective Daily Math Thinking Routines Build Math Power

The Effective Use of Routines Requires that Students Use the Mathematical Practices/Processes

Doing these routines is about more than just getting the answer. The students have to persevere. They must reason to themselves and out loud, and they must follow the reasoning of others and decide whether or not that reasoning makes sense. They are expected to talk with each other about their thinking. They should be accountable for their contributions. They are required to model their thinking with mathematical tools. Routines help students think about structure and pattern. Not only is thinking "promoted" but it is also "revealed," uncovered, seen in new ways, brought to light for everyone to discuss in helpful meaningful ways (Ritchhart, Palmer, Church, & Tishman, 2006). Through time, students learn that through their own thinking and the thinking of others, their knowledge base grows, their skills sets increase, and their understanding deepens.

The Effective Use of Routines Requires Students to Think about Problems in a Variety of Ways

Through routines, students begin to listen and learn from each other, seeing that there is more than one way to solve a problem, and understanding that although there might be more than one way, some ways are more efficient than others.

The Effective Use of Routines Requires that Students Make Connections between the Numbers

Daily Math Thinking Routines require that students think about the relationships among numbers. They go beyond "answer-getting" (Daro, n.d.). The purpose of a routine isn't for students to just give an answer, but to think about how does knowing 9×9 help me to think about $8\frac{1}{9}$? How does knowing $7 + 7$ help me to know $7 + 8$? The emphasis on routines is for students to reason about numbers and look at the structure and pattern of numbers.

Mental Math or Written Routines

There has to be a balance between developing mental agility with numbers and the written competencies where students are explaining their thinking on paper. Great math routines allow students to build competency with both. The routines are often recorded by the teacher, sometimes on chart paper, and other times on the board. There are also recording sheets for students to use sometimes. They can use their math thinking notebooks or white boards as well. Although the students may be doing the math in their heads at times, the teacher is always making "formal notations as a public record of the discussions and conclusions" (Resnick, Lesgold, & Bill, 1990, abstract).

Student Recording Sheets

Binders
Keep the routine recording sheets in a binder. Use separators so that they stay organized. These can actually be part of the general math toolkit, with a special section devoted to the routines.

Laminates/Page Protectors
Decide on a system that lets the students reuse the templates. You can either laminate them or put them in page protectors.

Where Do They Fit into the Curriculum?

RESEARCH NOTE

Freeing up Cognitive Space

Routines "take place in a focused, predictable, and fluid way" so students can focus on the actual math being discussed. "Routines free up cognitive processing space for both teachers and students by making automatic a subset of the cognitive processing tasks that would confront teachers and students if the problems for which these are solutions had to be solved anew each time" (Liendhardt, Weidman, & Hammond, 1987, pp. 135–136).

Routines should be taught from the beginning of the year (see Figure 1.4). They are used to review previously taught topics, preview new concepts, and practice current topics. For example, at the beginning of the year, third graders through fifth graders should start the *Fraction of the Day* routine. In this routine, students review fractions throughout the year, mainly reviewing much of what they learned in the prior year, but also being exposed to new ideas for the upcoming year. Then when the unit on fractions is taught, teachers add the new content to the ongoing routine. This way students "get on friendly terms with fractions."

When Do You Do Routines?

Routines can be done at any time of the day. Many teachers do them at the beginning of math class, but other teachers do them at the end of math class or at some other time in the day. Sometimes, people even put them on the menu in math workstations as something that must be done during that week. The important thing is that they are "used over and over again" so that they "support and scaffold specific thinking moves or actions" (Ritchhart, 2006, p. 1).

How Do You Know which Routine To Do?

There are a variety of routines (see Figure 1.5). Rotating through the routines gives students rigorous variety and keeps them engaged. There are certain routines that should be consistently done though. For example, *Problem of the Day* should be a routine that is done every day. This doesn't mean to do a different problem every day. It means to take a deep dive into problem solving every day and to work on the various parts of developing good problem solvers. On the other hand, a routine like *Number of the Day*, *Fraction of the Day* or *Decimal of the Day* should be done often but not every day.

 RESEARCH NOTE

The kinds of "tasks you choose to use in your classroom enhance or inhibit your ability to ask the kinds of questions that allow students to develop" deep thinking (Orrill, 2015).

How Do You Monitor Routines?

The teacher should monitor the routines as the students do them. Sometimes the routines are done out loud, and other times students write them down in their thinking notebook or on their white board. In this case, the teacher should roam around and observe what students are doing so that they might call up different examples of the work being done. Students should choose examples that help expand understanding of the number and build overall number sense.

The Yearlong Routine that Changes Over Time

 RESEARCH NOTE

"The presence of functioning activity structures and efficient supporting routines is one benchmark of a successful mathematics teacher."
(Leinhardt, Weidham, & Hammond, 1987, p. 135)

As the year progresses, students learn different things. So although the structure of the routine might stay basically the same, the actual routine does expand and change with a growing knowledge base. The simple routines grow to be more complex as the year progresses (see Figure 1.6). The routines "guide students' learning and intellectual interactions" (Ritchhart et al., 2006, p. 1). The discussion of the routines includes some examples for the beginning of the year and end of the year by grade level to reflect the expanding knowledge base. Routines are cognitively complex, coherent across time, relevant to the needs of the students, and challenging yet achievable. Routines are not random across the year; they are well-articulated opportunities for learning scaffolded throughout the year to promote student achievement. They are data-driven, differentiated, standards-based, cognitively demanding, engaging opportunities to learn more every day.

How Do They Help with Standardized Tests?

Purposeful practice helps students to reason about numbers (see Figure 1.7). It helps them think about the math they are seeing and whether it makes sense. It helps students to understand mistakes and error patterns, because these are explicitly discussed during routines. Students are better able to recognize distractors (which are usually designed to match error patterns that students make) and reason through problems.

Daily Math Thinking Routines Covered in this Book			
Always, Sometimes, Never	*Convince Me/Prove It*	*Disappearing Dan*	*Find and Fix the Error*
Guess My Number	*How Many More/Less To …?*	*Describe that Pattern*	*Input/Output Tables*
It Is/It Isn't	*I Was Walking Down the Street …*	*Model That!*	*Number Line It!*
Riddle Me This!	*3 Truths and a Fib*	*True or False?*	*What Doesn't Belong?*
What's Missing?	*Why Is It Not …?*	*Yes, But Why?*	*Count Around the Room*
Number Flexes			
I Love Math!	*Number of the Day*	*Subitizing*	*Fraction of the Day*
Decimal of the Day	*Number Talks (American style)*	*Number Talks (British style)*	*Over/Under/Same*
Virtual Dice Roll	*Virtual Cards*	*Do Not Solve!*	
Vocabulary Routines			
Alphabet Box	*Frayer Model*	*Brainstorm It!*	*Word Box*
Charades	*Mystery Word*	*Vocabulary Tic-Tac-Toe*	*Vocabulary Bingo*
Word of Mouth	*Math Scrabbo*	*1-Minute Essay*	
Problem Solving Routines			
Picture That!	*What's the Problem?*	*What's the Question?*	*Sort That!*
Two Arguments	*What's the Story?* (Reverse of *Model That!*)	*Template It!*	

Key Points

- Done daily
- Engaging formats
- Energizers are quick
- Routines are a bit longer
- High-level cognitive demand
- Practice does make perfect
- Practice gap
- Massed practice versus distributed practice
- Various math topics
- Importance of practices
- Mental math and written routines
- Routines are based on data
- Changing yearlong routine

- Provide practice for standardized tests
- Number flexes
- Problem of the day
- Rotating routines

Summary

Daily Math Thinking Routines are the linchpin of ongoing learning in the classroom. There are a variety of engaging formats. Energizers are quick and routines are a bit longer. As Shumway (2011) notes, the *dailyness* of doing the routine is part of the magic. It helps to fill the practice gap that is caused by the speed of the curriculum. The distributed practice over time allows for students to learn the concepts they were introduced to in the massed practice time (the unit of the study). The data-driven routines change over time. There are different types of routines, ranging from number flexes (that focus on fact fluency) to problem of the day (which works on problem solving) and rotating routines (which focus on reasoning about numbers). Done well, Daily Math Thinking Routines provide excellent practice for standardized tests.

Questions for Reflection

1. Do you currently do math routines? How often?
2. Do you have a plan around your routines? How do you pick them?
3. What stands out for you in this chapter?

References

Daro, P. (n.d.). Against answer-getting. Retrieved on December 11, 2016, from http://serpmedia.org/daro-talks/

Lappan, G., & Briars, D. (1995). How should mathematics be taught? In I.M. Carl (Ed.), *Prospects for school mathematics* (pp. 131–156). Reston, VA: National Council of Teachers of Mathematics.

Leinhardt, G., Weidman, C., & Hammond, K.M. (1987). Introduction and integration of classroom routines by expert teachers. *Curriculum Inquiry, 17*(2), 135–176. Retrieved December 20, 2016, from http://gaining.educ.msu.edu/resources/files/Leinhardt1987Introduction.pdf

Orrill, C.H. (2015, May 11). Tasks, questions, and practices. Retrieved December 13, 2016, from www.nctm.org/Publications/Teaching-Children-Mathematics/Blog/Tasks,-Questions,-and-Practices/

Resnick, L., Lesgold, S., & Bill, V. (1990). From protoquantities to number sense. Paper presented at the Psychology of Mathematics Education Conference (Mexico, July). Retrieved December 20, 2016, from http://files.eric.ed.gov/fulltext/ED335420.pdf

Ritchhart, R. (2002). *Intellectual character: What it is, why it matters, and how to get it.* San Francisco, CA: Jossey-Bass.

Ritchhart, R., Palmer, P., Church, M., & Tishman, S. (2006, April). Thinking routines: Establishing patterns of thinking in the classroom. Paper presented at American Educational Research Association, San Francisco.

Shumway, J. (2011). *Building number sense through routines.* Portland, ME: Stenhouse.

Silver, E. (2010). Examining what teachers do when they display their best practice: Teaching mathematics for understanding. *Journal of Mathematics Education at Teachers College, 1,* 1–6.

Society for Neuroscience. (2014). Does practice make perfect? Retrieved September 15, 2016, from www.brainfacts.org/ask-an-expert/does-practice-make-perfect

Visible Thinking. (n.d.) Introduction to thinking routines. Retrieved September 15, 2016, from www.visiblethinkingpz.org/VisibleThinking_html_files/03_ThinkingRoutines/03b_Introduction.html

2

Planning Thinking Routines

Not all tasks are created equal—different tasks promote different levels and kinds of student thinking.
—(Stein, Smith, Henningsen, & Silver, 2000, p. 139)

Classroom Vignette

Mrs. Mary is working on a geometry unit. She has planned for a series of rigorous routines throughout her unit of study that focus on her students talking and then solving. Here is a vignette from the True or False *routine.*

Mrs. Mary: OK, we are going to talk about some geometrical shapes today. Think about what we have been learning as you answer the questions. Use your tools to scaffold your thinking. **True or False: This is a hexagon.**

Mrs. Mary: Take some private think time. [*She gives them about 30 seconds.*] OK, now turn and talk with a neighbor. [*She gives them some more time.*] Who wants to explain how they thought about this?
Tomas: It's not a hexagon … because it is not like a circle.
Mrs. Mary: OK, what do you mean?
Tomas: You know, like it's usually a circle.
Mrs. Mary: Can you draw one?
Tomas: I think so.
Mrs. Mary: If you need to, get one and look at it to help you.
Kim: I agree with him.
Marta: I disagree. It is a hexagon. It has six sides.

Students start to count.

Mrs. Mary: Let's verify that. Marta, come up and count the sides out loud.
Reggie: It does have six sides. It also has six points.
Mrs. Mary: How many angles?

The students only count five and Mrs. Mary points out the sixth.

Mrs. Mary: So what do we think from what we have considered?
Katie: Well it's not a *hexagon* hexagon.
Mrs. Mary: What do you mean Katie?
Katie: Well it doesn't look like the one Tomas drew.
Mrs. Mary: Do all hexagons look alike?
Tim: I don't think so. Because both of those are hexagons and they look different.
Mrs. Mary: Given what we have discussed, I'd like everyone to draw two more hexagons.

Conversation continues. Mrs. Mary continues to ask questions and to push students to think about the difference between regular and irregular polygons. During the discussion she even has some students come up and draw other hexagons.

Clear Goals

Daily Math Thinking Routines are done to help guide students' thinking and learning and their "intellectual interactions" (Ritchhart, Palmer, Church, & Tishman, 2006, p. 1). It has been proven that teacher clarity has a strong impact on students' learning (Hattie, 2012). High expectations are great, but clarity is absolutely necessary. There are a variety of thinking routines but they each have very clear goals. Some of them – such as daily number flexes like *Number of the Day*, *Fraction of the Day*, or *Decimal of the Day* – are meant to develop fluency with operations and deep conceptual understanding of the concept. Other routines – such as *True or False* – are meant to engage students in reasoning about mathematical statements and to get them looking at the structure and pattern of numbers.

Teachers have to know what their students need, believe they can learn it, and then purposefully choose the routines that will help to scaffold their understanding, skill, and reasoning. Great routines have clear goals. Research shows that teachers who have clear goals and a plan have a higher impact on student learning. Have the plan and have a way to record what is happening as it happens. There are various ways to keep track of what is happening during the routine.

RESEARCH NOTE

"David Perkins has dubbed this ease-of-access quality 'action poetry,' indicating that there is a certain **brevity and elegance that helps the routine stick in our mind**."
(Ritchhart, 2002, p. 91, emphasis added)

Routines are explicit, named, and streamlined, and they have a familiar framework (Project Zero, 2010). When I say to the students that we are going to do *True or False*, they know it's different from *What Doesn't Belong?* They mentally adjust for the task. Each routine sets up and requires a specific "set of thinking moves" (Project Zero, 2010). Both the teachers and the students understand that they are not merely engaging in a activity, but rather this is a tool to help the students to know more, get better at doing something, and be able to discuss and explain the math they are engaged in (Project Zero, 2010). It is an explicit understanding that we all learn from each other and with each other.

RESEARCH NOTE

Repeating Routines

"While it seems axiomatic to say that routines are <u>used over and over again</u> in the classroom, **it is worth focusing on this repetitive quality with regard to thinking routines, as it is what separates them from single-use strategies and practices**."
(Richhart, Palmer, Church, & Tishman, 2006, p. 12, bold added)

During Daily Thinking Math Routines, teachers must use precise questioning and close listening to shape the routine into the cognitively demanding activity that it is meant to be. Teachers must listen intently in order to know what the next question will be. Killian (2016) notes that teachers should listen "to see if your students 'get it', whatever 'it' might be in a particular lesson." He reminds us that we have to "listen to the thinking *behind [our] students' responses*, and especially for any misconceptions that they may hold."

Mini-Tasks with High Cognitive Demand

If we want students to develop the capacity to think, reason, and problem solve, then we need to start with high-level, cognitively complex tasks (Stein & Lane, 1996). Small (2009) gives wonderful examples of the power of open tasks versus closed tasks. If we do routines where we ask students "yes or no" questions, that requires an entirely different type of thinking than if we ask questions where there is no specific correct answer. For example, if I ask students to round a series of numbers that I put on the board, that is an altogether different task than if I ask them to write down five possible numbers that could round to 50. If I ask them to use their centimeter paper to draw a rectangular figure that has a large perimeter and small area, that is very different from asking the students to solve perimeter problems (Small, 2009).

Low Floor High Ceiling Tasks

NRich Tasks has done a great deal of work on what they call Low Floor High Ceiling tasks (McClure, Woodham, & Borthwick, 2011). The basic idea is that there is an entry level for all students, and then the task can be scaffolded up to much higher levels for students that need it. This is a great framework for thinking about routines as well. You want routines that you can discuss at multiple levels. For example, I was in a second-grade classroom in Colorado Springs playing a game of *I Was Walking Down the Street* – in this game, the teacher says they heard a specific number being given as an answer (say, 1000) and the students have to state possible questions. In this particular classroom, while many of the second graders were saying things like "Was it 500 + 500?" or "Was it 1000 + 0?" one student raised his hand and said, "Was it 10 cubed?" Low Floor High Ceiling in action! I love this game because everybody can play. Now, I didn't give the boy who said it any more kudos for great thinking than I gave the other students, but he looked at me as if to say, "You know that I know some stuff that nobody else in here knows."

Planning for Big Ideas of Daily Math Thinking Routines

The research confirms that teachers who plan do better than teachers who don't (Leinhardt, Weidman, & Hammond, 1987). As you plan for routines throughout the year, you must consider several questions: What are the priority standards? What are the big ideas in the current unit of study? How do I plan to use routines in a purposeful way to reinforce, review, and preview these big ideas, enduring understandings, and skill sets throughout the year? For example, fractions and place value give students trouble all year long. So from third grade through seventh grade, teachers need to review fractions on a continuous basis starting at the beginning of the year.

When we are doing a unit of study, it is important to plan the routines for each day. The chart "Daily Lessons and Routines with Follow-Up" shows the daily lessons with the routines under them. The follow-up is in the guided math group and in the math workstations.

Fractions and Place Value Routines

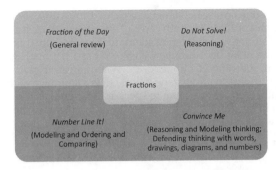

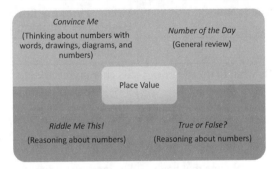

Daily Lessons and Routines with Follow-Up

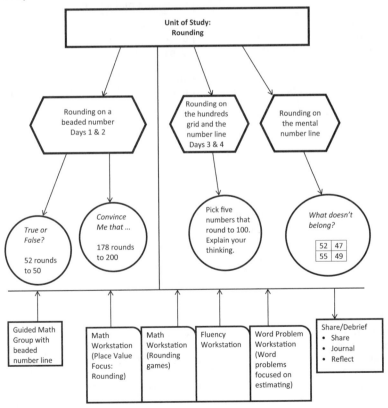

Language-Rich

Daily Math Thinking Routines must be "language-rich." I love this term. Rowan and Robles talk about how a language-rich approach to math can be "effective with all learners" (1998, p. 505). Language-rich routines hold students to a different standard. They require that students use math words always. So when someone refers to a number, I ask, "What's the math word?" It could be factor, dividend, divisor, addend, subtrahend, minuend, etc. When someone gives an answer, I ask, "What's the math word?" I want students to understand that math is a language with its own vocabulary, and if we are going to do math, then we are going to speak it. A language-rich classroom has vocabulary posted around the room in meaningful ways. For example, on the door are the words "vertical" and "horizontal" in the correct positions. On the window are signs that point to lines and angles. Students see the vocabulary in context. We also do vocabulary routines.

What a Thinking Routine Is Not Low-Level Tasks	What a Thinking Routine Is High-Level Thinking Tasks
Vignette 1	**Vignette 2**
Teacher tells the students what to do and how to do it. Closed Task. Is 7 odd or even? Round the number 54.	Teacher invites the students to ponder a question. Why is 7 not even? Name three numbers that can round to 50 and explain your thinking. Name a number that doesn't round to 50 and explain why not.
Students simply solve the problems that have been provided and modeled by the teacher.	Students must discuss, reason, and generate different answers. They justify their thinking by talking out loud, listening to the reasoning of others, and deciding whether or not that reasoning makes sense.
No discussion, thinking, or reasoning is involved. Students simply follow the learned procedure. No connections to number relationships, patterns, or structures. No emphasis on big ideas, understandings, or meaning of the math. Students are simply ANSWERING A QUESTION.	Students have to think about the problem and, often, discuss it with others. They have to reason. There isn't an instant answer. Students are encouraged to think about the big ideas, enduring understandings, and meaning of the math. Students are DOING MATH.

Key Points

- Clear goals are necessary.
- Tasks with high cognitive demand are required.
- Low Floor High Ceiling tasks allow everyone an entry point.
- Planning is essential.
- Language-rich classrooms scaffold access to the concepts.

Summary

Effective routines don't just happen – they are planned for. Teachers must analyze the data and decide what their students need to work on. Based on where the gaps, misunderstandings, and tricky parts are, teachers design Daily Math Thinking Routines to fill the gaps, correct misunderstandings, and clarify the tricky parts. Teachers also plan for the ongoing practice of the tough topics, like fractions and decimals. Moreover, teachers plan for the ongoing topics of fluency, vocabulary, and word problems. Throughout this planning, much thought should be given to tasks that are open-ended and require different levels of cognitive demand. Not only should teachers plan for the activities, but they must also plan for the vocabulary so that it doesn't get lost in the process. A well-planned routine can be extremely effective and help to move student achievement forward.

Questions for Reflection

1. Do you currently plan out your routines for the unit of study? What might you do differently after reading this chapter?
2. Do you plan Low Floor High Ceiling tasks? What new ideas do you have about this?
3. In what ways is your classroom language-rich?

References

Hattie, J. (2012). *Visible learning for teachers: Maximizing impact on learning.* London: Routledge.

Killian, S. (2016, July 12). Checking for understanding without creating mountains of markings. Retrieved December 11, 2016, from www.evidencebasedteaching.org.au/checking-for-understanding/

Leinhardt, G., Weidman, C., & Hammond, K.M. (1987). Introduction and integration of classroom routines by expert teachers. *Curriculum Inquiry, 17*(2), 135–176. Retrieved December 20, 2016, from http://gaining.educ.msu.edu/resources/files/Leinhardt1987Introduction.pdf

McClure, L., Woodham, L., & Borthwick, A. (2011). Using low threshold high ceiling tasks. Retrieved on September 15, 2016, from http://nrich.maths.org/7701

Project Zero. (2010). Research projects: Visible thinking. Harvard Graduate School of Education. Retrieved January 15, 2017, from www.pz.harvard.edu/resources/thinking-routines-visible-thinking

Ritchhart, R. (2002). *Intellectual character: What it is, why it matters, and how to get it.* San Francisco, CA: Jossey-Bass.

Ritchhart, R., Palmer, P., Church, M., & Tishman, S. (2006). Thinking routines: Establishing patterns of thinking in the classroom. Paper presented at American Educational Research Association, San Francisco, April.

Rowan, T.E., & Robles, J. (1998). Using questions to help children build mathematical power. *Teaching Children Mathematics, 4*(9), 504–509.

Small, M. (2009). *Good questions. Great ways to differentiate mathematics instruction.* New York; Reston, VA: Teachers College Press; NCTM.

Stein, M.K., & Lane, S. (1996). Instructional tasks and the development of student capacity to think and reason: An analysis of the relationship between teaching and learning in a reform mathematics project. *Educational Research and Evaluation, 2*(1), 50–80.

Stein, M.K., Smith, M.S., Henningsen, M.A., & Silver, E.A. (2000). *Implementing standards-based mathematics instruction: A casebook for professional development.* New York: Teachers College Press, Columbia University.

3

Creating a Community of Public Mathematicians

Never say anything a kid can say! This one goal keeps me focused. Although I do not think that I have ever met this goal completely in any one day or even in a given class period, it has forced me to develop and improve my questioning skills. It also sends a message to students that their participation is essential. Every time I am tempted to tell students something, I try to ask a question instead.

—(Reinhart, 2000, p. 480)

It is the teacher's role to create an environment that is friendly, supportive, and thoughtful for all students. Mistakes should be normed. Risk-taking should be an everyday affair. "Being stuck" should be familiar. Students have to be taught how to respect each other and work well together. This takes practice. I spend time role playing what happens when people get stuck, when they say the wrong answer, when they need help. This is the glue that holds learning together in your classroom. This is what makes progress possible. In the beginning teachers should do mini-lessons about talk in the classroom so that students know how to act and be during the routines and during learning in general (see Research Notes below).

RESEARCH NOTE

"Students need access to a pedagogy that helps them link new knowledge with prior knowledge" that interests them and takes them forward (Sánchez, 2010, p. 20).

RESEARCH NOTE

Student engagement is highly correlated to student achievement (Seidlitz & Perryman 2011, p. 24).

Daily routines are framed around the belief that when students are working with each other, communicating their thoughts, listening to each other, and truly trying to reason together, they learn more than if they were doing this on their own. The research shows that when students are paying attention and focus on a task, learning increases (Schmoker, 2006; Bickel and Bickel, 1986). Daily Math Thinking Routines provide "complex, hands-on learning experiences in low-threat/high-challenge context, as well as opportunities for active processing." They are responsive to students' needs, bridging the gap between what they know and what they need to know. Math routines should stimulate dialogue about learning and reflection. Math routines should also "nurture students' thinking dispositions" (Ritchhart, Hadar, & Turner, 2008, abstract). There is a great deal of research supporting the idea that thinking should be developed throughout the year and fostered with intentional activities so that students can share their thinking and make it visible for all to see and hear about (Ritchhart et al., 2008; Ritchart, Palmer, Church, & Tishman, 2006; Ritchhart & Perkins, 2000).

Introducing the Routines to Students

I really think it is important to have visual anchor charts that scaffold student thinking and speaking. It is one thing to have information on a chart, but another to have it organized in such a way that students have access to it through visual mapping. Figures 3.1-3.8 provide some examples of what this looks like.

Figure 3.1 Why Do Daily Routines?

Why Do We Do Daily Math Thinking Routines?

We do routines to get better at math. When we think about math daily, we build our math muscle. Our brain actually grows!
When: Daily
How: By working with each other on different math problems. By getting stuck and unstuck. By helping each other.

Figure 3.2 What Is In Daily Routines?

What Do We Do in Daily Math Thinking Routines?

We think out loud!
We share our ideas in partners and groups.
We talk about our strategies.
We show our models.
We rethink our ideas.
We change our minds.
We become competent, confident, flexible mathematicians!

Teaching Students How To Talk with Each Other

It is really important that students know how to have a discussion with each other. These are all skills that have to be taught and reinforced throughout the year. This means teaching students how to interact with each other's ideas and to talk about one another's ideas, not about each other. They need what Lucy Calkins calls "the language of engagement" to share their own ideas and to learn to respond to those of others in helpful ways. In our daily endeavors, we must "strive to make thinking valued, visible and actively promoted" (Project Zero, n.d.).

Seidlitz & Perryman (2011) maintain that "asking students to talk with each other using specific language about a clearly defined topic is called a structured conversation." Structured conversations provide a scaffold for student thinking and then communication of that thinking. They argue that when we are explicit with students about the ways they should be interacting and speaking with each other, they can better focus, stay on task, and delve deeper into the topic. One specific strategy that they discuss is called QSSSA (Question, Signal, Stem, Share, Assess). In this strategy, the teacher asks a question, the students give some sort of signal that they have thought about and know the answer (such as standing or raising their hand), and then when everyone is ready, they share with their partner but use a specific sentence stem. Then, after students have shared with a partner or a group, the class comes back together and some people share out and assess their thinking (Seidlitz & Perryman, 2011, p. 43).

For example:

(Question) Teacher names three numbers that round to 50, and asks students to explain why.

(Signal) Students think and then signal by standing that they have an answer.

(Students use Stems to Share Thinking) Justine says that "*There are several numbers that round to 50. One of them is 49. This rounds to 50 because it is only 1 away from 50. If we are rounding to the nearest ten, 49 would work.*" Mike says, "*There are several numbers that round to 50. One of them is 47. This rounds to 50 because it is only 3 away from 50. It is closer to 50 than 40.*"

(Assess) Teacher randomly picks students to hear their thinking and assess if they understand.

The posters in Figures 3.3–3.8 are to foster student talk in the classroom and to remind students to engage in civil discourse. These types of anchor charts provide a framework for student verbal and nonverbal interaction. I suggest that these are kept up throughout the year.

Figure 3.3 Talk with Each Other Respectfully

Words We Use to Talk with Each Other Respectfully				
Agree	Disagree Agreeably	Clarifying Questions	Thoughts and Connections	Comments to Explain Your Thinking and Justify Your Answers
I did it a similar way. I got the same answer. I agree with _____ because _____. My strategy was like yours. My model was like yours. I was thinking the same way. I want to piggyback on _____. I want to add _____.	I got a different answer. I don't agree with that answer. I disagree with _____ because _____. My strategy was different because _____. My model was different because _____. I thought this because _____. I kind of agree. I'm not sure if that is right.	Can you model that for me? Can you talk some more about your strategy? Can you explain it another way? Can you say that again? Can you give me another example? How do you know you are right? What do you mean by _____? I have a question about _____. What do you think? Why did you _____? How did you _____? Could you tell me more?	It looks to me like _____. I was thinking _____. In my opinion _____. I was wondering _____. I still don't understand. I need to see another way. I don't understand that answer. This reminds me of _____. I know this because _____.	I used this model. I used this strategy. I can prove it because _____.

Figure 3.4 Math Talk

Math Talk Moves					
Wait Time (private think time)	**Repeating (say what they said)**	**Revoicing (summarize, put in your own words)**	**Reasoning (think about what they said)**	**Adding On (connect to thoughts and ideas of others)**	**Revising Your Thinking (change your mind)**
		So, you are saying ...			
Give everyone time to think.	So you think ____. So you are saying ____.	So what you are saying is that ____. So you think that ____.	I agree. I disagree because ____.	I would like to add ____. I would like to piggyback ____.	I used to think ____. But now I think ____. I changed my mind. I am going to change my answer.

Adapted from Chapin, O'Connor, & Anderson (2009)

Figure 3.5 Partner Poster: Example 1

Partner Work		
Looks Like	**Sounds Like**	**Feels Like**
Both partners looking at each other

Partners facing each other / one might lean forward

Show they are listening by nodding and agreeing (even quick verbal agreement)

Making eye contact

Might be looking at notes or taking notes

Taking turns talking | Both partners talking to each other in low voices

Talking about the math they are doing

Responding to each other

Being helpful

Comparing and connecting what they both did | Good

Respectful

It's OK to take risks |

Figure 3.6 Partner Poster: Example 2

Adapted from Teacher Stuff: https://itsmyblogyall.wordpress.com/2012/10/14/teacher-stuff-dual-language/

Figure 3.7 Group Poster

Group Work		
Looks Like	**Sounds Like**	**Feels Like**
Everybody is paying attention Everyone is looking at the speaker Everyone is following along with the conversation One person is speaking at a time Some people might be taking notes or looking at their notes	One person is speaking at a time Each group is speaking in a low voice that only their group can hear Everyone is participating in the conversation by making clarifying statements or asking questions Students are taking turns to talk; everybody should get a chance Comparing and connecting what you both did	Good Respected Like it is OK to share our thinking even if we are not sure Sticking with it – even if it is tricky

Reflection Notes: Are you fully listening? Is everyone using the talk moves: repeating, rephrasing, wait time, piggybacking, and translating? Are mistakes being used as building blocks? The focus is on always helping each other get to the next level!

Figure 3.8 Super Participants

Be a Super Participant	
Look at the speaker	
Listen to the speaker	
Contribute to the conversation by asking questions or making statements	I was thinking ____. I showed my work this way ____. Could you draw a model to show me?
Maybe take notes or refer to your notes during the conversations	
Always be really respectful and helpful	I think you could ____. I don't understand what you mean.

Getting Stuck and Sticking with It

This is more than a conversation. It's a routine in and of itself. By routine, I mean that it is something you talk about explicitly with the students throughout the school year. The National Research Council (2001) states that having a productive disposition is one of the five elements of mathematical proficiency. There are so many resources out there to read now about developing a positive disposition or mindset. Teachers are launching lessons with books, poems, songs, videos, discussions, and more (see below).

Here are a few of my favorite resources:		
With math I can	Jo Boaler	Dr. Nicki's Pinterest Growth Mindset Board
https://www.amazon.com/gp/withmathican	https://www.youcubed.org/mathematical-mindsets/	https://www.pinterest.com/drnicki7/growth-mindsetperseverance/

Answering

There are a variety of ways that students can participate in the Daily Math Thinking Routines (see Figure 3.12). Teachers should use all these formats throughout the week. What is important is to find ways where everyone has an opportunity to participate – sometimes out loud as a public mathematician and other times with a partner or in a small-group discussion. Researchers have found that randomized questioning (using popsicle sticks or name cards) and using rotations (such as Kagan's [1992] numbered heads structure) can improve active student engagement, attentiveness, and even achievement (McDougall & Cordeiro, 1993).

Formats for Student Responses	
Volunteers	Students volunteer to answer. Although this can be used sometimes, Seidlitz & Perryman (2011) point out that students can get relaxed and uninvolved if the response system is all volunteer based. When we use random selection and cooperative structures like numbered heads or jigsaw, students attend to the conversation in a different way. Everybody is on high alert and ready to participate if they do not know who is going to be called on.
Random Select	The teacher randomly selects a student to answer. Teachers use index cards or popsicle sticks with each student's name and randomly choose students by pulling these items from a jar. Then the cards or sticks for students who have been called are placed in a different jar until everyone has had a turn. This can also be done electronically these days – for example, using: Random Name Picker (www.miniwebtool.com/random-name-picker/); Random Name Generator Tool (www.superteachertools.us/instantclassroom/random-name-generator.php#.WIgtDGQrJR1); or the Who's Next app.
Paired Response	A partner pair can respond together.
Turn and Talk	Students turn and talk with their neighbor. (Whoever wants to can then talk. Not everyone shares out.)
Choral Response	The class answers in unison.
Individual Pupil Response	Everyone answers with either their fingers, a response card, their white board, or in some other way.
Small Group Discussion	Students talk in a small group about their thinking.

Teaching Students to Evaluate their Conversations

It is just as important to get students to reflect on their conversations as it is to get them to have a conversation. Teachers should teach students how to evaluate their own work, their work with partners, and their group work. This can be done through making and then referring to rubrics as students engage with each other (see Figures 3.9-3.11).

Figure 3.9 Individual Reflection Checklist

Thinking about My Partner Work	
	How did I do?
	I turned to my partner.
	I looked at my partner.
	I listened to my partner.
	I asked a question or made a comment.
	My partner shared their thinking and their work.
	I talked. I shared my thinking and my work.

Figure 3.10 Partner Talk

Partner Talk Rubric				
0	**1**	**2**	**3**	**4**
Nobody said anything.	One person talked. Then we just sat and looked at each other.	I talked. My partner talked too. We listened to each other.	I talked and showed my work. My partner talked and showed their work. We talked some more. We compared our thinking.	I talked. My partner talked. We both talked some more and showed our work. We shared our models and our strategies. We thought of some new ideas.

Adapted from Marie Mounteer

Figure 3.11 Class Talk

Reflecting on Our Class Discussions						
Criteria	Day 1	Day 2	Day 3	Day 4	Day 5	Overall Week
We all 👀 watched the speaker.						
We all 👂 listened to the speaker.						
Everybody participated in a helpful way using our math words.						
We shared our thinking with words, numbers, tools, sketches, and diagrams. $3 \times 3 = 9$						
We asked questions about the work when we were confused. ???????????						
We gave ourselves permission to rethink our thinking.						
We made mistakes and learned from them. $6 \times 5 = 25$ $5 \times 5 = 25$						
Scores	4 – We rocked. We did it a lot. 3 – We were good. We did it often. 2 – We need to work on it. 1 – We need to make a plan on how to get better. We are not there yet.					

Inspired by https://litlearnact.wordpress.com/2014/03/12/accountable-talk-fuels-book-discussions/

Display of Student Thinking

Getting student thinking down is a skill. Teachers have to know how to follow and record precisely what students are saying so that others can follow their thinking. So it isn't random notations; it is precise recording. Sometimes teachers are tempted to hijack the student's language and thoughts, BUT never do this. Write exactly what the student is saying, and if you want to add, clarify, or question, you must actually do that and then ask permission to change anything. You must honor the thinking by accurately recording the thoughts.

Figure 3.12 Showing Student Thinking

Capturing and Recording Student Thinking				
Recording on the Interactive Board	**Recording on Chart Paper**	**Recording on Chart Paper** (Group response that is used in a "walk and talk" around the room. Sticky note comments from others are expected to be added to this.)	**Recording in Student Journals**	**Recording on a Recording Sheet** True or False What do you think? Why?
The benefit of this is that you can pull down all sorts of interactive tools (number lines, number frames, fraction and decimal bars, place value bars, etc.). The challenge is that unless you take a picture, when you take it down, it is gone.	The benefit is that you have a permanent record of what has been said when, where, and how. You can track learning and refer back to past conversations. However, the paper load can be too much.	This is a great way to get thinking down. The students work in small groups and record their thinking. The posters are then displayed around the room and everyone goes and visits them (in an orderly fashion) and comments on them with Post-its.	This is another great way to have a record of student thinking that students can refer back to over time. They simply date it and describe what they were doing.	This is yet another way to get the information down so that we can look at it, talk about it, and reflect on it.

There are different ways to capture and record student thinking. You should rotate the different methods (see Figure 3.12). They all have value.

Individual Pupil Response Systems

There are a variety of ways for students to respond. There is an extensive amount of research on the benefits of individual pupil response systems (Griffin & Ryan, 2016; Cooper & Robinson, 2000; Lambert, Cartledge, Heward, & Lo, 2006; Jerome & Barbetta, 2005). The research indicates that when all students are involved in the conversations through active participation systems, then motivation, engagement, student knowledge, and achievement increase (Lambert et al., 2006; Whitney, Cooper, & Lingo, 2015). Teachers should indicate different ways to respond throughout the week. The particular way depends on what the question is. There are written response signals, ready response signals, making choices signals, and self-evaluation signals (Seidlitz & Perryman, 2011; Marzano, 2004; Marzano, Pickering, & Pollock, 2001) (see below).

	Ways to Check for Understanding	
	Methods	**Explanation**
Written Responses	Mini white boards	Students write their answers on their mini white boards and then hold them up.

Ready Responses	Pencils up/pencils down	Students hold up their pencils if they are ready, and if they are still working, their pencils are still in use.
	Hands up/hands down	Students hold up their hands when they are ready, and if they are still working, their hands are down (doing the work).
	Envelope response	Students write on their response sheets: true or false, numbers, or letters.
Making Choices	Thumbs up	Students hold up their thumbs to indicate they have an answer. Often it is more detailed, with students holding their thumbs up or down, or sideways if they're not sure.
	True/false	Students hold up true or false cards to record their answers.
	Think, write, pair, share	Students turn and talk with their partners. They are responsible for sharing their thinking in such a way that partners can explain what they said.
	Answer sticks	Students show specific numbers to respond. Letters or numbers are on a ring or board so students can hold them up to respond.
	Number fans	Students show a specific number to respond.
	Yes/no cards	Students hold up these cards to indicate their response.
Self-Evaluation	Five fingers	Students use their fingers to represent their levels of understanding, usually with 1 being little understanding and 5 being a high level of understanding.
	Thumbs up/thumbs down	Students use their thumbs to show that they get it, kind of get it, or don't get it yet.
	Number rings/fans/cards	Students use these to indicate their level of understanding: For example: 1 – I get it/a green card 2 – I kind of get it/a yellow card 3 – I don't get it yet/an orange card

Key Points

- "Never say anything a kid can say!"
- Norm mistakes
- "Nurture thinking dispositions"
- Introduce the routines one by one
- Establish norms
- Teach "math talk"
- Discuss "language of engagement"
- Teach partner, small-group, and whole-group norms
- Teach students to reflect on their conversations
- Create different formats for student responses
- Display student thinking
- Have a variety of ways to check for understanding

Summary

Collaborative conversations are the bedrock of Daily Math Thinking Routines. Students must learn how to speak and listen to each other. They must be public mathematicians who will take risks, embrace mistakes, and learn to stick with it until they get it. Teachers must use a variety of formats for sharing responses, reflecting on thinking, and displaying thinking. Daily Math Thinking Routines give them a launch pad to engage in rigorous, standards-based, engaging conversations. Through these Daily Math Thinking Routines, we have a tremendous opportunity to "nurture thinking dispositions."

Questions for Reflection

1. In what ways do you currently "nurture thinking dispositions"?
2. Can your students describe and use the various talk moves that should occur in a discussion?
3. How well do your students work in partners, in small groups, and in the whole group?
4. How often do you give your students the opportunity to reflect on their participation?
5. What are different ways that you check for understanding?

References

Bickel, W.E., & Bickel, D.D. (1986). Effective schools, classrooms, and instruction: Implications for special education. *Exceptional Children, 52*(6), 489–500.

Chapin, S.H., O'Connor, M.C., & Anderson, N.C. (2009). *Classroom discussions: Using math talk to help students learn, grades K–6*. Sausalito, CA: Math Solutions.

Cooper, J.L., & Robinson, P. (2000). The argument for making large classes seem small. In J.L. Cooper & P. Robinson (Eds.), *New directions for teaching and learning: Energizing the large classroom* (pp. 5–16). San Francisco, CA: Jossey-Bass.

Griffin, C., & Ryan, M. (2016). Active student responding: Supporting student learning and engagement. *In Touch*, May. Retrieved January 25, 2017, from www.into.ie/ROI/Publications/InTouch/FullLengthArticles/Fulllengtharticles2016/ActiveStudentResponding_InTouchMay2016.pdf

Jerome, A., & Barbetta, P.M. (2005). The effect of active student responding in computer-assisted instruction on social studies learning by students with learning disabilities. *Journal of Special Education Technology, 20*(2), 13–23.

Kagan, S. (1992). *Cooperative learning*. San Juan Capistrano, CA. Kagan Cooperative Learning.

Lambert, M.C., Cartledge, G., Heward, W.L., & Lo, Y. (2006). Effects of response cards on disruptive behavior and academic responding during math lessons by fourth-grade urban students. *Journal of Positive Behavior Interventions, 8*(2), 88–99.

McDougall, D., & Cordeiro, P. (1993). Effects of random questioning expectations on education major's preparedness for lecture and discussion. *College Student Journal, 26*(2), 193–198.

Marzano, R.J. (2004). *Building background knowledge for academic achievement: Research on what works in schools*. Alexandria, VA: Association for Supervision and Curriculum Development.

Marzano, R., Pickering, D., & Pollock, J. (2001). *Classroom instruction that works: Research-based strategies for increasing student achievement*. Alexandria, VA: Association for Supervision and Curriculum Development.

National Research Council. (2001). *Adding it up: Helping children learn mathematics*. Washington, DC: The National Academies Press.

Project Zero. (n.d.). Ron Ritchhart. Retrieved on December 1, 2017, from www.pz.harvard.edu/who-we-are/people/ron-ritchhart

Reinhart, S. (2000). Never say anything a kid can say! *Mathematics Teaching in the Middle School, 5*(8), 478–483.

Ritchhart, R., & Perkins, D.N. (2000). Life in the mindful classroom: Nurturing the disposition of mindfulness. *Journal of Social Issues, 56*(1), 27–47.

Ritchhart, R., Palmer, P., Church, M., & Tishman, S. (2006). Thinking routines: Establishing patterns of thinking in the classroom. Paper presented at American Educational Research Association, San Francisco, April.

Ritchhart, R., Hadar, L., & Turner, T. (2008). Uncovering students' thinking about thinking using concept maps. Paper presented at American Educational Research Association, New York, March.

Sánchez, F. (2010). *Interactive classroom strategies and structures for success: Focus on English learners*. Retrieved December 15, 2016, from https://www.csustan.edu/sites/default/files/SAIL/documents/InteractiveClassroomStrategiesandStructuresforSuccess-Dr.FranciscaSanchez.pdf

Schmoker, M. (2006). *Results now*. Alexandria, VA: Association for Supervision and Curriculum Development.

Seidlitz, J., & Perryman, B. (2011). *7 Steps to a language-rich interactive classroom: Research-based strategies for engaging all students*. San Clememte, CA: Seidlitz Education.

Whitney, T., Cooper, J.T., & Lingo, A.S. (2015). Providing student opportunities to respond in reading and mathematics: A look across grade levels. *Preventing School Failure: Alternative Education for Children and Youth, 59*(1), 14–21.

4

The Art and Science of Questioning to Build Student Thinking During Daily Math Routines

There is a fine line between a question that encourages the student to think and one that provides the student with too much information or inadvertently solves the problem for the student. Being able to straddle this fine line comes with reflective practice.

—(Ontario Ministry of Education, 2006, p. 32)

Classroom Vignette

Mr. Marcus: OK, today we are going to play *Guess My Number*. Remember that you are going to try to find the number by asking place value questions.

Figure 4.1

1	2	3	4	5	6	7	8	9	10
11	12	13	14	15	16	17	18	19	20
21	22	23	24	25	26	27	28	29	30
31	32	33	34	35	36	37	38	39	40
41	42	43	44	45	46	47	48	49	50
51	52	53	54	55	56	57	58	59	60
61	62	63	64	65	66	67	68	69	70
71	72	73	74	75	76	77	78	79	80
81	82	83	84	85	86	87	88	89	90
91	92	93	94	95	96	97	98	99	100
101	102	103	104	105	106	107	108	109	110
111	112	113	114	115	116	117	118	119	120

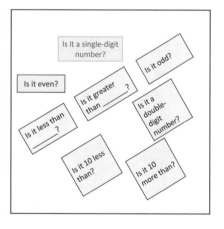

It's Kelly's turn to come up and either pick a number from the number jar or make up a number. She makes one up, writes it down, and shows it to Mr. Marcus.

Mr. Marcus: Who wants to start?
Timothy: Is it even?
Kelly: No.
Mike: Is it less than 50?
Kelly: No.
Tami: Is it greater than 80?
Kelly: Yes.
Maribel: Is it odd?
Kelly: Yes.
Mr. Marcus: So let's review what we know.
Taylor: We know it is odd and greater than 80.
Tiffany: Is it less than 100?
Kelly: No.
Mr. Marcus: OK, now we know that we are only looking at odd numbers greater than 100. Think about what kind of question can focus our range.
Clark: Is it greater than 109?
Kelly: No.
Marcos: Is it greater than 102?
Kelly: No.
Yasmin: It's 101, because that's the odd number that is in between 100 and 102.
Mr. Marcus: Class do you agree?

1	2	3	4	5	6	7	8	9	10
11	12	13	14	15	16	17	18	19	20
21	22	23	24	25	26	27	28	29	30
31	32	33	34	35	36	37	38	39	40
41	42	43	44	45	46	47	48	49	50
51	52	53	54	55	56	57	58	59	60
61	62	63	64	65	66	67	68	69	70
71	72	73	74	75	76	77	78	79	80
81	82	83	84	85	86	87	88	89	90
91	92	93	94	95	96	97	98	99	100
101	102	103	104	105	106	107	108	109	110
111	112	113	114	115	116	117	118	119	120

Most of the class says yes. Tiffany says she needs a minute to think about it. After a few minutes and a quick conversation with her math partner, she agrees. Kelly verifies that that was her number.

Questioning

The role of the teacher during the Daily Math Thinking Routines is to use a variety of questions to move through the routine (see Classroom Vignette and Figure 4.1). We want to know what students know, what they don't know, what they are confused about, what they kind of know. We ask questions to promote higher-level thinking. Our questions should be thoroughly planned so they are open-ended, thought-provoking, and scaffolded. They should "engage and guide students' thinking to deeper levels." They should allow students to see the math in a different way. They should push students to the edge of their reasoning. We want to have a low-stress, low-anxiety, risk-friendly, intellectually engaging learning environment.

> ### 🔍 RESEARCH NOTE
>
> "The teacher's skillful questioning plays a vital role in this context, helping students to identify thinking processes, to see the connections between ideas and to build new understanding as they work their way to a solution that makes sense to them."
> (Ontario Ministry of Education, 2011, p. 1)

Different questions do different things. Some questions are aimed at recall of facts or procedures, whereas others are aimed at problem solving or concept development. Questions can provoke student thinking, deepen conceptual understanding, lead to procedural fluency, and get students to reason and to reflect on their thinking. Manouchehri & Lapp note that

> In a general sense, teachers' questions control students' learning because they focus students' attention on specific features of the concepts that they explore in class. Moreover, these questions

establish and validate students' perceptions about what is important to know to succeed in mathematics class.

(2003, pp. 563–564)

The Importance of Wait Time

Rowe (1974) argues that it is important to give students wait time when they ask a question. We are all pretty good at that. She also says that once students answer a question, we should put the answer back out there and have students think about it some more in relation to what they did and then talk about that. Most of us could work on that part. It is important for students to learn to respect the thinking time of others. We have to explicitly teach them how to let others process the math that we are doing. I encourage everyone to make a Private Think Time poster and then require students to abide by those guidelines (see Figure 4.2). Let people think. That means don't raise your hand to give the answer, to shout out; don't sigh and make gestures showing that you are impatient. Just wait. Wait respectfully.

As teachers, we control this. We either create an environment where this is the norm or we do not. When students are thinking, I often go to another question with another student and I say I'm going to come back. I do go back. And if they are stuck, I don't give them the answer or ask anyone else to. I scaffold. I encourage them to use a tool, to think of a strategy or a way to model it. This means that everyone has toolkits, strategy maps, and thinking spaces.

Figure 4.2 Private Think Time Poster

Private Think Time

It means we wait.	We let them think about what they will use.
We let everyone gather his or her thoughts.	We are respectful of each other's thinking! We work together and learn from each other! It takes teamwork to make the dream work! We got this together.

The Question Crossroads

Whenever an answer is given, teachers come to a crossroads. Here is a visual map of what that looks like (see Figure 4.3).

When students know the answer, we can go to the next question or probe more. You can probe the level of understanding around that answer or move on and make more connections to that answer.

Figure 4.3 Visual Map of Answers

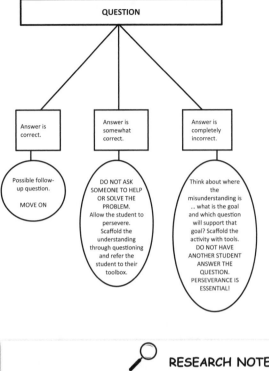

🔍 RESEARCH NOTE

"Using questions and prompts to cause children to make sense of, reason about, predict from, solve and apply mathematics is a powerful teaching strategy and may be the key to fostering self-reliance and success."

(Rowan & Robles, 1998, p. 504)

If the student gets the question wrong, the teacher should scaffold some more so that the student who has the question can answer it. Never snatch the question from the student and give it to someone else. We are trying to build perseverance, and you can't do that by taking a question from one student and passing it to another because this sends the opposite message: "You don't have to persevere. You don't have to stick with it. Because the minute you don't know it, I am going to send someone in to save you." Instead, ask the student to continue to think about the question and refer them to their toolkit (the one everybody should have).

If they are still stuck, then suggest a tool. But as Dan Meyers warns us, don't over-scaffold. If you say, "Hey Mike, maybe you could try the ten frame," that is very different from saying, "Hey Mike, take out your ten frame, put 5 yellow counters on the top and 2 red counters on the bottom, and count them and tell me how many there are." In the first case you are scaffolding; in the second you are clearly over-scaffolding. The first suggestion is sufficient.

Questions that Unearth Error Patterns and Misconceptions

In order to ask really good questions, teachers must have thought about the error patterns and misunderstandings that students have around the topic (see "Types of Error" chart, below). Questions should promote deeper thought and reflection. Questions should challenge students' thinking. Questions frame the math that we want students to engage with. Good questions help us to consider the big ideas and understandings. Good questions help to build and expand conceptual understanding and procedural knowledge. Good questions help students to reason out loud and think about the thinking of others.

Types of Error	
Ginsburg (1987) categorizes math errors as either slips or bugs	
Slip – careless error The student is going too fast or not paying attention to their work. Students can self-correct "slips."	**Bug – common error** There are a variety of math "bugs." These are the common errors that students make. There have been some excellent books written about common math errors (Ashlock, 2010; Spangler, 2010).
Conceptual Error Students don't understand the concept. For example, they don't understand that subtraction is to take away. They might not understand that fractions are part of a whole.	**Procedural Error** Procedural errors are computation errors such as ignoring the zeros when subtracting across zeros or adding denominators when adding fractions.
When thinking about the answers that students are giving, ask yourself: Is this a slip? Is this a bug? Is this a near-miss answer or a wild guess? (Sometimes students will give an answer that is near the answer, like saying 55 or 57 for 8×7). Do they know the answer but just can't verbalize their thinking? Do they know the answer but still don't really understand?	
As teachers become more familiar with which ideas are more complex for students and why, they are better able to ensure that their instruction is at the appropriate developmental level for students, and that it challenges students' mathematical conceptions in appropriate ways. This minimizes the likelihood of students developing mathematical misconceptions. (Small, 2009, p. 11)	

Questions Frame Daily Math Thinking Routines

Good questions don't just happen. We don't stumble upon them by talking. They are planned for. As we plan units of study, we should plan specific questions that will be asked throughout the unit. Specifically, we should plan what, when, where, and how we will ask engaging, informative, thinking questions. It is essential that we get better at planning power questions to move our pedagogy forward.

Questions are used throughout the routine to move it along. Before the routine, the questions set the students up for the math that they are about to do. During the routine, the questions push them forward, make them think, and encourage them to take risks. After the routine, the questions give students an opportunity to reflect on what they did. Students should reflect on both the activity itself and the math. See some sample questions in chart "Sample Questions: Before, During, and After the Routine".

Sample Questions: Before, During, and After the Routine		
BEFORE	**DURING**	**AFTER**
What can you do if you get stuck? How can your strategy mat help you? How can your model mat help you? What should you do when you're not sure?	How do you know that? Are you sure about that? Can you prove it? Can you give me an example? Does that make sense? Can you model that? How would you explain this to your friend who is stuck?	What was easy? What was tricky? Did you get stuck? What did you do when you got stuck? Did you have an "aha!" moment? What did you learn? Did you have an "ugh" moment?

BEFORE	DURING	AFTER
	Is there a pattern? What is it?/Why not?	Did you have an "uh-oh" moment?
	What can you do with what you have so far?	Are you still fuzzy about anything?
	Can we make this into an easier problem?	Which models did you use?
		Which strategies did you use?
		Did anyone get the same answer a different way?
		Did anyone get a different answer?
		Is there more than one way to do this?
		Is there a faster or easier way to do this?
Question Resources: http://mason.gmu.edu/~jsuh4/teaching/resources/questionsheet_color.pdf www.edu.gov.on.ca/eng/literacynumeracy/inspire/research/CBS_AskingEffectiveQuestions.pdf		

Toolkits

Tools help us to model our thinking. They are essential for all students. Many times teachers will tell me that "the students get it," but really they just get the how, not the why. Tools, when used appropriately and effectively, can help students to understand the why of math as well as the how. Therefore, all students should have access to math tools. Van de Walle (2007) says that they help to scaffold students' thinking. There are many types of tools, some store-bought, others handmade, and others digital. Different students will use different tools at different times. The chart "Tools for Students" lists some of the tools that students should have access to in their toolkits.

Tools for Students		
Concrete Tool	**Digital Tool**	**Templates**
Unifix Cubes	https://www.eduplace.com/cgi-bin/schtemplate.cgi?template=/kids/mw/manip/mn_popup.thtml&filename=connectingcubes&title=Connecting%20Cubes&grade=1	www.center.edu/BLACKLINES/001-061/028-032.pdf
Cuisenaire Rods	www.mathplayground.com/mathbars.html	1-inch centimeter paper https://www.hand2mind.com/pdf/gridpaper.pdf
1-inch tiles		1-inch paper www.math.kent.edu/~white/graphpaper/
Bears	www.glencoe.com/sites/common_assets/mathematics/ebook_assets/vmf/VMF-Interface.html (look under manipulatives)	

Continued

Tools for Students		
Concrete Tool	**Digital Tool**	**Templates**
Rekenreks	www.mathlearningcenter.org/web-apps/number-rack/	Rekenrek paper
Ten Frames	www.mathlearningcenter.org/web-apps/number-frames/	Five Frames/Ten Frames/Double Ten Frames https://sites.google.com/site/get2mathk5/home/templates-graphic-organizers
Base Ten Blocks	www.mathlearningcenter.org/web-apps/number-pieces/	http://lrt.ednet.ns.ca/PD/BLM/table_of_contents.htm
Beaded Number Line	http://mathsframe.co.uk/en/resources/resource/69/itp_beadstring	https://www.tes.com/teaching-resource/beaded-lines-0-30-6059835
Part-Part Whole Mat	http://lakeviewtcsd.weebly.com/glencoe-virtual-manipulative-work-mats.html	https://sites.google.com/site/get2mathk5/home/templates-graphic-organizers
Fraction Pattern Blocks	http://illuminations.nctm.org/activity.aspx?id=3577	https://www.eduplace.com/math/mthexp/g3/visual/pdf/vs_g3_47.pdf
Fraction Circles, Squares, Rectangles	www.glencoe.com/sites/common_assets/mathematics/ebook_assets/vmf/VMF-Interface.html (look under manipulatives)	http://domanmom.com/wp-content/uploads/2013/08/Fractions-Poster.pdf www.printable-math-worksheets.com/fraction-manipulatives.html
Fraction Bars	http://www.abcya.com/fraction_percent_decimal_tiles.htm www.mathplayground.com/Fraction_bars.html www.visualfractions.com/	www.printable-math-worksheets.com/fraction-manipulatives.html
Decimal Wheel		http://eworkshop.on.ca/edu/resources/guides/NSN_vol_6_Decimal_Numbers.pdf
Decimal Bars	www.abcya.com/fraction_percent_decimal_tiles.htm	http://theteacherscafe.com/decimal-percent-bars/
Decimal Number Line		http://fractionbars.com/CommonCore/Gd4Les/CCSShundthsNoLineGd4.pdf
Decimal Sliders	www.numeracyhelper.com/pvslider/	www.education.vic.gov.au/school/teachers/teachingresources/discipline/maths/continuum/Pages/numslide.aspx#example1
Decimal Grids	www.mhhe.com/math/ltbmath/bennett_nelson8e/VMK.html?initManip=decimalSquares	http://lrt.ednet.ns.ca/PD/BLM_Ess11/pdf_files/decimals/decimal_squares_sets.pdf
Geo boards	www.mathplayground.com/geoboard.html	

Tools for Students		
Concrete Tool	**Digital Tool**	**Templates**
Protractors	www.mathplayground.com/measuringangles.html www.amblesideprimary.com/ambleweb/mentalmaths/protractor.html	https://www.ece.k-state.edu/hkn/files/protractor.pdf http://sciencenotes.org/printable-protractors/
Variety of Tools	www.glencoe.com/sites/common_assets/mathematics/ebook_assets/vmf/VMF-Interface.html	http://lakeviewtcsd.weebly.com/glencoe-virtual-manipulative-work-mats.html www.mathematicalpractices.com/mp1e/content/printable-manipulatives/
Hundred Grid	www.abcya.com/interactive_100_number_chart.htm http://cwnumbergrid.herokuapp.com/	www.sparklebox.co.uk/maths/counting/100-squares.html#.WFSscWQrK8U
Hundredths Grid	https://my.hrw.com/math06_07/nsmedia/tools/Decimal_Fractions/Decimal_Fractions.swf	https://guidedmath.wordpress.com/2014/06/10/decimals-hundredths-grid/

 RESEARCH NOTE

Protocol For Math Thinking Routines

A. Keep them short, between 5 and 10 minutes.
B. Make sure that students have private think time.
C. Remind them to listen carefully and try to follow each other's thinking.
D. Encourage students to share their thinking out loud in a clear, organized manner so that everyone can follow their thinking.
E. Chart the thinking in a way that it can be saved and referred back to.
F. Record all answers in a neutral way. The teacher should not indicate whether or not answers are correct or incorrect.
G. Allow students to question each other.
H. Give students permission to rethink at all times.
I. Encourage double-checking of one's own thinking.
J. Use different formats:

- Students explain their own thinking
- Students explain each other's thinking
- Students share their thinking with a partner
- Students share their thinking in a small group

Key Points

- Questioning is key
- Wait time is crucial
- Private thinking time is essential
- Whoever has the question gets to answer it!

- Don't over-scaffold
- Have and use toolkits

Summary

Questioning shapes thinking. Students shape their thoughts around questions – the ones the teacher asks, the ones their classmates ask, and most importantly the ones they learn to ask themselves. Teachers must use wait time strategically, waiting not only while students think *of* the answer but also after the answer has been given so that the student can think *about* the answer. Students must learn to respect each other's private think time so that everyone can process the problems. When a student is stuck, it is important not to give up on them and let somebody else answer. Everybody should answer whatever question they have been asked. When students are stuck, it is important that teachers scaffold their thinking; however it is essential not to over-scaffold. Every student should have access to their own toolkit so that they can use it to scaffold their thinking.

Questions for Reflection

1. How do you use private think time in your classroom?
2. What do you do when students are stuck?
3. Does everyone have a math toolkit?

References

Ashlock, R. (2010). *Error patterns in computation: Using error patterns to improve instruction* (10th ed.) Columbus, OH: Pearson.

Ginsburg, H.P. (1987). How to assess number facts, calculation, and understanding. In D.D. Hammill (Ed.), *Assessing the abilities and instructional needs of students* (pp. 483–503). Austin, TX: PRO-ED.

Manouchehri, A., & Lapp, D.A. (2003). Unveiling student understanding: The role of questioning in instruction. *Mathematics Teacher, 96*(8), 562–566. Retrieved September 30, 2016, from http://helmut.knaust.info/class/201420_4303/Manouchehi_2003.pdf

Ontario Ministry of Education. (2006). *A guide to effective literacy instruction, Grades 4 to 6 – Volume 1.* Toronto: Queen's Printer for Ontario.

Ontario Ministry of Education. (2011). *Asking effective questions: Provoking student thinking/deepening conceptual understanding in the mathematics classroom.* Capacity Building Series, Special Edition No. 21. Retrieved on December 1, 2017, from www.edu.gov.on.ca/eng/literacynumeracy/inspire/research/CBS_AskingEffectiveQuestions.pdf

Rowan, T.E., & Robles, J. (1998). Using questions to help children build mathematical power. *Teaching Children Mathematics, 4*(9), 504–509.

Rowe, M.B. (1974). Pausing phenomena: Influence on the quality of instruction. *Journal of Psycholinguistic Research, 3*(3), 203–223.

Small, M. (2009). *Making math meaningful to Canadian students, K–8.* Toronto: Nelson Education.

Spangler, D.B. (2010). *Strategies for teaching whole number computations: Using error analysis for interventions and assessment.* Thousand Oaks, CA: Corwin.

Van de Walle, J.A. (2007). *Elementary and middle school mathematics: Teaching developmentally.* Boston: Pearson/Allyn and Bacon.

Part II

Daily Math Thinking Routines

5

Rotating Routines

It is the distributed practice across the year that builds mathematical confidence, conceptual understanding, procedural fluency, adaptive reasoning and strategic competence.

—Author

When students work with numbers every day in various ways, they become familiar, unafraid, confident, and thoughtful about the way they work. They learn not only to clearly communicate their thinking but also to listen intentionally to the thinking of others. It's a way of being that comes with time. It's a planned process. It doesn't just happen. Through a teacher's careful attention to the educational needs of students, the emotional responses that they show, and the affective cultural climate of the entire class, a whole world of learning can be constructed. The research tells us that the four biggest influences on a productive disposition, which directly shapes student learning, are: 1) past and present experiences; 2) teachers; 3) parents; and 4) culture (school and outside) (Koechler & Grouwns, 1988; Mutai, 2010). Daily Math Thinking Routines provide experiences, and the teacher and student responses inform dispositions. We have to make it all work together so our students can succeed. Here are a set of 20 daily routines that should be alternated throughout the year:

1. *Always, Sometimes, Never*
2. *Convince Me/Prove It*
3. *Disappearing Dan*
4. *Find and Fix The Error*
5. *Guess My Number*
6. *How Many More/Less To …?*
7. *Describe That Pattern*
8. *Input/Output Tables*
9. *It Is/It Isn't*
10. *I was walking down the street …*
11. *Model That!*
12. *Number Line It!*
13. *Riddle Me This!*
14. *3 Truths and a Fib*
15. *True or False?*
16. *What Doesn't Belong?*
17. *What's Missing?*
18. *Why Is It Not…?*
19. *Yes, But Why?*
20. *Count Around the Room*

Routine #1
Always, sometimes, Never

The *Always, Sometimes, Never* Routine	
The *Always, Sometimes, Never* routine makes students think about the generalizability of mathematical ideas. In this routine, they have to decide whether or not the idea is always, sometimes, or never true.	
Materials and Tools	**"I Can" Statement**
Students should have a variety of tools to think and reason about the numbers being discussed. They should use their toolkits. Students can use manipulatives, drawings, and mental math.	**I can** reason about numbers and explain and justify my thinking. I can listen to, understand, and respond to the thinking of others and decide whether or not their reasoning makes sense. I can explain why some math statements are always true, some statements are sometimes true, and other statements are never true.

Protocol	Purpose:
Overview: The teacher puts some mathematical concept on the board, and the students have to decide whether it is always, sometimes, or never true.	• Reason • Generalize math concepts • Defend thinking

Protocol

Overview: The teacher puts some mathematical concept on the board, and the students have to decide whether it is always, sometimes, or never true.

1. The teacher puts a mathematical concept on the board.
2. The teacher tells the students to take "private think time" to think about the concept.
3. After about 30 seconds, the teacher tells the students to "turn and talk to a neighbor."
4. Everyone comes back together, and students raise their hands and explain their thinking.

Purpose:

- Reason
- Generalize math concepts
- Defend thinking

Questions:

- Is this always, sometimes, or never true?
- How do you know that?
- Are you sure about that?
- Can you prove it?
- Can you give me an example?

What's the Math?

Always, Sometimes, Never should require students at different levels to explore:

Kindergarten
- Adding and subtracting
- Comparing two- and three-dimensional shapes
- Comparing measurable heights
- Decomposing numbers 2–20

First Grade
- Adding and subtracting
- Using properties of addition
- Using the inverse relationship between addition and subtraction
- Comparing two-digit numbers
- Measuring length of objects
- Partitioning circles and rectangles into two and four equal shares

Second Grade
- Even and odd
- Adding and subtracting
- Using properties of addition
- Doubling and halving
- Skip counting
- Comparing numbers

Third Grade
- Even and odd
- Doubling and halving
- Adding and subtracting
- Multiplying and dividing
- Using the inverse relationship between multiplication and division
- Using properties of addition and multiplication
- Rounding to the nearest 10 or 100

Fourth Grade
- Adding and subtracting, including fractions and decimals
- Multiplying and dividing, including fractions by whole numbers
- Multiples and factors
- Prime and composite
- Discussing attributes of quadrilaterals
- Equivalent fractions and decimals

Fifth Grade
- Prime and composite
- Multiples and factors
- Adding and subtracting, including fractions and decimals
- Multiplying and dividing, including fractions and decimals
- Attributes of quadrilaterals
- Equivalent fractions and decimals

Continued

- Attributes of quadrilaterals
- Equivalence of whole numbers written as fractions
- Equivalent fractions
- Comparing fractions can only occur when fractions refer to same whole
- Perimeter and area

- Comparing fractions and decimals
- Perimeter and area

- Comparing fractions and decimals
- Perimeter and area
- Volume

Classroom Vignette: **Always, Sometimes, Never**

Mr. Ted: Good morning class. Today for our routine we are going to do *Always, Sometimes, Never.*

The first statement is this:

Any time I add two numbers together, the sum gets bigger than the two numbers I added.

Kelly: Always.

Jennifer: Always.

Mr. Ted: Please explain and give examples.

Cliff: It gets bigger because adding is putting together. Like if you put together 4 and 4, you get 8. It is bigger.

Kenya is shaking her head yes.

Mr. Ted: Kenya, I see you agree. Can you give another example?

Kenya: Yes. If I add 5 and 5, I get 10. That's bigger.

Mr. Ted: OK, take out a tool and talk about it with your shoulder buddy. Remember the question is: Is this always, sometimes, or never true? So far we think it is always true. Does anybody think it is never true?

Mikey yells out that it's always true, and Mr. Ted looks at him with a caring smile.

Mr. Ted: Thank you for sharing. I appreciate your enthusiasm Mikey. Please remember to use your inside voice. OK right, now talk it out with your shoulder buddy and I'm going to come and listen. Remember to try different numbers on your number grid.

The children work together, and Mr. Ted chats with pairs and pushes thinking. He notices that Carla is working on adding 0.

Mr. Ted: Carla what are you exploring?

Carla: I'm thinking about what happens when I add 0. When I add 0 to 5, I still have 5. And that's not a bigger number. The number stays the same?? [*in a somewhat unsure voice*].

Mr. Ted: That's an interesting observation. When we come back to group, be sure to share that finding.

The children return to the whole group with several examples. Carla shares her finding and they discuss it. They decide that the statement is sometimes true.

Always, Sometimes, Never – Kindergarten	
Beginning of the Year	**End of the Year**
Counting and Cardinality; Operations and Algebraic Thinking • When you write your numbers, you always start at the top. • When counting objects, the last number you say is the total number of objects. • When you count by 10's, the answer has a zero in the ones place if you start at 10. • 5 is greater than 3. • 4 is less than 2. • The only way to break apart 5 is with a 4 and a 1. • Circles have straight sides. **Geometry** • Triangles have sides that are all the same length.	**Operations and Algebraic Thinking** • When you add 0 to a number, the answer is the same number you started with. • When you take away 0 from a number, the answer is the same number you started with. • When you add 1 to a number, the answer is the next counting number. • The only way to break apart 14 is to use a 10 and a 4. • Addition can be used to solve subtraction problems. **Geometry** • Circles are round. • A shape that has 4 corners is a rectangle. **Data and Measurement** • First graders are taller than kindergarteners.

Always, Sometimes, Never – First Grade	
Beginning of the Year	**End of the Year**
Operations and Algebraic Thinking • When you add 0 to a number, the sum is 0. • When you subtract 0 from a number, the difference is 0. • The answer can come first in a number sentence. • 15 is less than 30. • When I am adding, I have to count on from the first number. • The only way to break apart 16 is to use a 10 and a 6. • The only way I can break apart 10 is a 6 and a 4. • Addition can be used to solve subtraction problems. **Geometry** • Three triangles can be used to make a rectangle. • A shape that has 3 corners is a rectangle. **Measurement and Data** • 5-year-olds are taller than 4-year-olds.	**Operations and Algebraic Thinking** • Numbers can be added in any order. • Numbers can be subtracted in any order. • To subtract, you have to count back. • When a word problem has the word "more," then you can solve it by adding the numbers together. • The answer can appear on the left side of the equal sign in an equation. **Number and Operations in Base Ten** • The only way to break apart 42 is to use a 40 and a 2. • The number 38 has 8 ones (making sure students understand there are 38 ones). • 4 tens is less than 3 tens and 13 ones. • When you add 10 to a number, the answer always has a zero. **Measurement and Data** • The only way you can measure objects is to use a ruler. **Geometry** • When shading in one half of a circle or rectangle, the line must go up and down. • When breaking a rectangle into fourths, there will always be four smaller rectangles.

Continued

Continued

Always, Sometimes, Never – Second Grade	
Beginning of the Year	**End of the Year**
Operations and Algebraic Thinking • When you subtract, the difference is smaller than the number you started with. • When you add, the sum is bigger than the number you started with. • Numbers can be added in any order. • Numbers can be subtracted in any order. • When a problem uses the words "less than," then I have to subtract. • When I am adding, I can break apart numbers to make a 10. • I can use addition to solve a subtraction problem. **Geometry** • Triangles have curved edges. • Rectangles have 4 vertices.	**Operations and Algebraic Thinking** • If you add 2 even numbers, the sum is even. • If you add 3 numbers, the sum is odd. • Adding doubles makes an even number. **Place Value** • When you skip count by 2's starting on an even number, all the other numbers in the pattern are even. **Geometry** • Rectangles have 4 equal sides. • Triangles have 3 vertices and 3 angles.
Always, Sometimes, Never – Third Grade	
Beginning of the Year	**End of the Year**
Operations and Algebraic Thinking • If you add 3 numbers, the sum will be odd. • When you subtract, the difference is less than the number you started with. • If you double a number, the number is even. • If you halve a number, the number is even.	**Operations and Algebraic Thinking** • If you multiply by 0, you get the number you multiplied. • Multiples of 5 have a 5 in the ones place. • Multiples of 10 have a 0 in the ones place. • If you multiply a number by 1, you always get that number. • You can multiply numbers in any order. • When subtracting two numbers, you need to regroup. • I can use multiplication to solve a division problem. **Numbers Base 10** • Five rounds to the nearest ten. **Measurement** • We measure liquid with liters. • We measure mass in grams. • You count to calculate the perimeter of a figure.

Always, Sometimes, Never – Fourth Grade	
Beginning of the Year	**End of the Year**
Operations and Algebraic Thinking • When you divide 0 by a number, the quotient is zero. • You can multiply numbers in any order. • You can divide in any order. **Geometry** • Quadrilaterals are always rectangles. • Lines are parallel. • Polygons have straight sides.	**Operations and Algebraic Thinking** • A number has 2 factors. • When you multiply by 2, the product is even. • When you multiply by 3, the product is odd. • The digits in the multiples of 9 add up to 9. **A square number is even** • When you multiply, the product is larger than the number you started with. **Numbers Base 10** • When rounding a number to the nearest 10 and then nearest 100, the result will be the same. **Geometry** • Quadrilaterals are always parallelograms. • All squares are rectangles. • All rectangles are squares. • A square's area and perimeter are the same.
Always, Sometimes, Never – Fifth Grade	
Beginning of the Year	**End of the Year**
Operations and Algebraic Thinking • If you halve a number, the number will be even. • When you multiply a number, the product is a bigger number • Multiples of 4 are even. **Fractions and Decimals** • ¼ is less than ½ (without specifying for the students the size of wholes) **Geometry** • The lines of symmetry of a polygon are equal to the number of sides of the polygon. • The perimeter of a rectangle is larger than the area. • Quadrilaterals are always parallelograms. • All squares are rectangles. • All rectangles are squares. • A square's area and perimeter are the same.	**Operations and Algebraic Thinking** • When you multiply by 5, the product has a five in it. • When you put a zero after a number the number always gets bigger. • When you divide by a number, the quotient is a smaller number. • Composite numbers have an even number of factors. **Fractions and Decimals** • The decimal with the most amount of digits is the bigger number. **Geometry** • Triangles can have more than one right angle. • The volume of a rectangular prism will always be larger than the area of the base.

Continued

Continued

Anchor Chart

We do the math routine *Always, Sometimes, Never* so we can think about statements.

Statements can be *always* true, like: Even + even = even

Statements can be *sometimes* true, like:

When you add 2 numbers together, the number gets bigger.

Statements can be *never* true, like:

You can switch the order of the numbers in a subtraction equation.

Student Response Sheet

Name: Date:

Directions: Look at the following statements and determine if they are *always*, *sometimes*, or *never* true.

A. If you multiply by whole numbers, the number always gets bigger.
   Always, sometimes, or never true?

   Explain:

B. If you divide a number by 1, the quotient is the number.
   Always, sometimes, or never true?

   Explain:

C. If you add 2 even numbers, the sum is an even number.
   Always, sometimes, or never true?

   Explain:

Resources for *Always, Sometimes, Never*

https://nrich.maths.org/12672
https://mathednerd.wordpress.com/always-sometimes-never/
https://nrich.maths.org/12670
www.flaguide.org/tools/math/convincing/convincing1B.php
https://www.illustrativemathematics.org/content-standards/tasks/1941
https://www.tes.com/teaching-resource/always-true-sometimes-true-and-never-true-cards-6278314
https://www.tes.com/teaching-resource/reasoning-with-always-sometimes-or-never-statements-year-2-11303480
https://www.tes.com/us/teacher-lessons/properties-of-shape-always-sometimes-never-7553615
https://www.youtube.com/watch?v=znuAkeuxAOw
https://mathednerd.wordpress.com/2015/05/01/always-sometimes-never/

Routine #2
Convince Me/Prove It

The *Convince Me/Prove It* Routine

The *Convince Me* or *Prove It* routine requires students to justify their thinking. They are given information that they have to justify with numbers, words, and/or models. Students should often think about proving it in more than one way.

Materials and Tools	"I Can" Statement
Students should have a variety of tools to think and reason about the numbers being discussed. They should use their toolkits. Students can use manipulatives, drawings, and mental math.	**I can** justify my thinking with objects, drawings, diagrams, and words.

Protocol	Purpose:
Overview: The teacher puts some mathematical concept on the board, and the students are asked to convince everyone it is true. 1. The teacher puts a mathematical concept on the board. 2. The teacher tells the students to take "private think time" to think about the concept. 3. After about 30 seconds, the teacher tells the students to "turn and talk to a neighbor." 4. Everyone comes back together, and students raise their hands and explain their thinking.	• Justify their thinking • Defend their thinking • Convince others that the student's own thinking makes sense • Prove their answers **Questions:** • What do you think? • How can you justify your thinking? • How can you prove it? • Are you sure? • How will you model your thinking?

What's the Math?

Convince Me or *Prove It* should require students at different levels to explore:

Kindergarten	First Grade	Second Grade
• Adding and subtracting • Comparing two- and three-dimensional shapes • Comparing measurable heights • Decomposing numbers 2–20	• Adding and subtracting • Using properties of addition • Using the inverse relationship between addition and subtraction • Comparing 2 two-digit numbers • Measuring length of objects • Partitioning circles and rectangles into 2 and 4 equal shares	• Even and odd • Adding and subtracting • Using properties of addition • Doubling and halving • Skip counting • Comparing numbers • Partitioning circles and rectangles into 2, 3, or 4 equal shares • Recognizing shapes having specified attributes, such as a given number of angles or equal faces (triangles, quadrilaterals, pentagons, hexagons, and cubes) • Equal groups up to 5×5

Continued

Third Grade	Fourth Grade	Fifth Grade
• Even and odd • Doubling and halving • Adding and subtracting • Multiplying and dividing • Using properties of addition and multiplication • Using the inverse relationship between multiplication and division • Rounding to the nearest 10 or 100 • Equivalence of whole numbers written as fractions • Equivalent fractions • Comparing fractions can only occur when fractions refer to the same whole • Perimeter and area	• Adding and subtracting, including fractions and decimals • Multiplying and dividing, including fractions by whole numbers • Multiples and factors • Prime and composite • Equivalent fractions and decimals • Comparing fractions and decimals • Perimeter and area	• Prime and composite • Multiples and factors • Multiplying and dividing • Adding and subtracting, including fractions and decimals • Equivalent fractions and decimals • Comparing fractions and decimals • Perimeter and area • Volume

Classroom Vignette: *Convince Me/Prove It*

Mrs. Maribel: Good afternoon class. Today we are going to do the Convince Me routine to work on proving our thinking. Remember that in this routine, you have to provide evidence of your thinking. You can't just say it; you must prove it. You can prove it with manipulatives, numbers, words, sketches, or diagrams.

Number 1: Prove that ⅗ is greater than ⁶⁄₇.

Mrs. Maribel: First take some private think time. Work by yourself in your thinking notebook. [Three minutes pass.] OK, now turn to your math partner and talk about your thinking. I'm going to circulate and listen in to your thinking.

Tiffany: [Explaining to Cliff] I don't understand because ⁶⁄₇ is bigger. 6 and 7 are bigger than 5 and 5.

Cliff looks at her and then looks at the board and then looks at the math bar reference sheet. Mrs. Maribel asks them both to think about what they see on the sheet and what they know. Mrs. Maribel slowly states that she can see that ⅗ is bigger because it is the whole and ⁶⁄₇ is smaller than a whole. Mrs. Maribel asks them to keep thinking about this and to look at another model to compare (maybe the circles). She then listens in on Tami.

Tami: I just knew because ⅗ is a whole and we would need ⁷⁄₇ to make that one a whole. So it was easy.

Mrs. Maribel listens and then asks her could she prove it with a visual model. Tami tips her head to think about that.

When it is time to share out, Mrs. Maribel asks Tiffany to explain her thinking from start to finish. Next she calls on Tami. She continues to call on different students to Prove It in different ways (manipulatives, numbers, words, sketches, or diagrams).

Mrs. Maribel is thinking about a few different things that she saw during this routine. Her goal is to get the students to reason about fractions, and she realizes that the students still need a great deal of work. In the small guided math group she'll pull with Tiffany and Cliff, she will continue to build conceptual knowledge about fraction size. In the small guided math group with Tami, she will need to work on being able to model thinking. Tami had no difficulty reasoning the problem out with words, but she was stuck when it came to representing her thinking.

Convince Me/Prove It – Kindergarten	
Beginning of the Year	**End of the Year**
<ul><li>Convince me that 3 is greater than 2.</li><li>Convince me that 1 is less than 5.</li><li>Convince me that this is 3.</li></ul>	<ul><li>Convince me that 7 is greater than 5.</li><li>Convince me that 0 isn't worth anything.</li><li>Convince me that this is 8.</li></ul>

<ul><li>Convince me that this is a circle.</li></ul>

<ul><li>Convince me that this is not a circle</li></ul>

Convince Me/Prove It – First Grade	
Beginning of the Year	**End of the Year**

Operations and Algebraic Thinking

- Convince me that you can decompose 7 in different ways.
- Convince me that you need 3 more to get to 10 from 7.

Place Value

- Convince me that 10 is less than 20.
- Convince me that there are lots of ways to make 10.
- Convince me that 9 is 1 more than 8.

Geometry

- Convince me that this is a cylinder.

Operations and Algebraic Thinking

- Convince me that $2 + 3 + 5 = 5 + 5$
- Convince me that $7 + 8 = 8 + 7$
- Convince me that $7 + 7 + 1 = 14 + 1 = 15$

Place Value

- Convince me that 29 is less than 30.
- Convince me that 14 take away 6 is 8.
- Convince me that 10 more than 80 is 90.
- Convince me that $50 - 20$ is 30.

Geometry

- Convince me that this is a trapezoid.

Continued

Continued

Convince Me/Prove It – Second Grade	
Beginning of the Year	**End of the Year**
Operations and Algebraic Thinking • Convince me that $7 + 8 + 2 = 10 + 7$. • Convince me that $7 + 9 = 7 + 7 + 2$. • Convince me that $2 + 7 = 10 - 1$. **Place Value** • Convince me that 10 less than 30 is 20. • Convince me that there are lots of ways to make 25. • Convince me that 29 is 10 more than 19. **Geometry** • Convince me that this is a quadrilateral. 	**Operations and Algebraic Thinking** • Convince me that 7 is not even. • Convince me that 8 is even. • Convince me that $18 + 29 + 32 = 50 + 29$. **Place Value** • Convince me that you can add to find the answer to a subtraction problem. • Convince me that 700 is 100 less than 800. • Convince me that I can add 29 and 33 by making it $30 + 32$. **Geometry** • Convince me that this is a triangle.

Convince Me/Prove It – Third Grade	
Beginning of the Year	**End of the Year**
Operations and Algebraic Thinking • Convince me that 17 is not even. • Convince me that $60 - 39 = 60 - 40 + 1$. • Convince me that $60 - 45 = 3 \times 5$.	**Operations and Algebraic Thinking** • Convince me that $6 \times 7 = (3 \times 7) + (3 \times 7)$. • Convince me that $8 \times 1 = 64 \div 8$. • Convince me that you can't divide by 0.
Place Value • Convince me that you can add to find the answer to a subtraction problem. • Convince me that 1000 is 100 more than 900. • Convince me that I can add 79 and 24 by making it $80 + 23$. • Convince me that this is a cube. 	**Place Value** • Convince me that 9×20 is 180. • Convince me that 47 rounds to 50. • Convince me that $188 + 224$ can be made into an easier problem like $190 + 222$. • Convince me that this is a hexagon.

Convince Me/Prove It – Fourth Grade	
Beginning of the Year	**End of the Year**
Operations and Algebraic Thinking • Convince me that a number divided by itself is 1. • Convince me that 0 divided by a number is 0. • Convince me that $7 \times 7 = (5 \times 7) + (2 \times 7)$. • Convince me that $4 \times 6 = 6 \times 4$. **Place Value** • Convince me that 10×20 is 200. • Convince me that there are at least 5 numbers that round to 50. • Convince me that $288 + 324$ can be made into an easier problem like $290 + 322$. **Geometry** • Convince me that some shapes are not polygons. • Convince me that all quadrilaterals aren't parallelograms.	**Operations and Algebraic Thinking** • Convince me that prime numbers only have 2 factors. • Convince me that multiples of 5 have a 5 or a 0 in the ones place. • Convince me that remainders can be interpreted in different ways. **Place Value** • Convince me that 70 is ten times greater than 7. • Convince me that 455 rounds to 500. • Convince me that there is more than one way to divide 567 by 9. **Geometry** • Convince me that some quadrilaterials are not parallelograms. • Convince me that parallel lines never touch. • Convince me that the sum of the angles in a triangle is always equal to 180. • Convince me that sometimes a rectangle can have an area and perimeter that are equal.
Convince Me/Prove It – Fifth Grade	
Beginning of the Year	**End of the Year**
Operations and Algebraic Thinking • Convince me that 28 is a composite number. • Convince me that 3 tenths is equivalent to 30 hundredths. • Convince me that the product of an even number and an odd number is always an even number. • Convince me that remainders can be interpreted in different ways. • Convince me that sometimes when you multiply two numbers, you don't always get a larger product. **Geometry** • Convince me that a square can be classified as a rhombus.	**Operations and Algebraic Thinking** • Convince me that 0.4 is larger than 0.399. • Convince me that $20 - 2 \times 7 = 6$ **Fractions and Decimals** • Convince me that when you multiply fractions that are less than 1, the product is smaller. **Geometry** • Convince me that the way you calculate volume is to multiply the length by the width by the height.

Continued

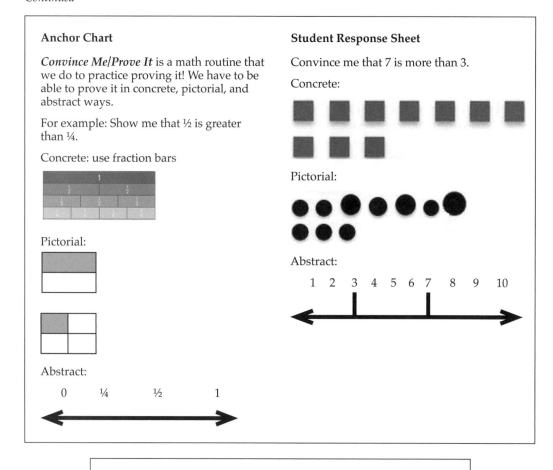

Anchor Chart

Convince Me/Prove It is a math routine that we do to practice proving it! We have to be able to prove it in concrete, pictorial, and abstract ways.

For example: Show me that ½ is greater than ¼.

Concrete: use fraction bars

Pictorial:

Abstract:

0   ¼   ½   1

Student Response Sheet

Convince me that 7 is more than 3.

Concrete:

Pictorial:

Abstract:

1   2   3   4   5   6   7   8   9   10

Resources for *Convince Me/Prove It*

https://nrich.maths.org/9169
https://www.youtube.com/watch?v=ye9XfMsscXk
www.educationworld.com/a_curr/mathchat/mathchat017.shtml

Routine #3
Disappearing Dan

The *Disappearing Dan* Routine

The *Disappearing Dan* routine is a fun, flexible, engaging routine that can be done with any mathematical topic. The basic idea of the routine is to draw a figure that contains different math concepts, and then as the students can answer questions about the concepts, the parts of the figure are erased. So Dan is disappearing. Teachers use Dan, Dana (his sister), or Dino (his dog). It is such a popular routine that teachers adapt the figure to the season. For example, during October they might make a "disappearing pumpkin," and in the spring they might have a "disappearing flower." This routine can be used to review something very specific or to do a spiral review of past topics.

Materials and Tools	"I Can" Statement
Students should have a variety of tools to think and reason about the numbers being discussed. They should use their toolkits. Students can use manipulatives, drawings, and mental math.	**I can** reason about numbers and explain and justify my thinking. I can listen to, understand, and respond to the thinking of others and decide whether or not their reasoning makes sense.

Protocol	Purpose:
Overview: The teacher draws a picture of Dan and writes various numbers or shapes on the figure.	• Identify error patterns • Discuss error patterns • Correct error patterns
1. The teacher puts the figure of Dan on the board with numbers in the figure. 2. As students choose a number or shape on the board, the teacher asks them a question related to that number or shape. The questions are differentiated based on the needs of the particular student. 3. When a student answers a question, that part of the figure is erased.	**Questions:** • The questions vary depending on the numbers. For example, if there is a number 20, the teacher might say: • Tell me two ways to make 20. • Tell me 10 more than 20. • Tell me the product of 20 × 20.

What's the Math?

Disappearing Dan should require students at different levels to explore:

Kindergarten	First Grade	Second Grade
• Adding and subtracting • Comparing two- and three-dimensional shapes • Comparing measurable heights • Decomposing numbers 2–20	• Adding and subtracting • Using properties of addition • Using inverse relationship between addition and subtraction • Comparing 2 two-digit numbers • Measuring length of objects • Partitioning circles and rectangles into 2 and 4 equal shares	• Even and odd • Adding and subtracting • Using properties of addition • Doubling and halving • Skip counting • Comparing numbers • Partitioning circles and rectangles into 2, 3, or 4 equal shares • Recognizing shapes having specified attributes such as a given number of angles or equal faces (triangles, quadrilaterals, pentagons, hexagons, and cubes)

Third Grade	Fourth Grade	Fifth Grade
• Even and odd • Doubling and halving • Adding and subtracting • Multiplying and dividing	• Adding and subtracting, including fractions and decimals • Multiplying, including fractions by whole numbers	• Prime and composite • Multiples and factors • Adding and subtracting, including fractions and decimals

Continued

Continued

- Using properties of addition and multiplication
- Using inverse relationship between multiplication and division
- Rounding to the nearest 10 or 100
- Discussing shared attributes of quadrilaterals
- Discussing equivalence of whole numbers written as fractions
- Discussing equivalent fractions
- Comparing fractions can only occur when fractions refer to the same whole
- Perimeter and area

- Multiples and factors
- Prime and composite
- Discussing shared attributes of quadrilaterals
- Equivalent fractions and decimals
- Comparing fractions and decimals
- Perimeter and area

- Multiplying and dividing, including fractions and decimals
- Discussing shared attributes of quadrilaterals
- Discussing equivalent fractions and decimals
- Comparing fractions and decimals
- Perimeter and area
- Volume

Classroom vignette: *Disappearing Dan*

Mr. Hong draws a heart on the board in celebration of the month of February. Then he tells students to raise their hands and pick a number. He reminds them that they are going to pick girl-boy-girl, etc. He tells them to look at the numbers and be ready to think about the answer. He reminds them that they can use any of their tools to scaffold their thinking. This particular day, Mr. Hong is reviewing different concepts.

Kelly: I pick 75.

Mr. Hong: Tell me how many more to 100?

Kelly: [*Looking at her hundreds grid*] 25.

Todd: I pick ½.

Mr. Hong: Draw a circle and shade ½.

Todd does this.

Maria: Square.

Mr. Hong: How many sides does a square have? What is special about these sides?

Maria: A square has 4 straight sides. They are all equal in length.

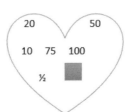

Conversation continues until all the items have been discussed and erased. Often on the last one Mr. Hong will have the students turn and talk with their neighbor about the number because usually there are about 10–12 items so everyone doesn't get to answer out loud to the group every time the routine is done.

* This is such a great routine because teachers can differentiate the questioning as they call on different students. Student A picks the number 20 and Mr. Hong says, "Give me 3 numbers that will make that number." Whereas, when Student B picks the number 20, Mr. Hong says, "How many more to make 100?"

Disappearing Dan – Kindergarten	
Beginning of the Year	

<table>
<tr><td>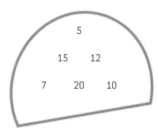</td>
<td>

Possible questions:

What comes before _____?

What comes after _____?

What does _____ come in between?

How many more to 10?

Give me 2 numbers that make that number when they are joined together.

Show me this number using your fingers. Now show me another way you can show me this number with your fingers.

</td></tr>
</table>

End of the Year	

<table>
<tr><td>

5

15   12

7   20   10

</td>
<td>

Possible Questions:

How many more to 10?

How many more to 20?

What number is 1 more than this number?

Count from this number up to 30.

Count backwards from this number until you reach 0.

How many tens and how many ones are in this number?

Break this number apart in a number bond.

</td></tr>
</table>

Disappearing Dan – First Grade	
Beginning of the Year	

<table>
<tr><td>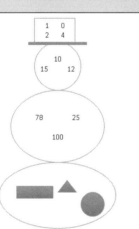</td>
<td>

Possible Questions:

How many more to 10?

What comes after this number?

Count from this number to 30.

How many tens and how many ones?

Break this number apart in a number bond.

Which number is greater, the number you picked or 25?

Count backwards from this number until I tell you to stop.

How many sides does this shape have?

</td></tr>
</table>

Continued

End of the Year

<table>
<tr>
<td>

7 10
20

45 99 120
1/4 1/2

</td>
<td>

Possible Questions:

How many more to 20?
How many more to 50?
What is 10 more than this number?
What is 10 less than this number?
How many tens and ones?
Represent this in a part-part-whole mat.
Start at _____. and count to _____.
Start at _____. and count back to _____.
Represent this fraction with a rectangle.
Represent this fraction with a circle.

</td>
</tr>
</table>

Disappearing Dan – Second Grade

Beginning of the Year

<table>
<tr>
<td>

</td>
<td>

Possible Questions:

How many tens and how many ones?
What is 10 more than this number?
What is 10 less than this number?
Use a math tool in our classroom to show how many this is.
Represent this number in a part-part-whole mat.
Start at _____ and count to _____.
Start at _____ and count back to _____.
Add 9 to this number.
Represent this fraction with a circle.
Represent this fraction with a rectangle.
Describe the shape.
Double this number.

</td>
</tr>
</table>

End of the Year

<table>
<tr>
<td>

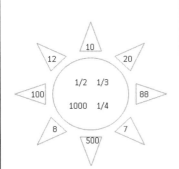

</td>
<td>

Possible Questions:

Make this number with coins.
Is this number even or odd?
How many more to 100?
What is 100 more?
What is 100 less?
How many tens, ones, and hundreds?
Represent this in a number bond.
Draw a base 10 sketch of this number.
What strategies can you use when you add 8 to a number?
Add 25 to this number and explain your thinking.
Represent this fraction with a circle.
Represent this fraction with a rectangle.
Double this number.
Half this number.

</td>
</tr>
</table>

Disappearing Dan – Third Grade	
Beginning of the Year	
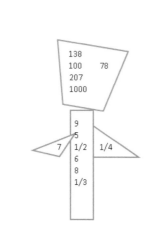	**Possible Questions:** Make this number with coins. How many more to 100? What is 100 more? What is 100 less? How many tens, ones, and hundreds? Represent this in a number bond. Draw a base 10 sketch of this number. What strategies can you use when you add 8 to a number? Add 25 to this number and explain your thinking. Represent this fraction with a circle. Represent this fraction with a rectangle. Double this number. Half this number. Is this number even or odd? How do you know? What shape is this? Describe the number of sides and the angles.
End of the Year	
	Possible Questions: Multiply this number by 10 (single-digit numbers). Multiply this number by itself (single-digit numbers). Make this number with coins. Round this number to the nearest 10. Round this number to the nearest 100. How many tens, ones, and hundreds? Represent this in a number bond. Is this number even or odd? How do you know? Draw a base 10 sketch of this number. Represent this fraction with a circle. Represent this fraction with a rectangle. Is this fraction more or less than ½? Is this fraction more or less than ¼? How much more do you need to make a whole? Double this number. Half this number.

Continued

Disappearing Dan – **Fourth Grade**

Beginning of the Year

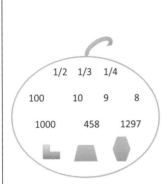

Possible Questions:

Multiply this number by 10 (single-digit numbers).

Multiply this number by itself (single-digit numbers). Explain your strategy.

Round this number to the nearest 10.

Round this number to the nearest 100.

Double this number.

Half this number.

Name a shape up here and describe its attributes.

Name a shape up here and draw a picture that shows a shape that is different from the one you picked.

Write a fraction that is equivalent to this amount.

End of the Year

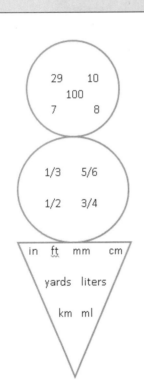

Possible Questions:

Round this number to the nearest 10 and the nearest 100.

Double this number.

Half this number.

Multiply this number by itself and explain your strategy.

Generate an equivalent fraction.

Compare this fraction with ½.

Name a fraction smaller than this fraction.

Name a fraction greater than this fraction.

Decompose this fraction. Now decompose the fraction another way.

How many more to 1?

How many inches are in a foot?

Name something about 8 inches long.

How many feet are in a yard?

Name something about a yard long.

How many milliliters are in a liter?

Name something that we buy in liters.

What do kilometers measure?

How many centimeters are in a meter?

How many millimeters are in a centimeter?

Disappearing Dan – Fifth Grade
Beginning of the Year

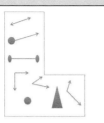

Possible Questions:

Pick a figure and name it. Justify why it is that type of figure.

Pick an angle and name it. Justify why it is that type of angle.

Name the shape and give two attributes and one nonexemplar.

End of the Year

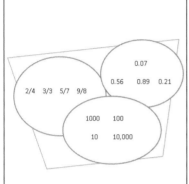

Possible Questions:

Generate an equivalent fraction.

How many more to 1 whole?

Add ½ to this fraction.

How many hundredths from 1 whole?

Write the decimal in expanded form.

Write the decimal in expanded notation.

Write the decimal in fraction form.

Pick a number and determine if it is less than, equal to, or greater than 1.

Pick a number and determine if it is less than, equal to, or greater than ½.

Pick a number and multiply it by 1000.

Pick a number and multiply it by 10.

Pick a number and multiply it by 100.

Pick a number and multiply it by 10,000.

Anchor Chart

Disappearing Dan is a fun routine where we have to think on our feet. There is a figure with numbers in it, and we take turns calling out a number. Then our teacher asks us to do something with that number.

For example: John picked the number 7.

- The teacher could say:
- Double that number.
- Multiply that number by 8.
- Divide 63 by that number.
- Is it odd or even?

Student Response Sheet

Although this routine doesn't have an activity sheet for the students to respond on, they interact on their white boards in class. For example, if the student picks 0.58, the teacher could say, "Come up to the board and write that in expanded notation." The student could also write it on his/her white board or thinking journal.

Student goes to the board and writes:

$5 \times \frac{1}{10} + 8 \times \frac{1}{100}$

Continued

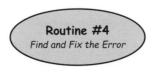

The *Find and Fix the Error* Routine
In the *Find and Fix the Error* routine, students are required to spot the errors in mathematical equations and then fix them. This routine works with student error patterns in the reverse. Error patterns or "math bugs" should be presented to students so that they can discuss and unpack them (Ginsberg, 1987; Ashlock, 2010). This way, they get to talk about them and address their misconceptions openly.

Materials and Tools	"I Can" Statement
Students should have a variety of tools to think and reason about the numbers being discussed. They should use their toolkits. Students can use manipulatives, drawings, and mental math.	**I can** reason about numbers and explain and justify my thinking. I can listen to, understand, and respond to the thinking of others and decide whether or not their reasoning makes sense. I can explain errors that I find and how they could be corrected.

Protocol	Purpose:
Overview: The teacher puts some mathematical concept on the board, and the students have to determine where the mistake was made. 1. The teacher puts a mathematical concept on the board. 2. The teacher tells the students to take "private think time" to think about the concept. 3. After about 30 seconds, the teacher tells the students to "turn and talk to a neighbor." 4. Everyone comes back together, and students raise their hands and explain their thinking.	• Identify error patterns • Discuss error patterns • Correct error patterns **Questions:** • Is this correct? • Do you agree with this? • Does anything look wrong? • Can you fix this? • What needs to be corrected?

What's the Math?
Find and Fix the Error should require students at different levels to explore:

Kindergarten	First Grade	Second Grade
• Adding and subtracting • Comparing two- and three-dimensional shapes • Comparing measurable heights • Decomposing numbers 2–20	• Adding and subtracting • Using properties of addition • Using the inverse relationship between addition and subtraction • Comparing 2 two-digit numbers • Measuring length of objects • Partitioning circles and rectangles into 2 and 4 equal shares	• Even and odd • Adding and subtracting • Properties of addition • Doubling and halving • Skip counting • Comparing numbers • Discussing that identical shares of same whole need not have same shape • Partitioning circles and rectangles into 2, 3, or 4 equal shares • Recognizing shapes having specified attributes, such as a given number of angles or equal faces (triangles, quadrilaterals, pentagons, hexagons, and cubes)

Third Grade	Fourth Grade	Fifth Grade
• Even and odd • Doubling and halving • Adding and subtracting • Multiplying and dividing • Using properties of addition and multiplication • Using inverse relationship between multiplication and division • Rounding to the nearest 10 or 100 • Discussing shared attributes of quadrilaterals • Discussing equivalence of whole numbers written as fractions • Discussing equivalent fractions • Comparing fractions can only occur when fractions refer to the same whole • Perimeter and area	• Adding and subtracting, including fractions and decimals • Multiplying and dividing, including fractions by whole numbers • Multiples and factors • Prime and composite • Discussing shared attributes of quadrilaterals • Discussing equivalent fractions and decimals • Comparing fractions and decimals • Perimeter and area	• Prime and composite • Multiples and factors • Multiplying and dividing, including fractions and decimals • Adding and subtracting, including fractions and decimals • Discussing shared attributes of quadrilaterals • Discussing equivalent fractions and decimals • Comparing fractions and decimals • Perimeter and area • Volume

Classroom Vignette

Mr. Sanchez: Good morning everyone. We are going to get started with our Daily Math Thinking Routine. Today we are doing *Find and Fix the Error*. We have been working on subtracting numbers with zeros and I noticed some interesting answers. Remember that it's OK to make mistakes, but we do have to find them and fix them. So here are some of our mistakes. I want you to take a close look and see if you can find the mistake that some of us are still making. This is actually a mistake a whole lot of kids in a whole lot of places make. But we gotta find it and fix it in here!

$$
\begin{array}{r}
2000 \\
-\ 875 \\
\hline
2875
\end{array}
$$

Mr. Sanchez: Turn and talk to your neighbor about what you see and what you think. Explain your thinking. That means tell them exactly what you see and where the error is. How would you help somebody who was doing this?

Class pairs off and students talk with their neighbors. Then they turn back for the whole-group discussion.

Marylou: [*Raising her hand*] Well, the error is that they didn't really subtract. You can't just drop the 875 because that doesn't make sense. You have to regroup. So you go to the 2 and then regroup all the way across to the 5.

Mr. Benson: Is everybody following the conversation. Remember we call it REGROUPING ACROSS ZEROS for a reason. We have to go across all the zeros. What else are you all thinking?

Marcus: I don't subtract. I drew an open number line and I added up. That's how I would tell them to do it because it is much easier that way. So if we jump 75 to 900 and then 100 more to 1000 and then 1000 more to 2000. Bam! There's the answer. All by adding. It's easier.

Mr. Benson: OK, I need both of you [*nodding to Marylou and Marcus*] to come up and show what you did on the board and be ready to explain it.

Continued

Continued

| Find and Fix the Error – Kindergarten ||
Beginning of the Year	End of the Year

• Counting Sequence
  1, 2, 4, 5, 6, 7
 	
• Representing an amount
  5
  ▪ ▪ ▪ ▪
	• $2 + 3 = 7$
	• $5 - 0 = 0$
	• Backward 5
	• Number bond showing 5 broken into a 3 and a 3

| Find and Fix the Error – First Grade ||
Beginning of the Year	End of the Year
• $10 - 9 = 2$ • $5 + 5 = 11$ • Number bond showing 8 broken into a 5 and a 4 • Counting errors to 100 • 7 is more than 5 • A triangle has 4 sides	• Number bond breaking 34 into 3 and 4 • $8 + 3 = 10$ • $14 = 9 + 6$ • $14 - 13 = 2$ • $5 + 1 = 6 + 2$ • $52 < 49$ • Counting errors

| Find and Fix the Error – Second Grade ||
Beginning of the Year	End of the Year
• Number bond breaking 56 into 5 and 6. • $8 + 7 = 16$ • $17 = 9 + 7$ • $10 + 4 = 6 + 7$ • $88 > 90$ • Count with errors and then have students explain what is wrong.	• $34 + 48 = 712$ • $14 + 24 = 24 + 13$ • $400 - 78 = 47$ • $398 > 401$ • Draw uneven fraction pieces and have students explain why they are not fractions.

| Find and Fix the Error – Third Grade ||
Beginning of the Year	End of the Year
• 78 is odd. • $36 + 48 = 714$ • $52 - 38 = 26$ • Half of 16 is 32. • If I had one quarter, two dimes, a nickle, and three pennies, I would have 55 cents. • $1000 - 456 = 1456$ • $179 > 201$	• 124 is odd. • $400 - 298 = 298$ • $5 \times 0 = 5$ • 46 rounded to the next 10 is 40. • 243 rounded to the nearest 100 is 300. • $6 \times 4 = 28$ • $\frac{4}{4} = 4$ • $\frac{1}{3} + \frac{1}{3} + \frac{1}{3} + \frac{1}{3} = 1$

Find and Fix the Error – Fourth Grade	
Beginning of the Year	**End of the Year**
• $10{,}000 - 5678 = 5678$ • $10 \times 0 = 10$ • $\frac{9}{9} = 9$ • 868 is odd. • $346 - 164 = 222$ • $4 \times 6 = 6 \times 5$ • 489 rounded to the nearest 10 is 480. • $\frac{1}{4} + \frac{1}{4} + \frac{1}{4} = 1$	• $\frac{4}{5} + \frac{3}{5} = 7/10$ • $3.6 - 1.8 = 2.2$ • $24 \times 12 = 28$ • $8 \times \frac{1}{4} = 3$ • 91 is prime. • $0.6 < 0.59$ • $\frac{4}{5} > \frac{5}{6}$

Find and Fix the Error – Fifth Grade	
Beginning of the Year	**End of the Year**
• $4000 - 2578 = 2578$ • $0/9 = 9$ • $\frac{3}{8} + \frac{4}{8} = \frac{7}{16}$ • $\frac{9}{12} - \frac{5}{12} = \frac{4}{0}$ • $5 - 3.8 = 2.8$ • $246 + 348 = 348 + 245$ • $\frac{3}{4} < \frac{2}{3}$ • $\frac{5}{9} < \frac{4}{10}$	• $\frac{2}{3} + \frac{2}{6} = \frac{4}{6}$ • $4.8 + 4.7 = 8.15$ • $4.2 - 2.98 = 2.78$ • $30 \times 200 = 15 \times 100$ • $0.27 \times 0.10 = 0.270$ • $13 \times (5 \times 3) = (13 \times 5) \times 2$ • $\frac{3}{5} \times \frac{4}{5} = \frac{7}{5}$

Anchor Chart	Student Response Sheet
Find and Fix the Error is a routine where we have to look for the mistake and then explain why it is a mistake. For example: $$\begin{array}{r} 200 \\ -\ 59 \\ \hline 259 \end{array}$$ Here is an error that a lot of kids make. They don't regroup! You could also just count up to 200 from 59.	$\frac{0}{7} = 7$ This is an error because if you have nothing and you divide it by any number, it is still nothing. The quotient will always be zero.

Resources for Find and Fix the Error

http://mathmistakes.org/
www.cpalms.org/Public/PreviewResourceAssessment/Preview/58067

The *Guess My Number* Routine

In the *Guess My Number* routine, students are required to guess a number using mainly place value questions. This routine focuses on place value, with some emphasis on algebraic thinking. Someone chooses a number or picks a number randomly. Then students guess that number through a series of mainly place value questions. As the students ask the questions, the numbers given as answers are recorded on either a hundreds grid or a number line.

Materials and Tools

Students mainly use a hundreds grid or a number line for this routine. The teacher marks off the clues with Post-it notes on a chart or highlighted areas on an interactive board.

"I Can" Statement

I can reason about numbers and explain and justify my thinking. I can listen to, understand, and respond to the thinking of others and decide whether or not their reasoning makes sense.

Protocol

Overview: The teacher puts up a number grid or a number line and a student picks a number, which other students then find by asking questions.

1. The student gets a number.
2. Students take turns asking questions about the number.
3. The teacher records the different clues.
4. Finally the number is identified.

Purpose:

- Place value
- Algebraic thinking
- Ordering numbers

Questions:

- Is the number odd or even?
- Is the number a one-digit or a two-digit number?
- Is the number greater than 50?
- Is the number less than 20?

What's the Math?

Guess My Number should require students at different levels to explore:

Kindergarten
- Numbers 1–20

First Grade
- Numbers 1–120

Second Grade

Numbers 1–1000

Third Grade
- Numbers through 10,000
- Fractions

Fourth Grade
- Numbers through 1 million
- Fractions
- Decimals

Fifth Grade
- Whole numbers
- Fractions
- Decimals

| | | | | | Digital Versions for *Guess My Number* | | | | |

<table>
<tr><td>Topmarks</td><td>Funbrain</td><td>Abcya</td><td>Ambleside Primary</td><td>Math Cats</td></tr>
</table>

Classroom Vignette: *Guess My Number*

Mrs. Choi: Good morning everyone. We are going to get started with our Daily Math Thinking Routine. Today we are going to do *Guess My Number*. I am thinking of a number between 1 and 300. Can you guess my number?

Tom: Is your number greater than 100?

Mrs. Choi: Yes.

Kelly: Is your number less than 200?

Mrs. Choi: No. So what do we know so far?

Class indicates that the number is between 200 and 300.

Mrs. Choi: OK, does everybody have that recorded on your grid so you can keep track? Who has the next place value question?

Carlos: Is your number odd?

Mrs. Choi: Yes.

Jamal: Is it greater than 250?

Mrs. Choi: Yes.

Carol: Is it in between 250 and 280?

Mrs. Choi: Yes. So what do we know now?

Number Chart
1-300

1	2	3	4	5	6	7	8	9	10
11	12	13	14	15	16	17	18	19	20
21	22	23	24	25	26	27	28	29	30
31	32	33	34	35	36	37	38	39	40
41	42	43	44	45	46	47	48	49	50
51	52	53	54	55	56	57	58	59	60
61	62	63	64	65	66	67	68	69	70
71	72	73	74	75	76	77	78	79	80
81	82	83	84	85	86	87	88	89	90
91	92	93	94	95	96	97	98	99	100
101	102	103	104	105	106	107	108	109	110
111	112	113	114	115	116	117	118	119	120
121	122	123	124	125	126	127	128	129	130
131	132	133	134	135	136	137	138	139	140
141	142	143	144	145	146	147	148	149	150
151	152	153	154	155	156	157	158	159	160
161	162	163	164	165	166	167	168	169	170
171	172	173	174	175	176	177	178	179	180
181	182	183	184	185	186	187	188	189	190
191	192	193	194	195	196	197	198	199	200
201	202	203	204	205	206	207	208	209	210
211	212	213	214	215	216	217	218	219	220
221	222	223	224	225	226	227	228	229	230
231	232	233	234	235	236	237	238	239	240
241	242	243	244	245	246	247	248	249	250
251	252	253	254	255	256	257	258	259	260
261	262	263	264	265	266	267	268	269	270
271	272	273	274	275	276	277	278	279	280
281	282	283	284	285	286	287	288	289	290
291	292	293	294	295	296	297	298	299	300

Kelly: It's an odd number between 250 and 280.

Mrs. Choi: So what might be a strategic question to ask me?

Melissa: Does it have 27 tens?

Mrs. Choi: Yes.

Larry: Would it round down to 270 or up to 280?

Mrs. Choi: It would round up to 280. So now think. What do you know?

Various students call out that it is either 275, 277, or 279.

Mrs. Choi: So what is a place value question you could ask me?

Taylor: Is it the odd number between 275 and 279?

Mrs. Choi: No.

Timothy: Is the sum of its digits 18?

Mrs. Choi: Yes.

Students indicate that it's 279.

Continued

Guess My Number – Kindergarten									

Beginning of the Year									

Teacher: I am thinking of a number. Can you guess what it is by using the number track?

1	2	3	4	5	6	7	8	9	10

Student: Is it less than 5?

Teacher: Yes.

Student: Is it more than 3?

Teacher: Yes.

Student: It's 4.

Teacher: Yep, it's 4.

End of the Year									

Teacher: I am thinking of a number. Can you guess what it is by using the number track?

1	2	3	4	5	6	7	8	9	10
11	12	13	14	15	16	17	18	19	20

Student: Is it more than 10?

Teacher: Yes.

Student: Is it less than 20?

Teacher: Yes.

Student: Is it more than or equal to 14?

Teacher: No.

Student: Is it more than 12?

Teacher: Yes.

Student: Is it 13?

Teacher: Yes.

Guess My Number – First Grade									

Beginning of the Year									

Teacher: I am thinking of a number. Can you guess what it is by using the number track?

1	2	3	4	5	6	7	8	9	10
11	12	13	14	15	16	17	18	19	20

Possible Questions:

Is it greater than _____?

Is it less than _____?

Is it a one-digit number?

Is it a two-digit number?

Is it in between _____ and _____?

End of the Year									

Teacher: I am thinking of a number. Can you guess what it is by using the number grid?

1. I'm thinking of a number between 1 and 50.
2. I'm thinking of a number between 1 and 100.

3　I'm thinking of a number between 1 and 120.

1	2	3	4	5	6	7	8	9	10
11	12	13	14	15	16	17	18	19	20
21	22	23	24	25	26	27	28	29	30
31	32	33	34	35	36	37	38	39	40
41	42	43	44	45	46	47	48	49	50
51	52	53	54	55	56	57	58	59	60
61	62	63	64	65	66	67	68	69	70
71	72	73	74	75	76	77	78	79	80
81	82	83	84	85	86	87	88	89	90
91	92	93	94	95	96	97	98	99	100
101	102	103	104	105	106	107	108	109	110
111	112	113	114	115	116	117	118	119	120

Possible Questions:

Is it greater than _____?

Is it less than _____?

Is it a one-digit number?

Is it a two-digit number?

Is it in between _____ and _____?

Guess My Number – Second Grade

Beginning of the Year

Teacher: I am thinking of a number. Can you guess what it is by using the number grid?

1. I'm thinking of a number between 1 and 10.
2. I'm thinking of a number between 1 and 20.
3. I'm thinking of a number between 1 and 50.
4. I'm thinking of a number between 1 and 100.
5. I'm thinking of a number between 1 and 120.

1	2	3	4	5	6	7	8	9	10
11	12	13	14	15	16	17	18	19	20
21	22	23	24	25	26	27	28	29	30
31	32	33	34	35	36	37	38	39	40
41	42	43	44	45	46	47	48	49	50
51	52	53	54	55	56	57	58	59	60
61	62	63	64	65	66	67	68	69	70
71	72	73	74	75	76	77	78	79	80
81	82	83	84	85	86	87	88	89	90
91	92	93	94	95	96	97	98	99	100
101	102	103	104	105	106	107	108	109	110
111	112	113	114	115	116	117	118	119	120

Possible Questions:

Is it greater than _____?

Is it less than _____?

Is it a one-digit number?

Is it a two-digit number?

Is it in between _____ and _____?

Continued

End of the Year

Teacher: I am thinking of a number. Can you guess what it is by using the number grid?

1. I'm thinking of a number between 1 and 200.
2. I'm thinking of a number between 1 and 300.
3. I'm thinking of a number between 1 and 500.
4. I'm thinking of a number between 1 and 1000.

Number Chart
1-300

1	2	3	4	5	6	7	8	9	10
11	12	13	14	15	16	17	18	19	20
21	22	23	24	25	26	27	28	29	30
31	32	33	34	35	36	37	38	39	40
41	42	43	44	45	46	47	48	49	50
51	52	53	54	55	56	57	58	59	60
61	62	63	64	65	66	67	68	69	70
71	72	73	74	75	76	77	78	79	80
81	82	83	84	85	86	87	88	89	90
91	92	93	94	95	96	97	98	99	100
101	102	103	104	105	106	107	108	109	110
111	112	113	114	115	116	117	118	119	120
121	122	123	124	125	126	127	128	129	130
131	132	133	134	135	136	137	138	139	140
141	142	143	144	145	146	147	148	149	150
151	152	153	154	155	156	157	158	159	160
161	162	163	164	165	166	167	168	169	170
171	172	173	174	175	176	177	178	179	180
181	182	183	184	185	186	187	188	189	190
191	192	193	194	195	196	197	198	199	200
201	202	203	204	205	206	207	208	209	210
211	212	213	214	215	216	217	218	219	220
221	222	223	224	225	226	227	228	229	230
231	232	233	234	235	236	237	238	239	240
241	242	243	244	245	246	247	248	249	250
251	252	253	254	255	256	257	258	259	260
261	262	263	264	265	266	267	268	269	270
271	272	273	274	275	276	277	278	279	280
281	282	283	284	285	286	287	288	289	290
291	292	293	294	295	296	297	298	299	300

Possible Questions:

Is it greater than _____?

Is it less than _____?

Is it a one-digit number?

Is it a two-digit number?

Is it a three-digit number?

Is it in between _____ and _____?

Is it odd?

Is it even?

Does it have a zero in the ones place?

Guess My Number – Third Grade

Beginning of the Year

Teacher: I am thinking of a number. Can you guess what it is by using the number grid?

1. I'm thinking of a number between 1 and 120.
2. I'm thinking of a number between 1 and 1000.

Possible Questions:

Is it greater than _____?

Is it less than _____?

Is it a one-digit number?

Is it a two-digit number?

Is it a three-digit number?

Is it in between _____ and _____?

Is it odd?

Is it even?

Does it have a zero in the ones place?

Does it round up?

Does it round down?

Is it half of _____?

Is it double _____?

If you skip count by _____, will you land on your number?

Is it a factor of _____?

Is it a multiple of _____?

End of the Year

Teacher: I am thinking of a number. Can you guess what it is by using the number grid?

1. I'm thinking of a number between 1000 and 10,000.
2. I'm thinking of a fraction between 0 and 1.

Possible Questions:

Is it greater than _____?

Is it less than _____?

Is it a one-digit number?

Is it a two-digit number?

Is it a three-digit number?

Is it in between _____ and _____?

Is it odd?

Is it even?

Does it have a zero in the ones place?

Does it round up?

Does it round down?

Is it half of _____?

Is it double _____?

If you skip count by _____, will you land on your number?

Is it a factor of _____?

Is it a multiple of _____?

Questions we can ask about fractions:

Is it greater than 1?

Is it near 0?

Is it less than half?

Is it equal to ½?

Is it more than ½?

Can it be written as a mixed number?

Guess My Number – Fourth Grade

Beginning of the Year

Teacher:

1. I'm thinking of a number between 1 and 1000.
2. I'm thinking of a number between 1000 and 10,000.
3. I'm thinking of a number between 2 million and 5 million?
4. I'm thinking of a fraction between 0 and 1.

0 ←————————————————→ 1

Possible Questions:

Is it greater than _____?

Is it less than _____?

Is it a one-digit number?

Is it a two-digit number?

Is it a three-digit number?

Is it in between _____ and _____?

Is it odd?

Is it even?

Does it have a zero in the ones place?

Does it round up?

Does it round down?

Is it half of _____?

Is it double _____?

If you skip count by _____, will you land on your number?

Is it a factor of _____?

Is it a multiple of _____?

Continued

Questions we can ask about fractions:

Is it greater than 1?
Is it near 0?
Is it less than half?
Is it equal to ½?
Is it more than ½?
Can it be written as a mixed number?

End of the Year

Teacher:

1. I'm thinking of a fraction between 0 and 1.
2. I'm thinking of a fraction between 0 and 2.
3. I'm thinking of a fraction between 0 and 10.
4. I'm thinking of a decimal between 0 and 1.

0   **2**

Questions we can ask about fractions:

Is it greater than 1?
Is it near 0?
Is it less than half?
Is it equal to ½?
Is it more than ½?
Can it be written as a mixed number?

Guess My Number – Fifth Grade

Beginning of the Year

Teacher:

1. I'm thinking of a number between 1 and 1000.
2. I'm thinking of a number between 1000 and 10,000.
3. I'm thinking of a number between 2 million and 5 million?
4. I'm thinking of a fraction between 0 and 1.
5. I'm thinking of a fraction between 0 and 10.
6. I'm thinking of a decimal between 0 and 1.

0   **2**

Questions we can ask about fractions:

Is it greater than 1?
Is it near 0?
Is it less than ½?
Is it equal to ½?
Is it more than ½?
Can it be written as a mixed number?

End of the Year

Teacher:

1. I'm thinking of a product between 1 and 100.
2. I'm thinking of a quotient between 1 and 100.
3. I'm thinking of a decimal between 0 and 1.
4. I'm thinking of a fraction between 0 and 5.

Hundredths Chart
0.01-1.00

0.01	0.02	0.03	0.04	0.05	0.06	0.07	0.08	0.09	0.10
0.11	0.12	0.13	0.14	0.15	0.16	0.17	0.18	0.19	0.20
0.21	0.22	0.23	0.24	0.25	0.26	0.27	0.28	0.29	0.30
0.31	0.32	0.33	0.34	0.35	0.36	0.37	0.38	0.39	0.40
0.41	0.42	0.43	0.44	0.45	0.46	0.47	0.48	0.49	0.50
0.51	0.52	0.53	0.54	0.55	0.56	0.57	0.58	0.59	0.60
0.61	0.62	0.63	0.64	0.65	0.66	0.67	0.68	0.69	0.70
0.71	0.72	0.73	0.74	0.75	0.76	0.77	0.78	0.79	0.80
0.81	0.82	0.83	0.84	0.85	0.86	0.87	0.88	0.89	0.90
0.91	0.92	0.93	0.94	0.95	0.96	0.97	0.98	0.99	1.00

Possible Questions:

Is it greater than _____?
Is it less than _____?
Is it _____ more?
Is it _____ less?
Is it odd?
Is it even?
Is it prime?
Is it composite?
Is more than ½?
Is it less than ½?

Anchor Chart

Guess My Number is a place value game where you have to guess a number in a certain range, but you can only ask place value questions. Then you use your hundred grid or number line to figure out the number based on the answers to those questions.

For example:
I am thinking of a number between 1 and 100. Guess my number.

Is it odd?
Is it even?
Is it a one-digit number?
Is it a two-digit number?
Is it greater than 50?
Is it less than 20?

Student Response Sheet

Kindergarten students would have a number track. The teacher would say, "I'm thinking of a number between 1 and 10." Then the students use their number track to figure out what it is.

Is it more than 2?	Yes
Is it less than 8?	No
Is it 9?	No
Then it must be 10!	YES!

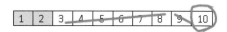

Resources for *Find and Fix the Error*
http://mathmistakes.org/
www.cpalms.org/Public/PreviewResourceAssessment/Preview/58067

The *How Many More/Less To ...?* Routine

The *How Many More/Less To ...?* routine helps students build their sense of the number line. In this activity, students have to tell how many more or less to a designated number. It helps students gain a sense of numbers up and down the number line (including whole numbers, fractions, and decimals).

Materials and Tools	"I Can" Statement
Students should have a variety of tools to think and reason about the numbers being discussed. They should use their toolkits. Students can use manipulatives, drawings, and mental math.	**I can** think about where numbers are on the number line. I can reason about how far or near numbers are to each other.

Protocol

Overview: The teacher puts a number on the board and then asks the students how many more to another number or how many less to another number.

1. The teacher puts a mathematical concept on the board.
2. The teacher tells the students to take "private think time" to think about the concept.
3. After about 30 seconds, the teacher tells the students to "turn and talk to a neighbor."
4. Everyone comes back together, and students raise their hands and explain their thinking.

Purpose:

- Gain a sense of fluency with the number line
- Work with tens, hundreds, thousands, and ten thousands as well as tenths, hundredths, and thousandths
- Explain mental calculations

Questions:

- What is a quick way to get there?
- What should you use as your benchmark numbers?
- Can you explain each step of your thinking out loud?

What's the Math?

How Many More/Less to ...? should require students at different levels to explore:

Kindergarten
- Numbers within 10

First Grade
- Numbers within 20

Second Grade
- Numbers within 100

Third Grade
- Numbers within 1000

Fourth Grade
- Numbers within 10,000
- Fractions
- Decimals to hundredths

Fifth Grade
- Multi-digit numbers
- Fractions
- Decimals to thousandths

Classroom Vignette: ***How many more to …?***

Mrs. Vo: Hey you guys. Today we are going to do *How many more to …?* Are you ready? If you need to, you can use anything in your toolkits.

Part I. *Some students pull out their fraction bar templates.*

A. From ½, how many more to 1?	Paul says that he knows ½ + ½ makes a whole.
B. From ¾, how many more to 1?	June says she knows you need 4/4 to make a whole, so ¼ is missing.
C. From 2/8, how many more to 1?	Maribel says she counted up to get to 8/8, and so she counted 6/8 up.
D. From 6/7, how many more to 1?	Trudi says that 7/7 makes a whole, so it is missing 1/7.

Part II. *Some students pull out their decimal hundredths grids.*

A. From 0.99, how many more to 1?	Marvin says if you have 99 cents, you only need a penny to get $1.
B. From 0.35, how many more to 1?	Yusef counts up on his decimals grid to get 0.65.
C. From 0.2, how many more to 1?	Rena says she used her money model and thought 20 + 80 makes $1.
D. From 0.08, how many more to 1?	Todd explains that first he thought 2 more cents, but then he thought again and noticed that that would only make a dime, so he needed 92 cents more to make $1.

* *Mrs. Vo is slowly fading out the use of the tools. Some days the students can use them, and other days they have to visualize the numbers in their head but can't refer to them physically with the tools.*

How Many More/Less to …? – **Kindergarten**	
Beginning of the Year	**End of the Year**
How many more or less to …? • 5, starting at 3 • 8, starting at 5 • 9, starting at 2	How many more or less to …? • 10, starting at 10 • 10, starting at 3 • 10, starting at 2

How Many More/Less to …? – **First Grade**	
Beginning of the Year	**End of the Year**
How many more or less to …? • 10, starting at 10 • 10, starting at 5 • 10, starting at 9	How many more or less to …? • 20, starting at 10 • 50, starting at 45 • 100, starting at 90

How Many More/Less to …? – **Second Grade**	
Beginning of the Year	**End of the Year**
How many more or less to …? • 15, starting at 9 • 20, starting at 7 • 35, starting at 28 • 50, starting at 20 • 100, starting at 50	How many more or less to …? • 82, starting at 68 • 102, starting at 99 • 126, starting at 100 • 500, starting at 448 • 1000, starting at 898

Continued

How Many More/Less to …? – Third Grade	
Beginning of the Year	**End of the Year**
How many more or less to …? • 92, starting at 76 • 100, starting at 79 • 205, starting at 190 • 1000, starting at 650	How many more or less to …? • 174, starting at 126 • 500, starting at 350 • 1000, starting at 735 • 10,000, starting at 5500
How Many More/Less to …? – Fourth Grade	
Beginning of the Year	**End of the Year**
How many more or less to …? • 279, starting at 219 • 413, starting at 398 • 700, starting at 450 • 1000, starting at 150 • 1, starting at ¾	How many more or less to …? • 1000, starting at 497 • 4000, starting at 2920 • 2, starting at ½ • 1000, starting at 250 • 1, starting at .75
How Many More/Less to …? – Fifth Grade	
Beginning of the Year	**End of the Year**
How many more or less to …? • 6000, starting at 4840 • 8002, starting at 7004 • 1, starting at ⁴⁄₆ • 2 ⅔, starting at 4 • 10,000, starting at 5400	How many more or less to …? • 3, starting at ⅝ • 2 ⁸⁄₁₂, starting at 5 • 1.3, starting at .72 • 1.2, starting at .52 • 4, starting at 2.78

Sample Anchor Chart	**Student Response Sheet**
We can figure out how many more to a number by using our tools. For example: How many more to 5? How many more to 10? How many more to 1 whole? 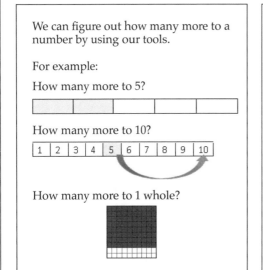	Use your tools to figure out how many more to 100? 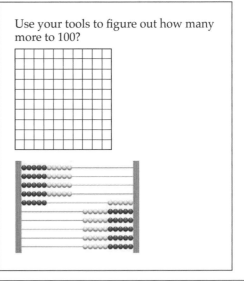

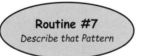

Routine #7
Describe that Pattern

The *Describe that Pattern* Routine	
The *Describe that Pattern* routine requires students to notice, recognize, describe, extend, and explain patterns.	
Materials and Tools	**"I Can" Statement**
Students should have a variety of tools to think and reason about the numbers being discussed. They should use their toolkits. Students can use manipulatives, drawings, and mental math.	**I can** describe patterns. I can extend patterns.
Protocol Overview: The teacher will put a pattern on the board. Students will determine what is happening in the pattern. 1. The teacher puts the pattern on the board. 2. The teacher tells the students to take "private think time" to think about the concept. 3. After about 30 seconds, the teacher tells the students to "turn and talk to a neighbor." 4. Everyone comes back together, and students raise their hands and explain their thinking.	**Purpose:** • Notice • Recognize • Describe • Extend • Explain
	Questions: • What do you notice? • Is it increasing, decreasing? • Is it adding, subtracting, doubling, or halving? • Is it doing more than one thing? • Is it growing?

Continued

What's the Math?

Describe that Pattern should require students at different levels to explore:

Kindergarten
- Adding and subtracting
- Shapes

First Grade
- Adding and subtracting
- Shapes

Second Grade
- Adding and subtracting
- Doubling and halving

Third Grade
- Even and odd
- Doubling and halving
- Adding and subtracting
- Multiplying and dividing
- Shapes

Fourth Grade
- Multiplying and dividing
- Multiples and factors
- Shapes

Fifth Grade
- Prime and composite
- Multiples and factors
- Multiplying and dividing
- Shapes

Classroom Vignette: *Describe that Pattern*

Mrs. Mayfield tells the class that today's thinking routine is **Describe that Pattern**. *She then proceeds to write a pattern on the board and asks what is happening in this pattern.*

Mrs. Mayfield: I need you to use your math words to describe what is happening with this pattern. If you need to refer to a tool to scaffold your thinking, you can.

1, 2, 4, 7, 11, 16, 22

Kevin: I used my number grid. I noticed that first I added 1 to get to 2, then I added 2 to get to 4, then 3 to get to 7, and then 4 to get to 11. So it is adding 1 more to the last number added each time.

Mrs. Mayfield: Can you come and show us that on the board?

Kevin goes up and explains his thinking, showing his work to the class on the board.

Lucia: It is a growing pattern. I did it on the number line.

Tommy: It is increasing. It is adding.

Mrs. Mayfield: Who can extend it? What comes next? What would be the tenth term in this pattern?

Describe that Pattern – Kindergarten	
Beginning of the Year	**End of the Year**
I can extend that pattern:	I can extend that pattern:
1, 2, 3, 4, 5, _____, _____, _____	10, 20, 30, _____, _____, _____
10, 11, 12, 13, _____, _____, _____	77, 78, 79, _____, _____, _____
12, 13, 14, 15, _____, _____, _____	10, 9, 8, 7, _____, _____, _____

Describe that Pattern – First Grade	
Beginning of the Year	**End of the Year**
I can extend that pattern:	I can extend that pattern:
27, 28, 29, _____, _____, _____	20, 30, 40, _____, _____, _____
10, 20, _____, _____, _____	9, 10, 11, _____, _____, _____
10, 9, 8, _____, _____, _____	77, 78, 79, _____, _____, _____

Describe that Pattern – Second Grade	
Beginning of the Year	**End of the Year**
I can extend that pattern: 70, 80, _____, _____, _____ 5, 10, 15, 20, _____, _____, _____ 2, 4, 6, _____, _____, _____	I can extend that pattern: 20, 19, 18, 17, 16, _____, _____, _____ 45, 55, 65, _____, _____, _____ 30, 32, 34, _____, _____, _____

Describe that Pattern – Third Grade	
Beginning of the Year	**End of the Year**
I can extend that pattern: 50, 49, 48, 47, 46, _____, _____, _____ 145, 155, 165, _____, _____, _____ 94, 96, 98, _____, _____, _____	I can extend that pattern: 106, 96, 86, _____, _____, _____ 3, 6, 9, _____, _____, _____ 8, 16, 24, _____, _____, _____ ⅓, ⅔, 1, _____, _____, _____ Describe the pattern with letters and words. When there are 5 triangles, how many circles will there be altogether?

Describe that Pattern – Fourth Grade	
Beginning of the Year	**End of the Year**
I can extend that pattern: 1000, 500, _____, _____, _____ 9, 18, 27, _____, _____, _____ 2, 7, 9, 14, 16, _____, _____, _____ ¼, ²∕₄, ¾, _____, _____, _____	I can extend that pattern: 100, 90, 92, 82, 84, _____, _____, _____ .25, .50, .75, _____, _____, _____ ⅔, ⁴∕₃, ⁶∕₃, _____, _____, _____

Continued

Describe that Pattern – Fifth Grade

Beginning of the Year	End of the Year
I can extend that pattern: 72, 81, _____, 99, _____ _____, 888, 444, 222, _____ 121, 110, 99, _____, _____, _____	I can extend that pattern: 0.25, 0.50, 0.75, _____, _____, _____ ⅔, 1 ⅓, 2, _____, _____, _____ ¾, 1 ½, 2 ¼, _____, _____, _____

Anchor Chart	Student Response Sheet
Use your decimal grid to think about the patterns.	Use your number grid to think about the patterns.

Anchor Chart decimal grid:

0.01	0.02	0.03	0.04	0.05	0.06	0.07	0.08	0.09	0.1
0.11	0.12	0.13	0.14	0.15	0.16	0.17	0.18	0.19	0.2
0.21	0.22	0.23	0.24	0.25	0.26	0.27	0.28	0.29	0.3
0.31	0.32	0.33	0.34	0.35	0.36	0.37	0.38	0.39	0.4
0.41	0.42	0.43	0.44	0.45	0.46	0.47	0.48	0.49	0.5
0.51	0.52	0.53	0.54	0.55	0.56	0.57	0.58	0.59	0.6
0.61	0.62	0.63	0.64	0.65	0.66	0.67	0.68	0.69	0.7
0.71	0.72	0.73	0.74	0.75	0.76	0.77	0.78	0.79	0.8
0.81	0.82	0.83	0.84	0.85	0.86	0.87	0.88	0.89	0.9
0.91	0.92	0.93	0.94	0.95	0.96	0.97	0.98	0.99	1.0

Student Response Sheet number grid:

1	2	3	4	5	6	7	8	9	10
11	12	13	14	15	16	17	18	19	20
21	22	23	24	25	26	27	28	29	30
31	32	33	34	35	36	37	38	39	40
41	42	43	44	45	46	47	48	49	50
51	52	53	54	55	56	57	58	59	60
61	62	63	64	65	66	67	68	69	70
71	72	73	74	75	76	77	78	79	80
81	82	83	84	85	86	87	88	89	90
91	92	93	94	95	96	97	98	99	100

Routine #8
Input/Output

The *Input/Output* Routine

The *Input/Output* routine is a common routine that is often underutilized. In the 21st century there are some great electronic input/output tables. Also, although we often use this for addition, subtraction, multiplication, and division, there are some great extensions of using this for measurement and geometry.

Materials and Tools	"I can" statement
Students should have a variety of tools to think and reason about the numbers being discussed. They should use their toolkits. Students can use manipulatives, drawings, and mental math.	**I can** reason about numbers and explain and justify my thinking. I can listen to, understand, and respond to the thinking of others and decide whether or not their reasoning makes sense. I can explain errors that I find and how they could be corrected.

Protocol	Purpose:
Overview: The teacher puts an input/output table on the board. Students are asked to determine what is done to the input value to make the output value.	• Identify patterns • Compose and decompose shapes

Protocol

Overview: The teacher puts an input/output table on the board. Students are asked to determine what is done to the input value to make the output value.

1. The teacher puts a mathematical concept on the board.
2. The teacher tells the students to take "private think time" to think about the concept.
3. After about 30 seconds, the teacher tells the students to "turn and talk to a neighbor."
4. Everyone comes back together, and students raise their hands and explain their thinking.

Purpose:

• Identify patterns
• Compose and decompose shapes

Questions:

• What do you see happening?
• What patterns do you notice?
• Is the output increasing or decreasing?
• Why do you think that?
• What models might help you figure this out?

What's the Math?

Input/Output Table should require students at different levels to explore:

Kindergarten
• Adding and subtracting

First Grade
Adding and subtracting

Second Grade
• Adding and subtracting
• Doubling and halving

Third Grade
• Doubling and halving
• Adding and subtracting
• Multiplying and dividing

Fourth Grade
• Multiplying and dividing
• Doubling and halving
• Adding and subtracting

Fifth Grade
• Multiplying and dividing
• Doubling and halving
• Adding and subtracting

Digital Versions

There are so many digital possibilities for this routine. I use the Ambleweb Primary Function Machine all the time. You can either pick a single-step operation, a two-step operation, or a random one. It is so cool and it makes sounds! The students love it. I usually will pick a function with the students, and then we decide on the input and the students have to tell me what the output is going to be. For the random setting, you never know what will come up. Sometimes they are too difficult for the grade, so I'll just say we aren't doing that one. Others are just great. Also, to do the random choice with them, I often will pick a function ahead of time and then just show them the machine and they have to decide what is happening. I have the students work on them, and then they have to tell me not what the rule is but, rather, give me a number and tell me what is going to come out. This is much more cognitively demanding for them to do and stretches their thinking.

Continued

Ambleweb Primary Function Machine	Math Playground	Topmarks	PBS Cyberchase	Commoncore Sheets
				Although I don't really promote the use of worksheets, these have some good activities. I would cut them up and have the students do a few of them because they are all different.

Classroom Vignette: *Input/Output Tables*

Mrs. Mayfield: Look at this input/output table and tell me what is happening? How do you know? Are you sure?

Input	½	¾	2	4 ¼
Output	1	1 ¼	2 ½	

Trini: I think the rule is to add ½. I think this because ½ + ½ = 1 and ¾ + ½ = 1 ¼.

Mark: I agree with her because the 2 becomes 2 ½, so the 4 would be 4 ¾.

Mrs. Mayfield: Who can prove this with a model?

Leti: I can show it on the number line …

½ ¾ 1 1 ¼ 1 ½ 1 ¾ 2 2 ¼ 2 ½

Input/Output Tables – **Kindergarten**
Beginning of the Year

Input	Output
2	3
3	4
5	6
7	8

Possible Questions:

Use your number track and tell me how far it is from _____ to _____?

What is the rule?

How do you know?

Are you sure?

A Add 1

B Add 2

End of the Year

Input	Output
5	10
4	8
3	6
1	2

A Add 1
B Add 0
C Doubling

Possible Questions:

Use your number track and tell me how far it is from _____ to _____?

What is the rule?

How do you know?

Are you sure?

Input/Output Tables – First Grade

Beginning of the Year

Input	Output
5	8
4	7
3	6
1	4

A Add 1
B Add 3
C Doubling

Possible Questions:

Use your number track and tell me how far it is from _____ to _____?

What is the rule?

How do you know?

Are you sure?

End of the Year

Input	Output
23	33
47	57
	88
92	

Possible Questions:

Use your number grid and tell me how far it is from _____ to _____?

What is the rule?

How do you know?

Are you sure?

Is the output increasing or decreasing?

Input/Output Tables – Second Grade

Beginning of the Year

Input	Output
7	14
8	16
5	10
	12
20	
	100

Possible Questions:

Use your number grid and tell me how far it is from _____ to _____?

What is the rule?

How do you know?

Are you sure?

Is the output increasing or decreasing?

Continued

End of the Year

Input	Output
250	500
100	200
700	1400
	300
	1000

Possible Questions:

Use your number grid and tell me how far it is from _____ to _____?

What is the rule?

How do you know?

Are you sure?

Is the output increasing or decreasing?

Input/Output Tables – Third Grade

Beginning of the Year

Input	43	52	68	74
Output	54	63	79	

Possible Questions:

Use your number grid and tell me how far it is from _____ to _____?

What is the rule?

How do you know?

Are you sure?

Is the output increasing or decreasing?

End of the Year

Input	4	6	7	9
Output	24	36	42	

Possible Questions:

Use your number grid and tell me how far it is from _____ to _____?

What is the rule?

How do you know?

Are you sure?

Is the output increasing or decreasing?

Input/Output Tables – Fourth Grade

Beginning of the Year

Input	⅓	2 ⅓	3 ⅓	
Output	1	3		5

Possible Questions:

Use your number line or fraction circle template and tell me how far it is from _____ to _____?

What is the rule?

How do you know?

Are you sure?

Is the output increasing or decreasing?

End of the Year

Input	25	42	78	
Output	250	420	780	900

Possible Questions:

What pattern do you see?

What is the rule?

How do you know?

Are you sure?

Is the output increasing or decreasing?

Input/Output Tables – Fifth Grade		
Beginning of the Year		

Beginning of the Year

Possible Questions:

What pattern do you see?

What is the rule?

How do you know?

Are you sure?

Is the output increasing or decreasing?

Input	◆ ⅓	▲ ⅙	⬡ 1 whole	?
Output	▱ ½	◆ ⅓	?	◆◆

End of the Year

Possible Questions:

What pattern do you see?

What is the rule?

How do you know?

Are you sure?

Is the output increasing or decreasing?

Input	0.25	0.42	0.78	
Output	2.50	4.20	7.80	9.20

Anchor Chart

An Input/Output Table routine is a quick routine where we look at a table and have to figure out what the rule is for what comes out. Sometimes we have to look at what came out and decide what went in.

We often do this with the digital tables, and they are fun because they have all kinds of sounds and gadgets.

For example:

Input	25	100	0.78	
Output	2.5	10	0.078	90

Student Response Sheet

Students do this activity orally.

It Is/It Isn't or Example/Counterexample Routine

The *It Is/It Isn't* or *Example/Counterexample* routine requires students to reason and then justify their thinking. Counterexamples are an important part of learning mathematics. This routine makes students deal with counterexamples. They have to explain why the given thing is a counterexample and not the actual thing. A great reasoning activity!

Materials and Tools	"I Can" Statement
Students should have a variety of tools to think and reason about the numbers being discussed. They should use their toolkits. Students can use manipulatives, drawings, and mental math.	**I can** reason about math concepts and explain and justify my thinking. I can listen to, understand, and respond to the thinking of others and decide whether or not their reasoning makes sense.

Protocol	Purpose:
Overview: The teacher puts a number or shape on the board. Students are asked to say what it is and then also what it isn't. 1. The teacher puts a mathematical concept on the board. 2. The teacher tells the students to take "private think time" to think about the concept. 3. After about 30 seconds, the teacher tells the students to "turn and talk to a neighbor." 4. Everyone comes back together, and students raise their hands and explain their thinking.	• Reason out loud • Think about counterexamples • Discuss the example and the counterexamples **Questions:** • Why is it not this? • What is it? • Do you agree with this?

What's the Math

It Is/It Isn't should require students at different levels to explore the following:

Kindergarten
- Adding and subtracting
- Geometry

First Grade
- Adding and subtracting
- Place value
- Geometry

Second Grade
- Even and odd
- Adding and subtracting
- Place value
- Measurement
- Geometry

Third Grade
- Even or odd
- Adding and subtracting
- Multiplying and dividing
- Place value
- Measurement
- Geometry

Fourth Grade
- Multiplying and dividing
- Multiples and factors
- Prime and composite
- Place value
- Fractions
- Decimals
- Measurement
- Geometry

Fifth Grade
- Prime and composite
- Multiples and factors
- Multiplying and dividing
- Place value
- Fractions
- Decimals
- Measurement
- Geometry

Classroom Vignette: *It Is/It Isn't*

Ms. Terri: This is a circle.

Tom: It is not a square.
Luke: It is not an oval.
Mary: It does not have straight sides.
Missy: It does not have any vertices.
Larry: It is not a triangle.

It Is/It Isn't – Kindergarten	
Beginning of the Year	**End of the Year**

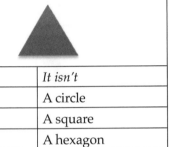

It is	It isn't
A triangle	A circle
	A square
	A hexagon
	Doesn't roll
	Doesn't have 4 sides

10	
It is	It isn't
The number 10	Smaller than 5
	Bigger than 20
	Close to 19

It Is/It Isn't – First Grade	
Beginning of the Year	**End of the Year**

It is	It isn't
A rectangle	A circle
	A triangle
	A hexagon
	Doesn't roll

100	
It is	It isn't
100	Greater than 120
	Less than 50
	A one-digit number
	A two-digit number

Continued

It Is/It Isn't – Second Grade

Beginning of the Year		End of the Year	

A hexagon		59	
It is	*It isn't*	*It is*	*It isn't*
A polygon	A 3d figure – like a cube	Odd	A single-digit number like 8
Has 6 sides	A triangle – more than 3 sides	10 less than 69	A three-digit number like 345
Has 6 angles	A quadrilateral	10 more than 49	It isn't even, like 58
Has 6 corners		Composed of 5 tens and 9 ones	

It Is/It Isn't – Third Grade

Beginning of the Year		End of the Year	

52		Trapezoid	
It is	*It isn't*		
Even	Odd, like 53		
10 more than 42	A three-digit number like 564	*It is*	*It isn't*
10 less than 62	Greater than 60 like 78	A trapezoid	A parallelogram like a square
Composed of 5 tens and 2 ones	Doesn't round to 60 like 58	A polygon	A circle – doesn't roll
	Less than 20	A quadrilateral	A 5-sided figure like a pentagon
			A 3d figure like a rectangular prism

It Is/It Isn't – Fourth Grade

Beginning of the Year		End of the Year	

1000		Acute angle	
It is	*It isn't*	*It is*	*It isn't*
Even	A two-digit number like 27	Measures less than 90 degrees	90 degrees – a right angle
A four-digit number	A three-digit number like 458	Formed at a vertex	180 degrees – a straight line
100 tens	Odd like 999		More than 90 degrees like an obtuse angle
10 hundreds	Prime like 7		

Fifth Grade – Beginning of the Year		Fifth Grade – End of the Year	

630	
It is	*It isn't*
Even	Odd
A multiple of 3, 5, 6, 9, or 10	Prime
63 tens	Greater than 800
Composite	Less than 500
	A multiple of 4 or 8

Scalene triangle	
It is	*It isn't*
A polygon	Isosceles
All sides of different length	Equilateral
3 angles, 3 sides, 3 vertices	A parallelogram
	A regular polygon

Anchor Chart

It Is/It Isn't

In this routine we are looking at something and giving counterexamples. We are saying what it is and what it is not.

Here is an example:

7	
It is	*It isn't*
Odd	Even
More than 5	Greater than 9
5 less than 12	Less than 5
	The sum of a doubles fact (whole numbers)

Student Response Sheet

It Is/It Isn't

Write about this shape. Give some counterexamples and explain your ideas.

Parallelogram

7	
It is	*It isn't*
A quadrilateral	A circle – not round
A figure with 360 degrees	A regular polygon – all the sides are not equal
A figure that has 2 pairs of parallel sides	A 3d shape like a rectangular prism

Routine #10
I was walking down the street ...

I was walking down the street ... Routine
The *I Was Walking Down the Street ...* or *I Was Walking Down the Hall ...* routine is about getting students to be flexible with their numbers. It requires them to compose and decompose numbers in a variety of ways quickly. The teacher tells a story in which an answer is given. The students have to think about and then discuss what the question was.

Materials and Tools	**"I Can" Statement**
Students should have a variety of tools to think and reason about the numbers being discussed. They should use their toolkits. Students can use manipulatives, drawings, and mental math.	**I can** think flexibly about numbers.

Continued

Protocol	Purpose:
Overview: The teacher tells the students a story about walking down the street one day and hearing someone say a number. Students are then asked to determine what the question that came before it could have been. 1. The teacher says: I was walking down the street. 2. A few students respond. 3. Teacher asks another question.	• Compose and decompose whole numbers • Compose and decompose fractions • Compose and decompose decimals

	Questions:
	• What could be the question? • What are some ways to make this number? • What are some ways to break this number up? • Are you sure?

What's the Math?

I Was Walking Down the Street … should require students at different levels to explore:

Kindergarten
- Adding and subtracting

First Grade
- Adding and subtracting
- Properties of addition

Second Grade
- Even and odd
- Adding and subtracting
- Properties of addition

Third Grade
- Adding and subtracting
- Multiplying and dividing
- Properties of addition and multiplication

Fourth Grade
- Adding and subtracting
- Multiplying and dividing
- Prime and composite

Fifth Grade
- Adding and subtracting
- Multiplying and dividing

Classroom Vignette: *I Was Walking Down the Street* …

In this routine it is important that students have a variety of manipulatives so they can think about the numbers. Students should have their templates and their tools with them. A few ideas for templates for this activity are part-part-whole mats, number bonds, five, ten, and twenty frames, and blank paper for drawing. Also number lines and number grids.

So, for example, if the teacher says, "I was walking down the street and I heard Carol say 10," the students might look at their ten frames and decide ways to make 10. The teacher would have previously taught the students that one way to find 10 is to shade in some and see what's left. Students could also use rekenreks for this activity, because they could break apart the beads and have some on one side and some on the other.

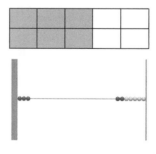

Another example is if the teacher says, "I was walking down the street and I heard Carol say 100." The students could use the blank hundred grid and shade in some numbers and see what's left. They could also use the 100-bead rekenrek.

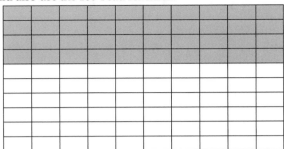

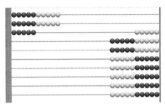

The same tools could be used to find parts of decimals. For example, the models above could just as well be 0.40 + 0.60 and 0.25 + 0.75.

I was walking down the street … – **Kindergarten**	
Beginning of the Year	**End of the Year**
I was walking down the street and I heard Jamal say:	*I was walking down the street and I heard Jamal say:*
• 3 Show me that many fingers. • 4 Draw that number on your white board. • 5 Shade that many in on your 5 frame.	• 5 Student asks: Was it 4 and 1? • 10 Student asks: Was it 5 and 5? • 2 Student asks: Was it 1 and 1?

I was walking down the street … – **First Grade**	
Beginning of the Year	**End of the Year**
I was walking down the street and I heard Kelly say:	*I was walking down the street and I heard Kelly say:*
• 8 Student asks: Was its 4 and 4? • 10 Student asks: Was it 5 and 5? • 3 Student asks: Was it 2 and 1?	• 10 Students say many different ways to make 10. • 9 *… and he didn't use any addition.* • 10 *… and he used three numbers.*

I was walking down the street … – **Second Grade**	
Beginning of the Year	**End of the Year**
I was walking down the street and I heard Jamella say:	*I was walking down the street and I heard Jamella say:*
• 10 *… and she didn't use addition.* • 12 *… and she used three numbers.* • 7 *Students find a variety of ways to make 7.*	• 50 *… and she didn't use addition.* • 100 *… and she used three numbers.* • 1000 *Students find a variety of ways to make 1000.*

Continued

I was walking down the street ... – Third Grade	
Beginning of the Year	**End of the Year**
I was walking down the street and I heard Marcos say: • 100 *... and he didn't use any addition.* • 1000 • 59 *... and he used three numbers.*	*I was walking down the street and I heard Kiyana say:* • 12 *... and she didn't use any addition or subtraction.* • 18 *... and she used 3 numbers.* • 4 *... and she only used division.*

I was walking down the street ... – Fourth Grade	
Beginning of the Year	**End of the Year**
I was walking down the street and I heard Grace say: • 18 *... and she didn't use any addition or subtraction.* • A factor of 24 *Students can refer to their multiplication grid.* • 10 *... and she only used division.*	*I was walking down the street and I heard Mike say:* • ⅝ *Students decompose this into fractions with the same denominator.* • ⅞ *... and he used 3 fractions.* • 5 *... and he only used division.* • 0.5 *Tell them to think money.*

I was walking down the street ... – Fifth Grade	
Beginning of the Year	**End of the Year**
I was walking down the street and I heard Miguel say: • 4/8 Students make it any way. • 9 *... and he didn't use any addition or subtraction.* • 10/10 *... and he used 3 numbers.*	*I was walking down the street and I heard Mary say:* • ¾ Students make it any way. • ½ *... and she didn't use any addition.* • 0.8 Think money. • 27/100 Any kind of way.

Anchor Chart

I Was Walking Down the Street ... is a routine where we have to think of different ways to make a number. You can add, subtract, multiply, or divide, but it has to make that number. You have to listen to the instructions of how to do it.

For example: I was walking down the street and I heard Todd say 100. He used 3 numbers.

Students say:

Was it 33 + 33 + 34?

Was it 102 – 1 – 1?

Was it 2 x 51 – 2?

Student Response Sheet

I was walking down the street and I heard Ricki say 15. I wonder what was the question?

Routine #11
Model That!

The *Model That!* Routine

Model That! is a quick routine that just works on modeling mathematics. Students are given an equation and told to model that! It works on building a repertoire of models. Each grade level has specific models that are required. This routine emphasizes those models while reviewing others from prior grades.

Materials and Tools	"I can" statement
Students should have a variety of tools and templates to think and reason about the numbers being discussed. They should use their toolkits. Students can use manipulatives, templates, drawings, and diagrams.	**I can** model math equations.

Protocol	Purpose:
The teacher shows an equation. The teacher asks the students to model it. Sometimes the teacher may name the model that students should use, but often it is left up to the students. 1. The teacher shows the equation. 2. Students model the equation. 3. Students share their thinking with a peer. 4. The whole class discusses their thinking.	• Practice with various models
	Questions:
	• What models did you use? • Why? • Was any of it tricky?

What's the Math?

Model That! should require students at different levels to explore:

Kindergarten
• Adding and subtracting

First Grade
• Adding and subtracting
• Properties of addition

Second Grade
• Even and odd
• Adding and subtracting
• Properties of addition
• Doubling

Third Grade
• Even and odd
• Doubling and halving
• Adding and subtracting
• Multiplying and dividing
• Properties of addition and multiplication

Fourth Grade
• Prime and composite
• Doubling and halving
• Adding and subtracting
• Multiplying and dividing
• Properties of addition and multiplication

Fifth Grade
• Prime and composite
• Doubling
• Adding and subtracting
• Multiplying and dividing
• Properties of addition and multiplication

Continued

Classroom Vignette: *Model That!*

Mrs. James: Good morning class. We are going to start our day off with *Model That!*

First expression: 3 × 3 Model that!

Claire:

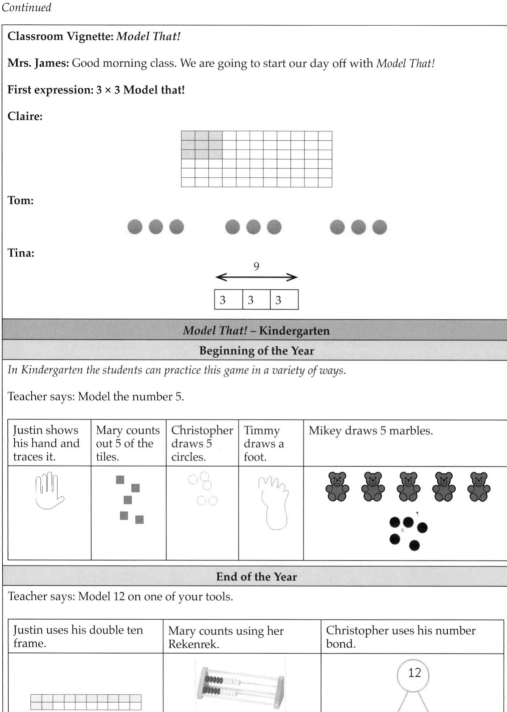

Tom:

Tina:

Model That! – Kindergarten

Beginning of the Year

In Kindergarten the students can practice this game in a variety of ways.

Teacher says: Model the number 5.

Justin shows his hand and traces it.	Mary counts out 5 of the tiles.	Christopher draws 5 circles.	Timmy draws a foot.	Mikey draws 5 marbles.

End of the Year

Teacher says: Model 12 on one of your tools.

Justin uses his double ten frame.	Mary counts using her Rekenrek.	Christopher uses his number bond.

Model That! – First Grade

Beginning of the Year

Teacher says: Model 34.

Luke uses his blank hundred grid.	Todd uses his Rekenrek.	Kylie draws a base 10 sketch.

End of the Year

Teacher says: Model 1 + 1 + 3 = 2 + 3

Left side of the equation	Right side of the equation

Model That! – Second Grade

Beginning of the Year

Teacher says: 78 + 10. Model that!

Luke uses his double ten frame.	Todd uses his Rekenrek.	Kylie draws a base 10 sketch.

End of the Year

Teacher says: 120 + 100. Model that!

Judy shaded it on her empty hundreds grids.	Mark drew a base 10 sketch.

Continued

Continued

Model That! – Third Grade		
Beginning of the Year		
Teacher says: 4 ÷ 2. Model that!		
Marline drew a rectangle cut into 4 pieces. She drew a circle around each group of 2 pieces.	Teddy drew some cookies divided by 2 friends.	Taylor drew a bar diagram.
		4
End of the Year		
Teacher says: ⅔. Model that!		
Lucia drew a rectangle divided into 3 parts with 2 parts shaded.	Bryan drew a circle divided into 3 parts with 2 parts shaded.	Michael drew a number line and plotted ⅔.
		⅓ ⅔

Model That! – Fourth Grade		
Beginning of the Year		
Teacher says: 12 × 12. Model that!		
Terri modeled it with the base 10 blocks.	Michael J. sketched it.	Katie shaded it in on the chart paper.
End of the Year		
The digital tools used for modeling come from apps.mathlearningcenter.org/number-pieces/		
Teacher says: ½ + ½ + ½ = 1 ½. Model that!		
Maya drew fraction circles.	Hong drew rectangles.	Trevor drew a number line.
		0 ½ 1 1 ½ 2

Beginning of the Year

Teacher says: 2 × ¼. Model that!

Yesenia drew a circle model.	Ted drew a rectangle model.	Luke drew a number line model.

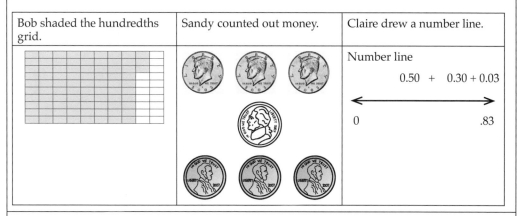

End of the Year

Teacher says: 0.83. Model that!

Bob shaded the hundredths grid.	Sandy counted out money.	Claire drew a number line.

Number line

0.50 + 0.30 + 0.03

0   .83

Anchor Chart

The routine *Model That!* is where we model math number sentences (equations).

For example:

7 − 5 = 2

Student Response Sheet

The routine *Model That!* is where we model math number sentences (equations).

For example:

I can model my mathematical thinking.

0.30 − 0.15 = 0.15

Continued

Continued

Student Response Sheets

Name:
Date:

I can model my thinking.

Number line
16 + 17

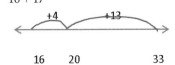

16   20   33

Name:
Date:

I can model my thinking with different tools:

Tools	
Counters	3
Number path	2 + 3
Number grid	30 – 10 = 20
Number frame	

Routine #12
Number Line It!

The *Number Line It!* Routine

The *Number Line It!* routine is fun. There are different versions. In one version, the students are given a bunch of numbers and a number line, and they have to order the numbers. In the other version, they are given a number line and asked to plot on it various numbers that the teacher either shows them or calls out.

Materials and Tools	"I Can" Statement
Template of number line or number grid.	**I can** think flexibly about numbers.

Protocol	Purpose:
The teacher tells the students which numbers to plot on the number line or a number grid. 1. Teacher gives the students a number line or a number grid and some numbers to order. 2. The students take a few minutes of private think time. 3. The students then share their thinking with a neighbor. 4. The whole class comes back together and talks about it.	• To build student flexibility • To build students' range of numbers
	Questions: • What are you thinking? • Are you sure about that? • Is there another way?

What's the Math?

Number Line It! should require students at different levels to explore:

Kindergarten/First Grade/Second Grade
- Students work with plotting whole numbers on the number line

Third Grade	Fourth Grade	Fifth Grade
• Whole numbers • Fractions	• Whole numbers • Fractions • Decimals	• Whole numbers • Fractions • Decimals

Digital Versions

www.sheppardsoftware.com/mathgames/earlymath/fruit_shoot_NumberLine.htm	www.funbrain.com/linejump/	www.abcya.com/number_line_fractions_percents_decimals.htm

Classroom Vignette: *Number Line It!*

Mrs. Lucy: Hey you all! We are going to do the *Number Line It!* routine today. Take out your number line templates.

All the students take out their laminated number line templates.

12 100 75 150 99 50

Mrs. Lucy: When ordering these numbers, what should we do? How should we think about this?

Yesenia: We need to find the beginning and the end.

Todd: And the middle.

Mrs. Lucy: OK, so what do we do with those numbers?

Tammy: Well, we should look at the big numbers like 100 and then 150.

Mrs. Lucy: So how does that help us?

Macy: Well we can order them then. Maybe we could put 200 up there and then 150 in the middle of 100 and 200.

Mrs. Lucy: Who agrees with that strategy and why?

Mason: It's good because then we could also put like 0 and 50 more ... then we could order the numbers.

Carol: Now that we know where 100 is, we can put 99.

The conversation continues until all the numbers are plotted. The students are doing this on their own individual number lines. The teacher and the students take turns recording the work on a big Class Number Line as well.

Continued

Continued

Number Line It! – Kindergarten	
Beginning of the Year	**End of the Year**
Number line it! 0 2 4 5 3	Number line it! 2 1 5 7 8 9 10 3 4 6
Number Line It! – First Grade	
Beginning of the Year	**End of the Year**
Number line it! 10 0 20 15 1 9 18	Number line it! 100 0 50 20 30 70 80 90 40 60 When all the numbers are plotted, the students then have to give other numbers that can go on the number line.
Number Line It! – Second Grade	
Beginning of the Year	**End of the Year**
Number line it! 120 10 100 50 5 90 When all the numbers are plotted, the students then have to give other numbers that can go on the number line.	Number line it! 1000 100 500 0 10 900 When all the numbers are plotted, the students then have to give other numbers that can go on the number line.
Number Line It! – Third Grade	
Beginning of the Year	**End of the Year**
Number line it! 10,000 1000 100 5000 10 When all the numbers are plotted, the students then have to give other numbers that can go on the number line.	Number line it! $\frac{3}{4}$ $\frac{1}{2}$ $\frac{1}{4}$ 1 $\frac{2}{4}$ $\frac{1}{5}$ When all the numbers are plotted, the students then have to give other numbers that can go on the number line.
Number Line It! – Fourth Grade	
Beginning of the Year	**End of the Year**
Number line it! $\frac{1}{4}$ $\frac{1}{3}$ $\frac{1}{6}$ $\frac{1}{8}$ $\frac{1}{9}$ $\frac{1}{1}$ When all the numbers are plotted, the students then have to give other numbers that can go on the number line.	Number line it! $\frac{3}{10}$ $\frac{7}{100}$ $\frac{5}{10}$ $\frac{4}{100}$ $\frac{2}{10}$ $\frac{10}{10}$ When all the numbers are plotted, the students then have to give other numbers that can go on the number line.
Number Line It! – Fifth Grade	
Beginning of the Year	**End of the Year**
Number line it! 10 0.9 0.3 0.7 0.5 When all the numbers are plotted, the students then have to give other numbers that can go on the number line.	Number line it! 0.4 $\frac{2}{4}$ 0.5 $\frac{100}{50}$ $\frac{10}{10}$ When all the numbers are plotted, the students then have to give other numbers that can go on the number line.

Anchor Chart

Number Line It! is where we plot numbers in order from least to greatest on the number line. We have a number line and a set of numbers. We have to quickly figure out what goes where. We do this by finding benchmark numbers on the number line. You have to look at the largest number and the smallest number.

50   80   90   5   10

First you look at the largest and the smallest numbers on the number line.

Plot those. Then work from there.

For example, we know that 0 and 100 is the range of this number line. So then we think which of the numbers is closest to 0 and which is closest to 100. Then we plot those and work from there.

Student Response Sheet

Name: Date:

Plot the numbers on a number line.

$\frac{2}{8}$ $\frac{1}{4}$ $\frac{3}{6}$ $\frac{5}{4}$ $\frac{2}{3}$

Routine #13
Riddle Me This!

The *Riddle Me This!* Routine
The *Riddle Me This!* routine is where the teacher thinks of a shape or number and then proceeds to give students hints so that they may find out what it is.

Materials and Tools	"I Can" Statement
Students should have a variety of tools and templates to think and reason about the numbers being discussed. They should use their toolkits. Students can use manipulatives, templates, or drawings.	**I can** reason about math topics.

Protocol	Purpose:
Overview: The teacher gives the students a description of something in the form of a riddle, and the students try to find out what it is. 1. Teacher gives the students a riddle. 2. The students take a few minutes of private think time. 3. The students then share their thinking with a neighbor. 4. The whole class comes back together and talks about it.	• Reason • Think in a step-by-step way • Understand statements and think about whether they make sense or not
	Questions: • What are you thinking? • Are you sure about that? • Is there another way?

Continued

What's the Math?

Riddle Me This should require students at different levels to explore:

Kindergarten
- Adding and subtracting

First Grade
- Adding and subtracting
- Fractions
- Measurement
- Geometry
- Place value

Second Grade
- Adding and subtracting
- Fractions
- Measurement
- Geometry
- Place value

Third Grade
- Adding and subtracting
- Multiplying and dividing
- Fractions
- Measurement
- Geometry
- Place value

Fourth Grade
- Adding and subtracting
- Multiplying and dividing
- Fractions
- Decimals
- Measurement
- Geometry
- Place value

Fifth Grade
- Adding and subtracting
- Multiplying and dividing
- Fractions
- Decimals
- Measurement
- Geometry
- Place value

Digital Versions

www.math-salamanders.com/math-riddles.html	http://thinkmath.edc.org/resource/who-am-i-puzzles

Classroom Vignette: *Riddle Me This!*

Mrs. Martinez: Hello! Today we are going to play *Riddle Me This!*

Riddle 1: I am a shape. I have 6 vertices. I am not a quadrilateral.

Ken: You have to be a hexagon, because hexagons are shapes that have 6 vertices.

Mrs. Martinez: Great thinking!

Riddle 2: I am an odd number between 1 and 20. I have 2 digits. The sum of my numbers is greater than 5.

Mrs. Martinez: OK what do we know?

Christopher: The number is a teen number. 13, 15, 17, 19.

Tiffany: The sum of the numbers is greater than 5, so that is 15, 17, or 19.

Kelly: Is the sum greater than 8?

Mrs. Martinez: No.

Todd: Then it is 15 or 17.

Grace: Is the sum greater than 6?

Mrs. Martinez: Yes.

Students call out that it's 17.

Mrs. Martinez: Tell me about your thinking. How did you all go about figuring it out?

Thalia: Well, we went number by number.

Alberto: We did it in a pattern. Like we said OK it's these numbers … so then is it these numbers?

Charlie: AND WE DIDN'T TAKE WILD GUESSES.

Everybody applauds and laughs because they have been talking about the difference between a "Wild Guess" and a "Thinking Guess."

Mrs. Martinez: [*Chuckling*] Yes, today you didn't take WILD GUESSES.

Riddle Me This! – Kindergarten

Beginning of the Year

I am a shape. I have 4 sides. The sides are all the same length.
I am a number between 1 and 5. I am bigger than 3.

End of the Year

I am a shape. I can roll. Sometimes I dress up like a can of soup.

Riddle Me This! – First Grade

Beginning of the Year

Mrs. Martin: I am a number between 0 and 50. I have 2 digits. The ones place has a zero. What do we do first so we can keep track of our thinking?
Students say write it down.
Mrs. Martin: What would we write down so far given what we know?
Trina: It has to be 10, 20, 30, or 40.
Charlie: Are you greater than 20?
Mrs. Martin: Yes, so now what do you know?
Kay: We can cross out 10 and 20.
Lili: Are you greater than 40?
Mrs. Martin: No.
Class says it has to be 30.
Mrs. Martin: Why?

End of the Year

Mrs. Johnson: I am a shape that has 6 sides, 12 edges, and 8 vertices. Who am I? Turn and talk with your neighbor. Look at your shape chart and try to figure it out. Remember you have to ask thinking questions; you can't just guess a shape!

Tommy: Are you a 3d shape?

Mrs. Johnson: Yes.

Michelle: Are your faces squares?

Mrs. Johnson: Yes.

Claire: We have enough evidence to know that this is a cube!

Mrs. Johnson: Does everybody agree with her, and if so, why?

Continued

Riddle Me This! – Second Grade
Beginning of the Year

Mr. H: I am a number between 0 and 100. I am even. The sum of my digits make 8. How do we go about thinking about that?

Luis: We need to ask some questions.

Tracie: Are you bigger than 20?

Mr. H: Yes.

Trevor: Are you bigger than 50?

Mr. H: No. OK, now what are you going to do with what you know?

Lucy: We have to block off the parts where the number could be.

Sam: We need to cross out the odd numbers too!

Rene: So we have to add up the 2 digits of all the even numbers. 22, 24, 26. We found it!

Mr. H: There are some more answers. Keep going.

Katie: 28, 30, 32, 34, 36, 38, 40, 42, 44. We found it!

Mr. H: Yes, you did! I want you to tell me about your thinking.

Hary: We did it in like a pattern. We went 1 by 1.

Mr. H: How is that helpful?

Corinne: Because otherwise we would just be guessing numbers wildly. We did a Thinking Guess!

End of the Year

Mr. Ted: I am a type of measurement. Each one of me is about as long as a lady bug. I could also be the length of an ant.

John: Are the letters cm?

Mr. Ted: Yes.

Class says that cm is centimeters, and they are the size of a ladybug or ant.

Riddle Me This! – Third Grade
Beginning of the Year

Ms. Tomas: I am a number between 0 and 1000. I am even. The sum of my digits is 5. There is more than one answer. Think about what you know just from the clues. Look at your thousand grid.

Mike: We don't know. We have to ask some questions first.

Ms. Tomas: Yes you do, but you already know something. What is it? Think about the clues.

Holly: The sum of the digits is 5, so it can't be more than 500 …

Ms. Tomas: OK.

Carol: Are you greater than 100?

Ms. Tomas: Yes.

Raul: Are you greater than 200?

Ms. Tomas: Yes.

Tami: Are you greater than 400?

Ms. Tomas: No.

Riley: So, it is in the 300's and it is even … 302 makes 5!

Ms. Tomas: Are you sure?

Riley: Yes, because it is even and it is the 300's. That's one of the numbers.

Ms. Tomas: Are there any more? How do you know?

End of the Year

I am a shape. I have 4 equal-length sides. I have 4 right angles. What shape am I?

I am a measurement. You use me to measure liquids. I am the measurement of a large bottle of soda or a big bottle of water. Who am I?

I am a two-digit number. I am an odd number. I am less than 7 × 3. I am more than 5 × 2. The sum of my digits is equivalent to 3 × 2.

Riddle Me This! – Fourth Grade
Beginning of the Year

I am a polygon. I am a quadrilateral. I have only 1 pair of parallel sides. What shape am I?

I am a prime number. I am more than 4 squared and less than 5 squared. The sum of my digits is the same as $^{48}/_6$.

I am a three-digit number. I am even. I am greater than 10×50 and less than 10×55. The sum of my digits is 7.   What numbers could I be?

End of the Year

I am not a composite number. I am greater than 1 and less than 20. I am more than 4 squared. The sum of my digits is 10. Who am I?

I am a unit of measurement. People use me to talk about how much something weighs. I would be used when talking about apples or someone's weight. I am part of the customary system. Who am I?

I am a two-digit number. I am not composite. I am greater than 7×6. I am less than 8×8. The difference between my two digits is 3. Who am I?

Riddle Me This! – Fifth Grade
Beginning of the Year

I am $2 \times \frac{1}{10} + 3 \times \frac{1}{100}$. Who am I?

I am less than half of 100. I am a composite number. If you round me to the nearest 10, I would round up. I am more than 6 squared. The sum of my 2 digits is equivalent to 3×4.

I am a unit of measurement. You use me when you are talking about distance. I am part of the metric system. Who am I?

End of the Year

I am a benchmark fraction. My equivalent is a tenth less than .60. Who am I?

I am a composite number. One of my factors is 5. My other factor is 1 more than 3 squared. I am more than 7 squared. I am even. I am less than 8 squared.

I am a decimal. I am less than $4 \times .02$. I am more than $3 \times .01$. I am less than the difference between .10 and .05. Who am I?

Continued

Anchor Chart	Student Response Sheet
Riddle Me This is a game where we have to use the clues to guess a number. For example: I am greater than 1 and less than 10. I am not even. I am bigger than the difference between 12 and 4. What am I? We have to break down each part. You can't take wild guesses. You have to think about it and take a "thinking guess." The number is greater than 1 and less than 10, but it can't be even. So we list those numbers. The number is bigger than the difference between 12 and 4, which is 8. So the number must be 9. 3, 5, 7, **9**	Name: Date: Use this template to show your thinking. Students can think on their individual white boards, journals, or thinking templates with pre-made models such as number lines, ten frames, or hundreds grids.

Routine #14
3 Truths and a Fib

The *3 Truths and a Fib* Routine	
The *3 Truths and a Fib* routine is a reasoning routine where students have to read a series of statements or facts and then decide which one isn't true. It really emphasizes students' understanding of math vocabulary.	
Materials and Tools Students should have a variety of tools and templates to think and reason about the numbers being discussed. They should use their toolkits. Students can use manipulatives, templates, drawings, or diagrams.	**"I Can" Statement** **I can** reason about math topics.
Protocol The teacher writes four statements on the board. Three are true and the fourth is false. Students need to select the false statement and support their thinking with evidence. 1. The teacher gives the students the statements. 2. The students take a few minutes of private think time. 3. The students then share their thinking with a neighbor. 4. The whole class comes back together and talks about it.	**Purpose:** • Reason • Think in a step-by-step way • Understand statements and think about whether they make sense or not

* In some versions, students have individual pupil response sticks that say "Fact" on one side and "Fib" on the other.

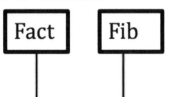

Questions:

- What are you thinking?
- Are you sure about that?
- Is there another way?

What's the Math?

3 Truths and a Fib should require students at different levels to explore:

Kindergarten
- Adding and subtracting
- Place value

First Grade
- Adding and subtracting
- Place value
- Fractions
- Geometry

Second Grade
- Adding and subtracting
- Place value
- Fractions
- Geometry
- Measurement

Third Grade
- Adding and subtracting
- Multiplying and dividing
- Place value
- Fractions
- Geometry
- Measurement

Fourth Grade
- Adding and subtracting
- Multiplying and dividing
- Place value
- Fractions
- Decimals
- Geometry
- Measurement

Fifth Grade
- Adding and subtracting
- Multiplying and dividing
- Place value
- Fractions
- Decimals
- Geometry
- Measurement

Digital Versions

www.hoodriver.k12.or.us/ cms/lib06/OR01000849/ Centricity/Domain/856/ three_facts_ad_a_fib_ template_example.pdf	http://mathequalslove. blogspot.com/2016/03/ two-truths-and-lie-parent-functions.html	http://teachingwithstowe. blogspot.com/2016/07/ two-truths-and-lie-writing-in-math-class.html
	[QR code]	[QR code]

Continued

Classroom Vignette: *3 Truths and a Fib*

Mrs. Haley: Good morning. Today we are going to do *3 Truths and a Fib*. Look at these statements and think about which one is incorrect. Remember to have your templates ready to help you think about these numbers if you need them.

• 50 is 10 more than 60.	• 77 is 3 less than 80.
• 105 is 100 less than 205.	• 67 is 10 less than 76.

Kate: We think it is 67 is 10 less than 76, because it looks true but it's not. 67 is 10 less than 77.

Mrs. Haley: Who agrees?

The class nods in agreement.

Mrs. Haley: Next one.

This is a square.	This is a triangle.	This is a hexagon.	This is not a polygon.

3 Truths and a Fib – Kindergarten
Beginning of the Year

10 is bigger than 5.	5 is bigger than 1.
1 is bigger than 2.	7 is in between 6 and 8

End of the Year

10 is bigger than 8.	12 is bigger than 10.
10 is bigger than 20.	11 is 2 more than 9

3 Truths and a Fib – First Grade
Beginning of the year

This is a square	This is a rectangle.	This is a hexagon.	This is a triangle.

End of the Year

20 is ten more than 40.	40 is 10 less than 50.
100 is 10 more than 90.	70 is 10 more than 60.

3 Truths and a Fib – Second Grade

Beginning of the Year

500 is 100 more than 600.	700 is 100 less than 800.
102 is in between 100 and 105.	670 is 10 less than 680.

5 is not even.	8 is even.
6 is not odd.	7 is not odd.

End of the Year

¼ is a fraction.	⅓ is a fraction.
2 is a fraction.	½ is a fraction.

2 groups of 5 is 10.	3 groups of 3 is 9.
5 groups of 3 is 15.	4 groups of 2 is 6.

3 Truths and a Fib – Third Grade

Beginning of the Year

3×3 is 6.	4×4 is 16.
5×5 is 25.	2×2 is 4.

Liters measure liquid.	Grams measure weight.
Centimeters measure length.	Meters measure liquid.

End of the Year

This is a special type of rectangle.	This is a parallelogram.	This is a polygon.	This is not a parallelogram.

3 Truths and a Fib – Fourth Grade

Beginning of the Year

$^{16}/_4 = 4$	$^{25}/_5 = 5$
$^{50}/_5 = 10$	$^{64}/_8 = 7$

Continued

This is a quadrilateral.	This is a parallelogram.	This is not a polygon.	This a parallelogram.

End of the year

Quarts measure liquid.	Pounds measure weight.
Pints measure length.	Cups measure liquid.

7 is not composite.	28 is composite.
13 is not prime.	15 is composite.

3 Truths and a Fib – Fifth Grade

Beginning of the Year

12 × 12 = 144	11 × 11 = 121	¼ is smaller than ⅓.	⅓ is greater than ⅙.
12 × 11 = 133	10 × 10 = 100	²⁄₂ is the same as 2.	¾ is less than ⁵⁄₄.

End of the Year

0.574 rounds to 0.6	0.481 rounds to 0.5	L × W × H = volume	A = L × W
0.829 round to 0.9	0.333 round to 0.3	P = 2w + 2L	P = w + 1

Anchor Chart

3 Truths and a Fib is a routine where we have to think about statements and then decide which one is incorrect.

For example:

16 is bigger than 15.
5 is not even.
6 is not odd.
20 is 10 less than 40.

Then we have to think about each one. The last one is not correct. Sometimes we use our templates to help us think about the statements.

Student Response Sheet

Name: Date:

Make up 3 truths and a fib.

The *True or False* Routine

True or False is a routine that focuses on reasoning. Students are presented with mathematical statements that are either true or false. They must reason about those statements themselves, in pairs, in small groups, and as a whole group to determine whether or not the statements make mathematical sense.

Materials and Tools

Students should have a variety of tools to think and reason about the numbers being discussed. They should use their toolkits. Students can use manipulatives, drawings, and mental math.

"I Can" Statement

I can reason about numbers and explain and justify my thinking. I can listen to, understand, and respond to the thinking of others and decide whether or not their reasoning makes sense.

Protocol

Overview: The teacher puts some mathematical concept on the board, and the students have to vote whether or not it is true or false.

1. The teacher puts a mathematical concept on the board.
2. The teacher tells the students to take "private think time" to think about the concept.
3. After about 30 seconds, the teacher tells the students to "turn and talk to a neighbor."
4. Everyone comes back together and students raise their hand with:
   a. thumbs up if they think it is true
   b. thumbs down if they think it is false
   c. thumbs sideways if they are not sure.
5. The teacher calls on various students to explain their thinking.

Purpose:

- Reason alone
- Reason with others and follow their thinking
- Determine whether something is true or false
- Defend one's own thinking
- Defend the thinking of another

Questions:

- How do you know that?
- Are you sure about that?
- Can you prove it?
- Can you show me another way?
- Does that make sense?
- Does this always work?

What's the Math?

True or False? should require students at different levels to explore:

Kindergarten
- Adding and subtracting
- Decomposing numbers
- Finding how many more to 10
- Counting
- Measurement
- Place value

First Grade
- Adding and subtracting
- Properties of addition
- Relationship between addition and subtraction
- Addition and subtraction strategies
- Understanding the meaning of the equal sign
- Determining if equations are true or false
- Measurement
- Place value
- Fractions

Second Grade
- Even and odd
- Adding and subtracting
- Properties of addition
- Relationship between addition and subtraction
- Addition and subtraction strategies
- Understanding the meaning of the equal sign
- Determining if equations are true or false
- Measurement
- Place value
- Fractions

Continued

Continued

Third Grade	Fourth Grade	Fifth Grade
• Even and odd • Doubling and halving • Adding and subtracting • Multiplying and dividing • Properties of addition and multiplication • Fractions • Decimals • Geometry	• Multiplying and dividing • Multiplicative comparison • Multiples and factors • Prime and composite • Measurement • Place value • Fractions • Decimals • Geometry	• Prime and composite • Multiples and factors • Multiplying and dividing • Writing and interpreting numerical expressions • Analyzing patterns and relationships • Measurement • Place value • Fractions • Geometry

Classroom Vignette: True or False?

Dr. Nicki: We are going to do True or False today.

Trapezoids are parallelograms. True or False?

Some students give a thumbs-up, others a thumbs sideways, and some a thumbs-down.

Dr. Nicki: OK, I have a question after looking at your responses: Who can explain what a trapezoid is and what a parallelogram is?

Trina: A trapezoid is the red one.

Dr. Nicki: What do you mean?

Trina: You know, in the blocks … a trapezoid is the red one.

Dr. Nicki: Oh, OK. Can you go get one? Let's take a look at it and think about this question using that model.

Trina: [Gets the trapezoid] It has four sides.

Dr. Nicki: What else?

Grace: It has four straight sides but two of them will touch, and a parallelogram has two pairs of parallel sides.

Dr. Nicki: Who agrees with Grace?

The entire routine takes about 10 minutes.

True or False? – Kindergarten	
Beginning of the Year	**End of the Year**
Operations and Algebraic Thinking • This is the number one. $$\boxed{1}$$ • $3 + 2 = 4$ • 3 squares are shaded:	**Operations and Algebraic Thinking** • This is the number twelve. $$\boxed{12}$$ • $5 + 5 = 10$ • 6 squares are not shaded:

This is 5 cats:

Geometry
- A circle has no straight sides.
- A triangle has 4 sides.
- A rectangle has 3 sides.

The number that goes in the other circle is 5.

- When you add 0 to a number, the number stays the same.
  Examples:
  $5 + 0 = 5$
  $12 + 0 = 12$
  - Is this always true?

Place Value
- $18 = 10 + 8$
- $10 + 5 = 18$
- $18 = 10 + 8$

Geometry
- A circle has 1 curved side.
- This is a triangle:

True or False? – First Grade	
Beginning of the Year	**End of the Year**
Operations and Algebraic Thinking • This is the number 20. `20` • $3 + 2 = 5$ • 1 more than 5 is 7 • $19 = 10 + 8$ • When you subtract a number from itself, you get 0. **Place Value** • $15 = 10 + 5$ • $10 + 8 = 18$ **Geometry** • Circles have no straight sides. • Triangles have 3 sides. • Squares have 5 sides.	**Operations and Algebraic Thinking** • This is the number 82. `82` • $4 + 6 = 10$ • $2 + 5 = 3 + 4$ • $2 + 2 + 6 = 4 + 6$ • To find $8 - \_\_\_ = 6$, I can think $6 + 2$ • $8 + 9$ is a near doubles or neighbor numbers fact • $4 + 3 = 4 + 4 - 1$ **Place Value** • $20 + 80 = 100$ • $25 + 40 = 90$ • $45 + 9 = 45 + 5 + 4$ **Geometry** • Circles have no straight sides. • Circles are polygons. • Triangles have to have all equal sides.

Continued

True or False? – Second Grade	
Beginning of the Year	**End of the Year**

Operations and Algebraic Thinking

- $8 + 9 = 4 + 4 + 9$
- $10 - 7 = 2$
- $3 - 1 = 4 - 2$
- $3 + 4 + 1 = 8$

Place Value

- $21 > 76$
- $42 < 50$
- $33 + 8 = 33 + 7 + 1$

Geometry

These are all triangles:

Operations and Algebraic Thinking

- 7 is odd.
- 18 is even.
- 40 is the double of 20.
- 8 doubled is 16.
- $15 = 6 + 9$
- When adding two numbers, I can add the tens first and then the ones.

Examples:

- $24 + 39 = 20 + 30 + 13$
- $35 + 49 + 20 = 34 + 50 + 20$

Place Value

- 200 has 20 tens.
- When you skip count by 5's, the number always ends in 5 or 0.
- 540 is greater than 430.
- $40 + 11 + 29 = 40 + 40 = 80$

Measurement

- A ruler is longer than a yardstick.
- A centimeter is shorter than an inch.
- A pencil is about 8 inches long.
- A pen is about 4 cm long.
- 5 dimes is worth more than 2 quarters.

Geometry

- This is a pentagon:

True or False? – Third Grade	
Beginning of the Year	**End of the Year**

Algebraic Thinking

- 14 is not odd.
- Half of 100 is 50.
- $29 + 33 = 30 + 32$
- $4 + 3 + 47 = 10 + 4$

Place Value

- $257 + 100 = 267$

Algebraic Thinking

- $15 \div 3 = 3 \times 5$
- $2 \times 7 \times 2 = (2 \times 7) + (2 \times 7)$
- 133 is even.
- Half of 114 is 57.
- When you multiply a number times zero, you get zero.
- $2 \times 7 = 1 \times 14$

Geometry

- This is a triangle:

- A meter stick has 100 cm.
- An inch is longer than a centimeter.
- A door is about 8 ft tall.
- A desk is about 3 cm long.
- 10 nickels and 2 quarters is more than $1.

Place Value

- $202 \times 8 = (102 \times 8) + (102 \times 8)$
- 254 has 25 tens and 4 ones.
- 54 rounds to 50.

Fractions

- $\frac{2}{2} = 1$
- $\frac{2}{3} > \frac{1}{2}$

Geometry

- This is a hexagon:

- A trapezoid is a quadrilateral.

Measurement

- You can measure liquid in grams.
- You can meausure weight in liters.
- You can find the perimeter by adding the sides.
- You can find the area by multiplying the sides.

True or False? – Fourth Grade

Beginning of the Year	End of the Year
Operations and Algebraic Thinking	**Operations and Algebraic Thinking**
• 17 is the product of 4×4	• 32 is a prime number
• 32 is the quotient of 9×4	• 16 is a factor of 16
• $6 \times 8 = (6 \times 4) + (6 \times 4)$	• 33 is a multiple of 8
Place Value	• $7 \times 2 = 2 \times 7$
• $40 \times 9 = (20 \times 9) + (20 \times 9)$	**Place Value**
• 1000 has 10 hundreds	• $45 \times 15 = (45 \times 10) + (45 \times 5)$
• 5489 rounds to 6000	• $\frac{92}{5} = (\frac{60}{5}) + (\frac{30}{5})$ with a remainder of 2
Fractions	• $5678 = 500 + 60 + 7 + 8$
• $\frac{5}{10} = \frac{3}{6}$	• $673 > 763$
• $\frac{1}{4} > \frac{1}{2}$	**Fractions**
• $\frac{5}{5} = 1$	• $\frac{3}{6} = \frac{4}{8}$
Measurement	• $\frac{5}{6} = \frac{2}{6} + \frac{1}{6} + \frac{1}{6} + \frac{1}{6}$
• We measure a door in grams	• $\frac{2}{4} + \frac{2}{4} = \frac{4}{8}$
• A baby elephant weigh about 40 grams	• $\frac{5}{8} - \frac{3}{8} = \frac{2}{16}$
• A regular glass holds about 4 liters	• $\frac{3}{10} = \frac{30}{100}$
Geometry	• $0.45 = \frac{45}{10}$
• A hexagon has 6 sides	**Measurement**
• This is a triangle	• We can measure a door in kilometers
• This is a hexagon	• A baby elephant weighs about 4 oz
• A rectangular prism has 6 sides	• There are 3 feet in a yard
• A cube has 12 edges	• 2 quarters and 4 nickels are less than $1
	• An obtuse angle is greater than 90°
	• This is a ray
	• These are not perpendicular lines

Continued

Do lots of unit of measurement questions. Students always do poorly with these questions. Do them throughout the year.

Geometry

- This is a trapezoid (Show a right-angled trapezoid)
- This is a hexagon (Show an irregular one)
- All quadrilaterals are parallelograms
- All parallelograms are quadrilaterals

True or False? – **Fifth Grade**	
Beginning of the Year	**End of the Year**
Operations and Algebraic Thinking - 79 is prime - 9 is a factor of 3 - 10 is a multiple of 2 - $5 \times 6 \times 10 = 560$ - You can break apart numbers to make problems easier. Justify your thinking and give me an example. **Fractions and decimals** - 3 halves is equivalent to 1 and ½ - 6 thirds is equivalent to 2 **Measurement** - An obtuse angle is over 180 degrees. - An acute angle is 90 degrees. - A right angle is 90 degrees. **Geometry** - A square is a rectangle. - There are different types of trapezoids. - Trapezoids are parallelgrams.	**Operations and Algebraic Thinking** - A way to multiply 29 and 28 is to round 29 to 30 and then subtract a set - 497 is a multple of 7 - 15 is a factor of 45 - $12 \times 15 = 6 \times 30$ **Fractions and Decimals** - $\frac{1}{2} \times \frac{1}{2} = \frac{2}{4}$ - $\frac{1}{3} + \frac{1}{6} = \frac{1}{2}$ - $3 \div \frac{1}{3} = 9$ thirds **Measurement** - The formula for perimeter is $2l + 2w$ - The formula for area is $2l \times 2w$ - The formula for volume is $l \times w \times h$ **Geometry** - All quadrilaterals have right angles. - All quadrilaterals are parallelograms. - A square is a rhombus but a rhombus isn't a square.

Anchor Chart

We can think about whether math ideas are *True or False*. We can use math tools to help.

Example: Is this true or false?

$$2 + 2 = 5 - 1$$

Student: Yes this is true, because when you do the math it comes out the same on both sides. I used counters to do it.

Student Response Sheet

We can think about whether math ideas are *True or False*. We can use math tools to help.

Example: Is this true or false?

$^{30}/_{100} = {}^{3}/_{10}$

Student: Yes this is true. You can use hundred grids to prove it. First you shade in 30 hundredths on one grid. Then on the other grid color in 3 tenths. Then you can see they equal the same amount.

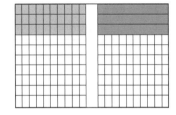

Student Response Sheets

Name:
Date:

Is it true or false?
$9 + 8 = 8 + 8 + 1$

Justify your thinking with numbers, words, and/or pictures.

Yes this is true, because 9 + 8 is a doubles plus one fact. It is 8 + 8 + 1 more.

Name:
Date:

Is it true or false? $3 \times 2 = 6$

I can use:

Counters	▣ ▣ ▣ ▣ ▣ ▣
Number path	1 2 3 4 5 6 7 8 9 10
Number grid	
Drawing	●● ●● ●●

Continued

Name:
Date:

Instructions: Pick a box and explain your thinking.

1. When you multiply by zero, you always get 0.

True	False

2. When you divide by 1, you get 1.

True	False

3. When you multiply 2 even numbers, you get an even number.

True	False

True	False

True	False

*Adapted from Silver, Brunstung, & Walsh (2008)

Anchor Chart

We can think about whether math ideas are *True or False*. We can use math tools to help.

Example: Is this true or false?

$$2 + 2 = 5 - 1$$

Student: Yes this is true, because when you do the math it comes out the same on both sides. I used counters to do it.

Student Response Sheet

We can think about whether math ideas are *True or False*. We can use math tools to help.

Example: Is this true or false?

$$\tfrac{30}{100} = \tfrac{3}{10}$$

Student: Yes this is true. You can use hundred grids to prove it. First you shade in 30 hundredths on one grid. Then on the other grid color in 3 tenths. Then you can see they equal the same amount.

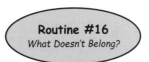

The *What Doesn't Belong?* Routine
The *What Doesn't Belong?* routine focuses on reasoning across different mathematics topics. Students are presented with a variety of options, and they have to figure out *which one is not like the others*. They can work by themselves, in pairs, in small groups, and as a whole group to determine what doesn't belong. Another version involves the inverse of this game, where you give the students three boxes filled in with something and then ask them what else belongs? Even when playing the first version of this game, once the students have figured out what doesn't belong, I have them tell me what else could go in the box.

Materials and Tools	"I Can" Statement
Students should have a variety of tools to think and reason about the ideas being discussed. They should use their toolkits. Students can use manipulatives, drawings, and mental math.	**I can** reason about numbers and explain and justify my thinking. I can listen to, understand, and respond to the thinking of others and decide whether or not their reasoning makes sense.

Protocol	Questions:
Overview: The teacher puts some mathematical concept on the board, and the students have to decide which one of the boxes doesn't belong and why.	<ul><li>How do you know that?</li><li>Are you sure about that?</li><li>Can you prove it?</li><li>Can you show me another way?</li><li>Does that make sense?</li><li>Does this always work?</li></ul>

1. The teacher puts a mathematical concept on the board.	
2. The teacher tells the students to take "private think time" to think about the concept.	
3. After about 30 seconds, the teacher tells the students to "turn and talk to a neighbor."	**Purpose:**
4. They have to pick the one they think doesn't belong and justify their reasoning with their neighbor.	<ul><li>Reason alone</li><li>Reason with others and follow their thinking</li><li>Determine whether something is true or false</li></ul>
5. Everyone comes back together and students raise their hands.	<ul><li>Defend one's own thinking</li></ul>
6 The teacher calls on various students to explain their thinking.	<ul><li>Defend the thinking of another</li></ul>

Continued

What's the Math?

What Doesn't Belong? should require students at different levels to explore:

Kindergarten

- Adding and subtracting
- Decomposing numbers
- Finding how many more to 10
- Counting

First Grade

- Adding and subtracting
- Properties of addition
- Relationship between addition and subtraction
- Addition and subtraction strategies
- Understanding the meaning of the equal sign
- Determining if equations are true or false

Second Grade

- Even and odd
- Adding and subtracting
- Properties of addition
- Relationship between addition and subtraction
- Addition and subtraction strategies
- Understanding the meaning of the equal sign
- Determining if equations are true or false

Third Grade

- Even and odd
- Doubling and halving
- Adding and subtracting
- Multiplying and dividing
- Properties of addition and multiplication
- Measurement
- Geometry

Fourth Grade

- Multiplying and dividing
- Multiplicative comparison
- Multiples and factors
- Prime and composite
- Measurement
- Geometry

Fifth Grade

- Prime and composite
- Multiples and factors
- Multiplying and dividing
- Writing and interpreting numerical expressions
- Analyzing patterns and relationships
- Measurement
- Geometry

The Digital Connection

What Doesn't Belong – Twitter	What Doesn't Belong – website	Downey Unified School District resources	For Kindergarten, be sure to Google the *Sesame Street* songs that go: "One of these things …." (There are several with different themes.)
▣ QR code	▣ QR code	www.dusd.net/cgi/files/2014/10/3-of-these-things-examples.pdf www.dusd.net/cgi/files/2012/12/OneofTheseThings.pdf	https://www.youtube.com/watch?v=6b0ftfKFEJg https://www.youtube.com/watch?v=aFbK0mE06FY https://www.youtube.com/watch?v=GC3AIV7CmVk

Classroom Vignette: *What Doesn't Belong?*

Mrs Shakhira: Good morning. Today we are going to start with the math routine *What Doesn't Belong?* We have been studying fractions, so let's begin with this.

½	⅔
2⁄4	5⁄10

Students think by themselves and then turn and talk with a neighbor.

Jamal: I think ⅔ doesn't belong, because it is not equivalent to half and all the others are.

Kelly: I agree that ⅔ doesn't belong, but I would add that it is the only fraction that is more than half.

Kim: I think ⅔ doesn't belong but for different reasons. It is the only one that doesn't have a denominator that is a multiple of 2.

Mrs. Shakhira: Great ideas. Can anyone tell me another fraction that would not belong and why?

Kylie: ⅘ would not belong because it is not equivalent to ½.

Mrs. Shakhira: Great warm-up you guys. Good thinking. Keep it up.

What Doesn't Belong? – Kindergarten

Beginning of the Year	End of the Year

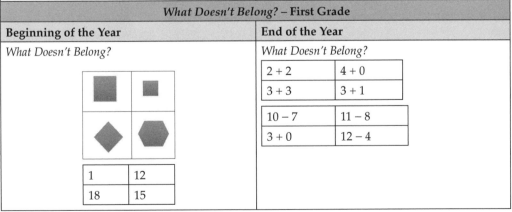

What Doesn't Belong? – Second Grade	
Beginning of the Year	**End of the Year**
What Doesn't Belong?	*What Doesn't Belong?*

<table>
<tr><td>

2 + 3	4 + 5
3 + 4	3 + 1

14 − 4	4 + 0
7 − 3	10 − 6

</td><td>

12	14
13	50

</td></tr>
</table>

What Doesn't Belong? – Third Grade	
Beginning of the Year	**End of the Year**
What Doesn't Belong?	*What Doesn't Belong?*

<table>
<tr><td>

12	36
18	7

40	41
38	49

</td><td>

$\frac{5}{3}$	$\frac{1}{2}$
$\frac{3}{4}$	$\frac{2}{4}$

</td></tr>
</table>

What Doesn't Belong? – Fourth Grade			
Beginning of the Year		**End of the Year**	

What Doesn't Belong?

m	km
cm	l

16	48
24	33

What Doesn't Belong?

cups	oz
lb	l

⅛	¼
½	⅙

What Doesn't Belong? – Fifth Grade			
Beginning of the Year		**End of the Year**	

What Doesn't Belong?

4/4	3/6
2/12	2/3

(use your pattern blocks)

16	48
24	33

5/6 − 6/6	½ + ⅔
2/6 + 3/6	2 + 3 + ⅙

What Doesn't Belong?

(Use your hundredths grids or decimal circles to reason about this.)

2 × ¹⁄₁₀ + 0.5	20 × ¹⁄₁₀₀ + 0.5
200 x ¹⁄₁₀₀₀ + 0.5	20 × ¹⁄₁₀ + 0.5

0.78	0.81
0.79	0.88

Anchor Chart

In the *What Doesn't Belong?* routine, we have to look at all four boxes and decide which one doesn't belong.

For example:

56	58
61	68

When we look at these numbers, we could think different things:

One thing is that 68 doesn't belong because it doesn't round to 60 and all of the others do. However, we could look at it a different way and pick 61 because it is the only odd number. Somebody else might say that 61 is the only one that when you add the numbers together, it is less than 10 (or that the sum of those two numbers is the only one that is a single-digit number).

Student Activity Sheet

What Doesn't Belong?

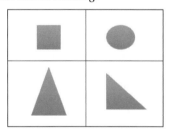

Explain your thinking. Use numbers, words, drawings, or diagrams to make your points.

Routine #17
What's Missing?

The *What's Missing?* Routine

The *What's Missing?* routine requires students to look at a sequence of numbers or an equation and determine what is missing. In some cases, students have to reason about the pattern. In other cases, they have to reason about the missing number.

Materials and Tools	**"I Can" Statement**
Students should have a variety of tools to think and reason about the numbers being discussed. They should use their toolkits. Students can use manipulatives, drawings, and mental math.	**I can** determine the missing number in a counting sequence. (K, 1) **I can** determine the missing number in an equation. (1–5)
Protocol Overview: The teacher puts a sequence of numbers or an equation on the board. Students are asked to find the missing number in the pattern or equation. 1. The teacher puts a pattern or equation on the board. 2. The teacher tells the students to take "private think time" to think about the concept. 3. After about 30 seconds, the teacher tells the students to "turn and talk to a neighbor." 4. Everyone comes back together, and students raise their hands and explain their thinking.	**Purpose:** • Work with a missing number • Reason about the missing number • Reason about a pattern • Explain thinking out loud **Questions:** • Are the numbers increasing or decreasing? By how much? • Are we multiplying or dividing? • What is it? • Do you agree with this?

What's the Math?

What's missing? should require students at different levels to explore:

Kindergarten
- Adding and subtracting

First Grade
- Adding and subtracting
- Properties of addition

Second Grade
- Even and odd
- Adding and subtracting
- Properties of addition
- Doubling and halving

Third Grade
- Adding and subtracting
- Properties of addition
- Doubling and halving
- Multiplying and dividing
- Properties of addition and multiplication

Fourth Grade
- Adding and subtracting
- Properties of addition
- Doubling and halving
- Multiplying and dividing

Fifth Grade
- Adding and subtracting
- Properties of addition
- Doubling and halving
- Multiplying and dividing

Classroom Vignette: *What's Missing?*

Mr. Benson: Good afternoon everyone. Today we are going to start with What's Missing?

      Problem 1: _____, _____, 42, 49, _____, 63, _____

Mr. Benson: Look at the numbers and think about a possible pattern. [*He leaves a couple of minutes.*] Now turn and talk to your neighbor. Tell them what you think and why.

Everyone is stuck. Mr. Benson asks them which tool could they possibly use to help them. Carol calls out the number line or the hundred grid. Students begin to study their tools and think. Mr. Benson looks around and asks someone to tell the class what they are thinking.

Dan: I am trying to figure out the pattern.

Telly: Is it 5?

Mr. Benson: How did you come up with 5?

Telly: I guessed.

Mr. Benson: Well, check your guess to see if 5 works. Look closely at the numbers and then calculate.

Sharon: [*Shouts out excitedly*] I think I got it.

Mr. Benson: OK, check it first at your table. Then don't tell me the answer … tell me what are two of the missing terms only.

Sharon: OK, 56 and 70.

Mr. Benson: Based on what Sharon said, who can see the pattern? … Give me the other two missing terms.

Many more students now raise their hands.

Kylie: 28 and 35.

Mr. Benson: OK, don't tell me the pattern yet … I want somebody to add to the sequence, either before or after.

Hong: We could put 77 and 84.

Mr. Benson: What would be the 20th term?

Class looks puzzled.

Marta: [*Raising her hand*] That's easy … it would be 140.

Mr. Benson: Why?

Marta: Because we are just multiplying by 7, so 7 times 2 is 14, and 7 times 20 would be 175.

Continued

Continued

What's Missing? – Kindergarten	
Beginning of the Year	**End of the Year**
What's Missing?	*What's Missing?*
1, 2, 3, 4, 5, _____ 7, 8 10, 11, 12, 13, _____ 15, 16 14, 15, 16, 17, _____, _____, _____, _____, 22	10, 20, 30, _____, _____, _____, 70 27, 28, 29, _____, _____, 32 55, 56, 57, _____, _____, _____, _____

What's Missing? – First Grade	
Beginning of the Year	**End of the Year**
What's Missing?	*What's Missing?*
87, 88, 89, _____, _____, _____, 93, 94 10, 20, _____, _____, _____, 60 $5 +$ _____ $= 10$	$10 = 7 +$ _____ $19 = 9 +$ _____ $7 = 14 -$ _____ $3 + 1 = 1 +$ _____ 40, _____, _____, _____, 80

What's Missing? – Second Grade	
Beginning of the Year	**End of the Year**
What's Missing?	*What's Missing?*
$10 =$ _____ $+ 6$ $5 = 10 -$ _____ $3 + 3 + 4 =$ _____ $+ 4 + 3$ $4 + 2 + 8 = 8 +$ _____	$20 = 8 +$ _____ $500 = 1000 -$ _____ $100 = 10 + 40 +$ _____ 100, 200, 300, _____, _____, _____, 700 45, 55, 65, _____, _____, _____, _____, 115 $1000 =$ _____ $+ 900$

What's Missing? – Third Grade	
Beginning of the Year	**End of the Year**
What's Missing? $499 = 500 -$ _____ $100 = 10 + 40 +$ _____ 100, 200, 300, _____, _____, _____, 700 45, 55, 65, _____, _____, _____, _____, 115 $1000 =$ _____ $+ 900$ $55 = 30 +$ _____ _____ $= 250 + 250$	*What's Missing?* $10 = 5 \times$ _____ _____ $= 12 \div 3$ $20 = 2 \times$ _____ $10,000 = 5,000 +$ _____

What's Missing? – Fourth Grade	
Beginning of the Year	**End of the Year**
What's Missing? $1000 = 500 + 250 +$ _____ _____ $= 72 \div 8$ $64 = 8 \times$ _____	*What's Missing?* $\frac{1}{2} + \frac{1}{2} + \frac{1}{2} =$ _____ $\frac{2}{4} = \frac{3}{4} -$ _____ $\frac{2}{10} +$ _____ $= 1$

What's Missing? – Fifth Grade	
Beginning of the Year	**End of the Year**
What's Missing?	*What's Missing?*
$4 \times \frac{1}{2} =$ _____	$0.25 + 0.25 +$ _____ $= 1$
$\frac{3}{5} = \frac{7}{5} -$ _____	_____ $= \frac{5}{6} - \frac{1}{2}$
_____ $= 99 \div 11$	$\frac{2}{10} +$ _____ $= 1$
$60 = 5 \times$ _____	$(5 \times 4) \times 6 = (5 \times$ _____ $) \times 4$
_____ $= 132 \div 11$	$5 + 3 \times 6 = 33 - 2 \times$ _____

Anchor Chart

> In the **What's Missing?** routine, we have to figure out What's Missing? There are two ways we play. One is to find the missing number in a pattern. The other is to fill an empty space. So we look at the empty space and figure out what is missing. Here again you have to focus on the equal sign. The equal sign means "is the same as," so you have to think about what numbers will make both sides the same.
>
> For Example:
>
> Fill it in:
>
> $\frac{2}{3} -$ _____ $= \frac{1}{3}$
>
> The answer is $\frac{1}{3}$, because if you have $\frac{2}{3}$ and you take away something and you only have $\frac{1}{3}$ left, then you took away $\frac{1}{3}$. So the equation should be $\frac{2}{3} - \frac{1}{3} = \frac{1}{3}$.

Student Response Sheet

> **What's Missing? Fill it in!**
>
> $1 = 0.25 + 0.35 +$ _____
>
> What number is missing?
>
> How do you know?
>
> Can you justify your thinking?

The *Why Is It Not ...?* Routine

The *Why Is It Not ...?* routine requires students to reason and then justify their thinking. Counterexamples are an important part of learning mathematics. This routine makes students deal with counterexamples. They have to explain why the given thing is a counterexample and not the actual thing. A great reasoning activity!

Materials and Tools	"I Can" Statement
Students should have a variety of tools to think and reason about the numbers being discussed. They should use their toolkits. Students can use manipulatives, drawings, and mental math.	**I can** reason about numbers and explain and justify my thinking. I can listen to, understand, and respond to the thinking of others and decide whether or not their reasoning makes sense. I can explain errors that I find and how they could be corrected.

Protocol	Purpose:
Overview: The teacher puts some mathematical concept on the board together with some possible answers. The teacher will pick an incorrect answer and ask, "Why is it not ...?"	<ul><li>Reason out loud</li><li>Think about counterexamples</li><li>Discuss the example and the counterexamples</li></ul>

Protocol (cont.)	Questions:
1 The teacher puts a mathematical concept on the board with some possible answers. 2 The teacher tells the students to take "private think time" to think about why one of the options is not the answer. 3 After about 30 seconds, the teacher tells the students to "turn and talk to a neighbor." 4 Everyone comes back together, and students raise their hands and explain their thinking.	<ul><li>Why is it not this?</li><li>What is it?</li><li>Do you agree with this?</li><li>Does anything look wrong?</li><li>What needs to be corrected?</li></ul>

What's the Math?

Why Is It Not ...? should require students at different levels to explore:

Kindergarten	First Grade	Second Grade
<ul><li>Adding and subtracting</li><li>Place value</li><li>Measurement</li><li>Geometry</li></ul>	<ul><li>Adding and subtracting</li><li>Properties of addition</li><li>Place value</li><li>Measurement</li><li>Geometry</li><li>Fractions</li></ul>	<ul><li>Even and odd</li><li>Adding and subtracting</li><li>Properties of addition</li><li>Doubling and halving</li><li>Place value</li><li>Measurement</li><li>Geometry</li><li>Fractions</li></ul>

Third Grade	Fourth Grade	Fifth Grade

- **Third Grade**
  - Even and odd
  - Doubling and halving
  - Adding and subtracting
  - Multiplying and dividing
  - Properties of addition and multiplication
  - Place value
  - Measurement
  - Geometry

- **Fourth Grade**
  - Multiplying and dividing
  - Multiples and factors
  - Prime and composite
  - Place value
  - Measurement
  - Geometry
  - Fractions
  - Decimals

- **Fifth Grade**
  - Prime and composite
  - Multiples and factors
  - Multiplying and dividing
  - Adding and subtracting
  - Place value
  - Measurement
  - Geometry
  - Fractions
  - Decimals

Classroom Vignette: *Why Is It Not …?*

Mr. Jamal: Good morning class. We are going to do *Why Is It Not …?* We have been working on missing number problems and lots of folks have been messing up [he smiles]. That's OK because our mistakes truly make us better mathematicians. But we have to think about them and catch them so we get better. We want to learn from them. So let's look at some of these and talk about them.

Problem 1: $2 \times \underline{\hspace{1cm}} = 12$

A. 14

B. 10

C. 6

D. None of the above

Mr. Jamal: Many people picked 14. Why is it not 14? Look at this problem. Think about it for a few minutes. Be ready to explain your thinking. [*After a few minutes …*] Turn and talk with a buddy. [*A few minutes later …*] Who wants to share out?

Tom: It's not 14 because 2×14 is 28. We are looking for a number that when you multiply it by 2, you get 12 … you have to get 12. So that number would be 6.

Mr. Jamal: Who agrees with him and would like to add to his explanation?

Rosalinda: I agree with him and I would like to add that you have to remember that it is an EQUAL SIGN [*she says this with exaggerated emphasis*].

We talk about how the equal sign means that it has to be the same on both sides.

Rosalinda: [*Looking at the class and reaching out her hands in an exaggerated fashion*] The SAME, people … the SAME!

Everyone laughs because Mr. Jamal says this and makes this gesture all the time.

Why is it not …? – Kindergarten	
Beginning of the Year	**End of the Year**
<ul><li>1, 2, 3, 5? Why is it not 5?</li><li>If I had 2 cookies and a friend gave me 1 more, why do I not have 4 cookies?</li></ul>	<ul><li>$2 + 3 = \underline{\hspace{1cm}}$ Why is it not 1?</li><li>$5 - 0 = \underline{\hspace{1cm}}$ Why is it not 0?</li><li>$4 + 1 = \underline{\hspace{1cm}}$ Why is it not 3?</li><li>Why is it not a circle?</li></ul>

Continued

Why is it not ...? – First Grade	
Beginning of the Year	**End of the Year**
• $5 + 3 =$ ____ Why is it not 10? • $9 - 0 =$ ____ Why is it not 0? • $8 - 5 =$ ____ Why is it not 4?	• $10 - 0 =$ ____ Why is it not 0? • $2 +$ _____ $= 5$ Why is it not 7? • $10 -$ _____ $= 7$ Why is it not 17?

Why is it not ...? – Second Grade	
Beginning of the Year	**End of the Year**
• $20 - 0 =$ _____ Why is it not 0? • $4 +$ _____ $= 8$ Why is it not 12? • $10 -$ _____ $= 9$ Why is it not 19?	• 8 Why is it not odd? • $24 =$ _____ $+10$ Why is it not 34? • Kate had 4 rings. Lucy had 1 more than Kate. How many do they have altogether? Why is it not 5? • Why is it not a polygon? • Why is it not a quadrilateral?

Why is it not ...? – Third Grade	
Beginning of the Year	**End of the Year**
• Why is it not 1456? $$\begin{array}{r} 1000 \\ -\ 456 \\ \hline 1456 \end{array}$$ • Kelly had 27 marbles. Mike had 10 more than she did. How many marbles did they have altogether? Why is it not 37? • $14 =$ _____ $+ 6$ Why is it not 20?	• $5 \times$ _____ $= 5$ Why is it not 0? • $3 = 12 \div$ _____ Why is it not 15? • $5 \div 5 =$ _____ Why is it not 5? • Why is it not a parallelogram?

Why is it not ...? – Fourth Grade	
Beginning of the Year	**End of the Year**
• Why is it not 5678? $\begin{array}{r} 10,000 \\ -\ 5678 \\ \hline \end{array}$ • Round 678 to the nearest 100. Why is it not 688? • $30 = \underline{\hspace{1cm}} \times 5$ Why is it not 35? • 9 Why is it not even? • Why is it not a polygon? • Why is it not a quadrilateral?	• 7 Why is it not composite? • 12 Why is it not prime? • John had 10 marbles. He had 2 times as many as Tim. How many did Tim have? Why is it not 20? • 500 ml Why is it not the same as a liter? • Why is it not a line? $\longrightarrow$ • Why is it not an obtuse angle? • Why is it not a parallelogram?
Why is it not ...? – Fifth Grade	
Beginning of the Year	**End of the Year**
• Why is it not 2578? $\begin{array}{r} 4,000 \\ -\ 2578 \\ \hline \end{array}$ • 55 Why is it not a multiple of 2? • $0 \div 12 = \underline{\hspace{1cm}}$ Why is it not 12? • John had 16 marbles. He had 2 times as many as Tim. How many did Tim have? Why is it not 32? • < Why is it not a 90-degree angle? • Why is it not a polygon?	• $0.27 \times 0.10 = \underline{\hspace{1cm}}$ Why is it not 0.27? • $4 = \underline{\hspace{1cm}} \div 12$ Why is it not 16? • $3 + 5 \times 2$ Why is it not 30? • $\frac{1}{2} \neq \frac{3}{4}$ Why is it not an equal sign?

Continued

Anchor Chart

In the *Why is it not ...?* routine, we are thinking about when students give the wrong answer and then explaining why it is not the right answer.

Here is an example:
5 = 2 + _____ Why is it not 7?

It's not 7 because the equation is 5 is the same as 2 + ?, and that wouldn't be 7. You have to look at and think about the = sign.

Student Response Sheet

Why is it not ...?

5 = 10 ÷ _____ Why is it not 15?

Justify your thinking with numbers, words, drawings, or a diagram.

Routine #19
Yes, But Why?

The *Yes, But Why?* Routine

The *Yes, But Why?* routine is a reasoning routine where students have to read a series of statements or facts and then defend why they are true.

Materials and Tools	"I Can" Statement
Students should have a variety of tools to think and reason about the numbers being discussed. They should use their toolkits. Students can use manipulatives, drawings, and mental math.	**I can** reason about math topics.

Protocol	Purpose:
The teacher will put a mathematical concept on the board that is a true statement. Students are asked to give statements to support why the statement is true. 1. The teacher gives the students the statements. 2. The students take a few minutes of private think time. 3. The students then share their thinking with a neighbor. 4. The whole class comes back together and talks about it.	• Reason • Think in a step-by-step way • Understand statements and think about whether they make sense or not
	Questions: • What are you thinking? • Are you sure about that? • Is there another way?

What's the Math?

Yes, But Why? should require students at different levels to explore:

Kindergarten
- Adding and subtracting
- Geometry
- Measurement
- Place value

First Grade
- Adding and subtracting
- Geometry
- Measurement
- Place value

Second Grade
- Adding and subtracting
- Geometry
- Measurement
- Place value

Third Grade
- Adding and subtracting
- Multiplying and dividing
- Geometry
- Measurement
- Place value
- Fractions

Fourth Grade
- Adding and subtracting
- Multiplying and dividing
- Geometry
- Measurement
- Place value
- Fractions
- Decimals

Fifth Grade
- Adding and subtracting
- Multiplying and dividing
- Geometry
- Measurement
- Place value
- Fractions
- Decimals

Classroom Vignette: *Yes, But Why?*

Mrs. Williams: Good morning. We are going to start today with the routine Yes, But Why? I love this routine. I love to hear you all thinking out loud and justifying your answers! Get your toolkits out. Remember that you can use either the tools or the templates.

This is a hexagon! Yes, but why?

Todd: It is a hexagon because it has 6 straight sides.

Mattie: It is a hexagon because it has 6 vertices.

Lucy: It is a hexagon because it has 6 angles.

Mrs. Williams: Great thinking! Next one:

$2 \times 3 = 3 \times 2$ **Yes, but why?**

Kelli: Because they are the same numbers.

Todd: Because 2×3 is 6 and 3×2 is 6.

Yes, But Why? – Kindergarten	
Beginning of the year	**End of the year**
<ul><li>If I have 1 cookie and you give me 1 more cookie, then I have 2 cookies. Yes, but why?</li><li>If I have 2 toy trucks and I give you 1, then I have 1 toy truck. Yes, but why?</li><li>This is a circle! Yes, but why?</li></ul>	<ul><li>$5 - 1 = 4$ Yes, but why?</li><li>$2 + 3 = 5$ Yes, but why?</li><li>$10 + 8 = 18$ Yes, but why?</li></ul>

Continued

Continued

| Yes, But Why? – First Grade ||
Beginning of the Year	End of the Year
<ul><li>3 + 4 = 7 Yes, but why?</li><li>6 = 4 + 2 Yes, but why?</li><li>8 − 4 = 4 Yes, but why?</li><li>This is not a square. Yes, but why?</li></ul> 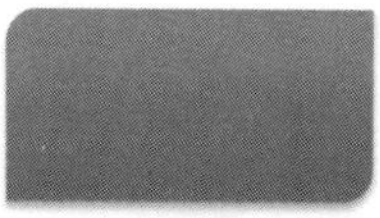	<ul><li>7 + 5 = 12 Yes, but why?</li><li>2 + 3 + 5 = 5 + 5 Yes, but why?</li><li>12 − 4 = 8 Yes, but why?</li><li>7 = 15 − 8 Yes, but why?</li><li>This is a triangle. Yes, but why?</li></ul> 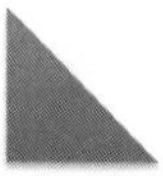

| Yes, But Why? – Second Grade ||
Beginning of the Year	End of the Year
<ul><li>6 + 8 = 14 Yes, but why?</li><li>4 + 5 = 5 + 4 Yes, but why?</li><li>14 = 15 − 1 Yes, but why?</li><li>2 + 2 + 4 = 4 + 4 Yes, but why?</li><li>This is a not a polygon. Yes, but why?</li></ul> 	<ul><li>We can say that ¼ of the square is shaded in. Yes, but why can we say that?</li></ul><ul><li>We use inches to measure a pencil. Yes, but why?</li><li>24 + 35 = 59 Yes, but why?</li><li>37 + 46 = 46 + 37 Yes, but why?</li><li>4 = 52 − 48 Yes, but why?</li><li>7 + 9 = 10 + 6 Yes, but why?</li></ul> 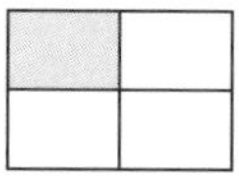

| Yes, But Why? – Third Grade ||
Beginning of the Year	End of the Year
<ul><li>2 × 3 = 3 × 2 Yes, but why?</li><li>54 + 36 = 36 + 54 Yes, but why?</li><li>55 + 78 = 53 + 80 Yes, but why?</li><li>88 is even. Yes, but why?</li><li>This is not a parallelogram. Yes, but why?</li></ul> 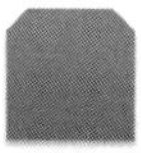	<ul><li>If we are rounding to the nearest 100, 105 rounds to 100. Yes, but why?</li><li>¼ is less than ¾. Yes but why?</li><li>⅓ is larger than ¼. Yes, but why?</li><li>⁴⁄₄ is equal to 1. Yes, but why?</li></ul>

| Yes, But Why? – Fourth Grade ||
Beginning of the Year	End of the Year
¾ = ¼ + ¼ + ¼ Yes, but why? 425 + 326 = 326 + 425 Yes, but why? When given 75 − x = 52, I can think 52 + x = 75. Yes, but why? 6 × 4 = 4 × 6 Yes, but why? If rounding 449 to the nearest hundred, it would be 400. Yes, but why?	<ul><li>4 × 8 = 2 × 16 Yes, but why?</li><li>91 is not composite. Yes, but why?</li><li>³⁄₁₀ + ⁴⁄₁₀₀ = ³⁴⁄₁₀₀ Yes, but why?</li><li>0.4 = 0.40 Yes, but why?</li><li>¾ = ⁶⁄₈ Yes, but why?</li></ul>

| Yes, But Why? – Fifth Grade ||
Beginning of the Year	End of the Year
<ul><li>2 × 4 × 8 = 4 × 8 × 2 Yes, but why?</li><li>⁵⁄₂ is greater than ⁶⁄₃. Yes, but why?</li><li>0.8 > 0.799 Yes, but why?</li><li>4.52 × 10 = 45.2 Yes, but why?</li><li>32 = (3 x 10) + (2 x 1) Yes, but why?</li></ul>	<ul><li>12 x 15 = 6 x 30 Yes, but why?</li><li>144/12 = 72/6 Yes, but why?</li><li>7 ¼ - 2 ¾ = 7 ½ - 3 Yes, buy why?</li></ul>

Anchor Chart

Yes, But Why? is a routine where we are given a mathematical statement and we have to say why it is true. Some are pretty easy, but others are really tricky. We have to think step by step as we build a case for why.

For example:
$8 \times 4 = (4 \times 4) + (4 \times 4)$

This is true because you can break apart factors. So here we broke apart the 8 and made it into 4's. So now we just have to multiply the two new factors by the other factor.

Student Response Sheet

Name: Date:

This is an octagon. Yes, but why? Explain your thinking.

This is an octagon because an octagon has 8 sides. This closed figure has 8 straight sides, 8 angles, and 8 vertices.

Routine #20
Count Around the Room

The *Count Around the Room* Routine
The *Count Around the Room* routine makes students think about the pattern of numbers.

Materials and Tools	"I can" statement
Students should have a variety of tools to think and reason about the numbers being discussed. They should use their toolkits. Students can use manipulatives, drawings, and mental math.	**I can** reason about numbers and explain and justify my thinking. I can listen to, understand, and respond to the thinking of others and decide whether or not their reasoning makes sense. I can see structure and pattern in math.

Protocol	Purpose:
Overview: The teacher discusses the count that students will do.	• Reason • Generalize math concepts • Defend thinking
1. The teacher puts a mathematical concept on the board. 2. The teacher tells the students to take "private think time" to think about the concept. 3. After about 30 seconds, the students begin to count around the room.	**Questions:** • What pattern do we see? • How do you know that? • Are you sure about that? • Can you prove it? • Can you give me an example?

Continued

What's the Math?

Count Around the Room should require students at different levels to explore:

Kindergarten	**First Grade**	**Second Grade**
• Counting within 100	• Counting within 120	• Counting by 1's to 1000 • Skip counting

Third Grade	**Fourth Grade**	**Fifth Grade**
• Students should be fluent working with multi-digit numbers and skip counting by whole numbers.	• Students should be fluent working with multi-digit numbers and skip counting by whole numbers, and fractions.	• Students should be fluent working with multi-digit numbers and skip counting by whole numbers, fractions, and decimals.

Classroom Vignette: *Count Around the Room*

Mrs. Webster: Good morning class. Today for our routine we are going to *Count Around the Room*. We are going to skip count by ½'s. We are starting at ¾. Who can tell me when we would do this in real life?

Students take a while to think about it.

Ricardo: When telling time.

Mrs. Webster: Yes, telling time, cooking, sewing … a lot of measurement activities. I want you to take out your pattern block squares and work with your table to figure out the count. Get as close to 4 as you can.

Students begin to work together.

Mrs. Webster: OK, what patterns did we visually see?

Maribel: That it goes 1 ¼, then 1 ¾ , then 2 ¼, and keeps going.

Jamal: Like using the squares made it easier because you can just see how to break down ½.

Grace: I agree because like ½ seems tricky, but when we did it by fourths, it was easier.

Mrs. Webster: You all are absolutely correct. I wanted you to see this pattern. Now, let's count it out around the room.

Students count it out … ¾, 1 ¼, 1 ¾, 2 ¼, 2 ¾, etc.

Mrs. Webster: Let's look at that pattern now on our number lines.

She pulls up a virtual number line from Math Learning Center and calls a volunteer to come and make the jumps. All the students follow along on their laminated fraction number lines.

Mrs. Webster: So, what can we say is a big takeaway from this Count Around the Room lesson today?

Lyle: You can take big numbers and break them down.

Mrs. Webster: And why would we want to do that?

Lyle: Because it makes it so much easier!

Mrs. Webster: Also, I want to know if exploring the pattern with a model helped you?

Claire: Yes. You can see it! Like we could see how to break the halves into fourths.

Mrs. Webster: Yes, and I want you to notice how we started with a concrete model and then we connected it to the number line.

Count Around the Room – Kindergarten	
Beginning of the Year	**End of the Year**
Counting by 1's to specific numbers like 5 and then 10 and then 20 and so on. *Class sing alongs:* • Jack Hartmann Videos	By the end of the year, students should be able to start at any number and count up to 100, and they should be able to skip count by 10's to 100.

Count Around the Room – First Grade	
Beginning of the Year	**End of the Year**
Counting by 1's from any number up to 100 and skip counting by 10's to 100. *Counting backwards* Use the virtual hundreds grid to track the counting: www.abcya.com/interactive_100_number_chart.htm *Class sing alongs:* • Jack Hartmann Videos • Heidi Songs • Number Rock Videos	By the end of the year, students should be able to start at any number and count up to 120, and they should be able to skip count by 10's to 120. In some states, students also learn to skip count by 2's and 5's as well as by 10's.

Count Around the Room – Second Grade	
Beginning of the Year	**End of the Year**
Students should be able to start at any number and count up to 120, and they should be able to skip count by 10's to 120. *Counting backwards* In some states, students in first grade also learn how to skip count by 2's and 5's as well as by 10's. *Class sing alongs:* • Jack Hartmann Videos • Heidi Songs • Number Rock Videos	By the end of the year, students should be able to start at any number and count up to 1000, and they should be able to skip count by 2's, 5's, 10's, and 100's through 1000. Playing the "**I have/Who has**" game is also a great way to practice skip counting. <table><tr><td>I have 5. Who has 5 more?</td><td>I have 10. Who has 5 more?</td><td>I have 15. Who has 5 more?</td></tr></table>

Count Around the Room – Third Grade	
Beginning of the Year	**End of the Year**
Students should be able to start at any number and count up to 1000, and they should be able to skip count by 2's, 5's, 10's, and 100's through 1000. *Class sing alongs:* • School House Rock • Jack Hartmann Videos • Heidi Songs • Number Rock Videos	By the end of the year, students should be able to skip count by numbers from 1 to 10 through 100. They should play around with skip counting by fractions of the same denominator. Use interactive hundred grids to show the patterns: www.hellam.net/maths2000/100square.html

Continued

Continued

Count Around the Room – Fourth Grade	
Beginning of the Year	**End of the Year**
Students should be able to skip count by numbers from 1 to 10 through 100. They should also be able to skip count by benchmark numbers like 25, 50, and 75. They should play around with skip counting by fractions of the same denominator. A great skip counting game is Bizz Buzz, or any variation thereof. Students skip count around the room and they have to say Bizz for multiples of 2 and Buzz for multiples of 3 and Bizz Buzz for multiples of both. I start it out by having the students highlight the numbers on their hundreds grids and then they can use those number grids as a scaffold for the game. Eventually we play without the scaffold. When students mess up, they aren't out; rather, we just have to start over. Here is a great video of a fourth-grade teacher using a counting stick to teach multiples of 4: https://www.teachingchannel.org/videos/teaching-multiplication	By the end of the year, students should be able to skip count by numbers from 1 to 12 through 144. They should be comfortable with skip counting by fractions of like denominators.
Count Around the Room – Fifth Grade	
Beginning of the Year	**End of the Year**
Students should be able to skip count by numbers from 1 to 12 through 144. They should be comfortable with skip counting by fractions of like denominators. For example, have the students count by fourths, and then ask them if they count by eighths where they might land given where they landed when counting by fourths.	By the end of the year, students should be able to skip count by whole numbers, fractions, and decimals.
* Remember that the FOCUS is on the relationships between the numbers! So for example, count around the room by 5's and then by 10's. Ask the students to talk about what they noticed. Have the students count by 2's and then ask them where they think they will land if they count by 4's given the relationship between those two numbers. Have the students count by 1's and then ask them where they think they will land if they count by twos.	

Anchor Chart

The *Count Around the Room* routine helps us to look at structure and pattern in our number system. One of the big ideas is that our base ten system has a specific pattern and we need to understand that pattern and be able to count using it.

1	2	3	4	5	6	7	8	9	10
11	12	13	14	15	16	17	18	19	20
21	22	23	24	25	26	27	28	29	30
31	32	33	34	35	36	37	38	39	40
41	42	43	44	45	46	47	48	49	50
51	52	53	54	55	56	57	58	59	60
61	62	63	64	65	66	67	68	69	70
71	72	73	74	75	76	77	78	79	80
81	82	83	84	85	86	87	88	89	90
91	92	93	94	95	96	97	98	99	100
101	102	103	104	105	106	107	108	109	110
111	112	113	114	115	116	117	118	119	120
121	122	123	124	125	126	127	128	129	130
131	132	133	134	135	136	137	138	139	140
141	142	143	144	145	146	147	148	149	150
151	152	153	154	155	156	157	158	159	160
161	162	163	164	165	166	167	168	169	170
171	172	173	174	175	176	177	178	179	180
181	182	183	184	185	186	187	188	189	190
191	192	193	194	195	196	197	198	199	200

Student Response Sheet

Name: Date:

Directions: Use the pattern blocks to help you solve the skip counting problems.

A. Use the rhombi to skip count by $\frac{2}{3}$. What is the 7th term in the pattern?

B. Draw it out.

C. Show this pattern on the number line.

Summary

Daily Math Thinking Routines are a group of activities that should be rotated throughout the year to help build thinking mindsets. Each one has its own protocol. It is important to think about where your students' strengths and challenges are so that you can decide on which routines to do. Remember that routines are about creating and maintaining a culture of thinking in which students are discussing standards-based, academically rigorous content. The routines should have entry points so that everyone can get started, and students should be able to climb to different levels within the routine.

Questions for Reflection

1. Which routine in this chapter stands out for you the most? Why?
2. Where are your students struggling the most? Which routines might you start doing immediately?
3. Which routine would you like to incorporate into a math workstation as well?

References

Koechler, M., & Grouwns, D.A. (2006). Mathematics teaching practices and their effects. In D.A. Grouwns (Ed.), *Handbook of research on mathematics teaching and learning* (pp. 115–126). Reston, VA: NCTM.

Mutai, J.K. (2010) Attitudes towards learning and performance in mathematics students in selected secondary schools in Bureti District Kenya. Masters thesis, Kenyatta University.

Silver, H., Brunsting, J., & Walsh, T. (2008). *Math tools. Grades 3–12: 64 ways to differentiate instruction and increase student achievement.* Thousand Oaks, CA: Corwin Press.

6

Number Flexes

Only if children come to believe that there are <u>always</u> multiple ways to solve problems, and that they, personally, are capable of discovering some of these ways, will they be likely to exercise—and thereby develop—number sense.

—(Resnick, Lesgold, & Bill, 1990, p. 4)

Number flexes are routines that happen often. They are called number flexes because they build flexibility. These routines in particular go right for the flexibility muscle. The goal is to build fluency with an emphasis on accuracy, flexibility, and efficiency. Throughout this chapter, there are different number flexes. Many of the routines described below show what they can look like at the beginning of the year and at the end of the year. It is important to think about the models and the strategies that students should be working with throughout the year as their knowledge base is expanded. Some number flexes are routines for everybody, such as *Number of the Day* or *Number Talks*. A few number flexes, such as *Fraction of the Day* and *Decimal of the Day*, are only for the upper elementary grades.

The number flex routines in this chapter are:

1. *I Love Math*
2. *Number of the Day*
3. *Subitizing*
4. *Fraction of the Day*
5. *Decimal of the Day*
6. *Number Talks (American Style)*
7. *Number Talks (British Style)*
8. *Over/Under/SameVirtual Dice Roll*
9. *Virtual Cards*
10. *Do Not Solve*

> **Routine #1**
> *I Love Math*

The *I Love Math* Routine	
The *I Love Math* routine is a quick game for students to work on their basic fact fluency. It is played like rock-paper-scissors. Instead of throwing rock, paper, or scissors, the students throw numbers. Depending on the grade, the winner is decided in different ways. For example, in kindergarten the students each throw out a number on one hand, and whoever says the sum of the two numbers first wins. They just keep playing over and over again. In fifth grade, students would each throw out a hand or two and then they have to multiply those numbers. Whoever says the product first wins.	
Materials and Tools	**"I can" statement**
Students.	**I can** state my math facts.
Protocol	**Purpose:**
Overview: The students get in pairs (often with direction from the teacher) and they play. 1. Students get in pairs. 2. They say "I Love Math."	• Identify patterns • Compose and decompose shapes

3. Then they throw out one hand. (Start with one hand and then work up to two hands.)
4. Whoever calls out the sum or product first wins.

* There are variations of this game, which are described in the grade-level sections.

Questions:

- What strategies did you use today?
- What facts were easy?
- What facts were challenging?

What's the Math?

I Love Math should require students at different levels to explore:

Kindergarten
- Adding and subtracting

First Grade
- Adding and subtracting
- Properties of addition

Second Grade
- Even and odd
- Adding and subtracting
- Properties of addition
- Doubling

Third Grade
- Even and odd
- Doubling and halving
- Adding and subtracting
- Multiplying and dividing
- Properties of addition and multiplication

Fourth Grade
- Prime and composite
- Even and odd
- Doubling and halving
- Adding and subtracting
- Multiplying and dividing
- Properties of addition and multiplication

Fifth Grade
- Prime and composite
- Even and odd
- Doubling and halving
- Adding and subtracting
- Multiplying and dividing
- Properties of addition and multiplication

Classroom Vignette: *I Love Math*

Mrs. Todd: Today we are going to play *I Love Math*. Remember to whisper the answer to your partner. That means nobody else can hear you. Also remember to think about your strategies so you can add more quickly. Also you must throw out your numbers at the same time. Try to name your strategies after you have said the answer. And if you think your partner said the wrong answer, challenge them and check it. Last thing – remember that each throw must be a new number.

Tina and Luke: Luke says 5. 5 × 1 is 5.

Mari and Jenn: Mari says 0. 0 × any number is zero.

Dave and John: John says 9. 3 × 3 is 9.

Continued

Play continues and then Mrs. Todd brings everybody back together.

Mrs. Todd: Who wants to share some of their facts?

Mari: We threw 0 × 3 and so that was 0 because anything multiplied by 0 is zero.

Carol: We threw 5 × 5 and that was 25. It is also a square number fact.

Jamal: We threw 4 × 5 which is 20. I just know that.

Mrs. Todd: What if someone didn't know that? What strategy could we tell them?

Maribel: They could use their 2's and then double them.

Carl: Yep, anytime you get stuck on your 4's think about your 2's. So 2 × 5 is 10. Double that for 4 × 5 and you get 20.

Mrs. Todd: Great strategy work you all.

I Love Math – **Kindergarten**	
In Kindergarten the students can practice this game in a variety of ways.	
Beginning of the Year	**End of the Year**
Way 1: One person puts up a hand and the other person says how much that is. 5 **Way 2:** Throw up one hand each. Whoever has the largest number wins. If the numbers are the same, it is a tie.	**Way 2:** Throw up one hand each. Add the two numbers together, and whoever says the sum first wins. 8

I Love Math – **First Grade**	
Beginning of the Year	**End of the Year**
Way 1: Throw up one hand each. Whoever has the largest number wins. **Way 2:** Throw up one hand each. Add the two numbers together. Whoever says the sum first wins. 8	By the end of the year, students can throw up two hands and they have to add all the numbers. Encourage them to think strategically and add numbers together. In the example here, the students could think 2 and 3 are 5 and then 5 more is ten. The teacher should model this with the students so they can learn to think efficiently.

I Love Math – Second Grade	
Beginning of the Year	**End of the Year**
Way 1: Throw up one hand each. Add the two numbers together and whoever says the sum first wins. 8 **Way 2:** By the end of the year, students can throw up two hands and they have to add all the numbers. Encourage them to think strategically and add numbers together. In the example, the students could think 3 and 3 is 6 and then 5 and 5 is 10, so that's 16. 16	**Way 1:** Throw up one hand each. The students have to add the numbers and then determine if the sum is odd or even. even

I Love Math – Third Grade, Fourth Grade, Fifth Grade

These are all together because all the students need to practice basic addition and basic multiplication. There are some grade-level challenge versions in the notes.

Beginning of the Year	**End of the Year**
Way 1: Throw up one hand each. Add the two numbers together, and whoever says the sum first wins. **Way 2:** Students throw up two hands and they have to add all the numbers. Encourage them to think strategically and add numbers together. In the example, the students could think 3 and 3 is 6 and then 5 and 5 is 10, so that's 16. 16 **Way 3:** The students have to add the numbers and then determine if the sum is odd or even. even	**Way 1:** Students multiply the numbers. 25 **4th challenge level:** Students throw up a number and they have to decide if it is prime or composite. **5th challenge level:** Students multiply all of the four numbers together. $6 \times 10 = 60$ (multiply sum of 1 hand by the other) **5th grade** *The teacher should be working on strategies. For example, 9×25 is the same as 10×25 minus one group of 25.* $3 \times 3 \times 5 \times 5 =$ $9 \times 25 = 225$ (multiply the product of 1 hand by the product of the other)

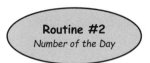

The *Number of the Day* Routine

Number of the Day builds number competence across mathematical topics. During this routine, students have to think about numbers in many different ways. They work on representing the number, naming the number, place value concepts, and operations as well as algebraic thinking. The number of the day can be generated by choosing the number randomly, or generating the number. Here are some number generators:

Dice	Cards	Spinners
* www.curriculumbits.com/mathematics/virtual-dice/ (with sound effects – a personal favorite) http://dice.virtuworld.net/ https://www.random.org/dice/?num=2 https://www.freeonlinedice.com/#dice	http://playingcards.io/hvvz	http://nrich.maths.org/content/id/6717/Spinners.swf

Materials and Tools	"I can" statement
Students should have a variety of tools to think and reason about the numbers being discussed. They should use their toolkits. Students can use manipulatives, drawings, and mental math.	I can reason about numbers and explain and justify my thinking. I can listen to, understand, and respond to the thinking of others and decide whether or not their reasoning makes sense.

Protocol

Overview: The teacher puts a number on the board and the students have to do grade-level-appropriate activities with that number. In kindergarten, teachers often spend time working on numbers within 10 at the beginning of the year and then work up to larger numbers. In first and second grades, teachers will use the number of days students have been in school. In the upper elementary grades, teachers will use the number of school days or random numbers that they choose or that the students choose. Students can either do this as an oral routine or write it on their white boards or in their thinking notebooks.

1. The teacher writes a number on the white board, on the interactive board, or on chart paper.
2. The teacher tells the students to take "private think time" to think about the concept.
3. After about 30 seconds, the teacher tells the students to "turn and talk to a neighbor."
4. Everyone comes back together, and students raise their hands and explain their thinking.

Purpose:

- Reason
- Generalize math concepts
- Defend their thinking

Possible Questions:

BEFORE

- What can you do if you get stuck?
- How can your strategy mat help you?
- What should you do when you're not sure?

DURING

- How do you know that?
- Are you sure about that?

AFTER

- Did you get stuck?
- What did you do when you got stuck?
- Are you still fuzzy about anything?
- Which models did you use?
- Which strategies did you use?

What's the Math?

Number of the Day should require students at different levels to explore:

Kindergarten
- Adding and subtracting

First Grade
- Adding and subtracting
- Properties of addition

Second Grade
- Even and odd
- Adding and subtracting
- Properties of addition
- Doubling and halving
- Skip counting
- Comparing numbers

Third Grade
- Even and odd
- Doubling and halving
- Adding and subtracting
- Multiplying and dividing
- Properties of addition and multiplication
- Rounding

Fourth Grade
- Multiplying and dividing
- Multiples and factors
- Prime and composite

Fifth Grade
- Prime and composite
- Multiples and factors
- Multiplying and dividing
- Decimals

The Models

In the early grades there is an emphasis on number frames, the hundreds grid, and drawings. Also, in kindergarten and first grade, be sure to use number "tracks" or "paths" because this allows the children the space that they need to look at and consider those numbers. This is not to say that you don't show the students number lines or ladders, but that you do much of the work on number tracks and paths. In first and second grades, start to use the hundred grid and the number grid "snapshot" (where students put the target number in the middle and then write the number above and below it as well as the numbers on both sides of it). Part-Part-Whole mats and number bonds should also be a big part of the *Number of the Day* routine because you want students flexible with composing and decomposing numbers.

In the upper elementary grades, it is important to continue using number bonds and having students do visual models and sketches of their thinking. Students should work with both horizontal and vertical number lines as well as marked and unmarked number lines.

Ball and Fullerton (2013, p. 18) have written about talk frames that can be used with Number of the Day routines. Here are a few of them:

_____ is too many _____.
_____ is too few _____.
_____ is just enough _____.

Shumway (2011) talks about asking when the number would be big and when would it be small. For example, 4 elephants in a room would be a lot of elephants, but 4 ants in a room would be a really small amount.

_____ in a room would be a lot.
_____ in a room would be a small amount.

In the upper elementary grades, you could use frames for rounding and estimating as suggested by Ball and Fullerton (2013):

_____ is about _____.
_____ is close to _____ but far from _____.

These are excellent frames for students to think about and discuss numbers.

Continued

Classroom Vignette: *Number of the Day*

Mr. T puts 12 on the board for his first-grade class. He then asks the students to:

- Write the word form: **twelve**
- Represent the number with a drawing:

- Represent the number in the double ten frames:

 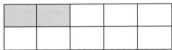

- Put it on a number line: #Before the number, the number, #after the number

11 12 13   20

- Say when the number would be big and when it would be small

  12 *hippos* are a lot but 12 *ants* are a little.

Number of the Day – Kindergarten

In kindergarten students are familiarizing themselves with the different aspects of numbers. At the beginning of the year, they should be writing the number, drawing it, representing it in a number frame, using tallies, and eventually breaking it apart into number bonds. By the end of the year, they should be representing numbers up to 20 using the double ten frame and working on number paths (a variation of the number line). Students can also be working on number lines and ladders but number paths give them more room to see and explore the numbers. They should be plotting the number and looking at what comes before the number and what comes after it.

Beginning of the Year	End of the Year
Draw a picture.	Draw a picture.
Show the number on the ten frame.	Show the number on the twenty frame.

$10 + \underline{\hspace{1.5cm}} = \underline{\hspace{1.5cm}}$

Circle the number.

1	2	3	4	5	6	7	8	9	10
11	12	13	14	15	16	17	18	19	20

Number of the Day – First Grade

In first grade students are working on the numbers to 120. They should be thinking about representing numbers between 0 and 120, determining how many tens and ones and adding, what comes before and after the number, as well as ten more and ten less than the number. Students also begin to work on spelling number words.

Beginning of the Year

Base Ten Sketch

Tens	Ones

Break apart the number.

_____ + _____ = _____

Represent the number on ten frames.

End of the Year

Number Word

_____ > _____
_____ < _____
_____ = _____

Put the number on the number line.

Make the number with an addition sentence.

_____ + _____ = _____

Base ten sketch

Tens	Ones

Fill in the hundred grid piece.

Number of the Day – Second Grade

In second grade students are working on numbers within 1000. They should be thinking about representing numbers to 1000 in many ways, understanding the place and value of numbers within 1000, adding and subtracting within 1000 using a variety of strategies and models and thinking about whether the number is odd or even.

Continued

Beginning of the Year

Base Ten Sketch

Hundreds	Tens	Ones

Break apart the number.

_____ + _____ = _____

Word Form: Expanded Form:

_____ > _____

_____ < _____

_____ = _____

End of the Year

Number Word   Put the number on the number line.

_____ > _____

_____ < _____   Make the number with an addition sentence.

_____ = _____

_____ + _____ = _____

Base ten sketch   Fill in the hundred grid piece.

Tens	Ones	Hundreds

Number of the Day – Third Grade

In third grade students are working on numbers within 10,000. They should be thinking about representing numbers to 10,000 in many ways, understanding the place and value of numbers within 10,000, and adding and subtracting within 10,000 using a variety of strategies and models.

Beginning of the Year

Base Ten Sketch

Hundreds	Tens	Ones	Thousands

Break apart the number. You can add more legs throughout the year.

_____ + _____ = _____

Word Form: Expanded Form:

_____ > _____
_____ < _____
_____ = _____

Have students break apart the number in different ways.

Write the number in word form:

Is it odd or even?

Expanded form:

_____ > _____
_____ < _____
_____ = _____

Show the money in coins two different ways
(for numbers under 100):

Put the number on the number line. Have
the students start with recording benchmark
numbers.

←————————————————————→

Round the number to the nearest 10. _____
Round the number to the nearest 100. _____
Round the number to the nearest 1000. _____

Make the number with an addition sentence
and a subtraction sentence.

_____ + _____ = _____
_____ − _____ = _____

10 more _____
10 less _____
100 more _____
100 less _____
1000 more _____
1000 less _____

Number of the Day – Fourth Grade

In fourth grade students are working on numbers within millions. They should be thinking about representing numbers in many ways, understanding the place and value of numbers within 10,000, and adding and subtracting multi-digit numbers fluently.

Beginning of the Year

Word form:

Is it odd or even?

Is it prime or composite?

Expanded form:

_____ > _____
_____ < _____
_____ = _____

Put the number on the number line.

←————————————————————→

Round the number to the nearest 10. _____
Round the number to the nearest 100. _____
Round the number to the nearest 1000. _____

Make the number with an addition sentence
and a subtraction sentence.

_____ + _____ = _____
_____ − _____ = _____

Continued

Name 2 multiples of the number. Name 3 factors of the number.	10 more _____ 10 less _____ 100 more _____ 100 less _____ 1000 more _____ 1000 less _____ 10,000 more _____ 10,000 less _____

End of the Year

Word form:

Is it prime or composite?

Expanded form:

_____ > _____

_____ < _____

_____ = _____

10 × _____ = _____

100 × _____ = _____

1000 × _____ = _____

Put the number on the number line.

⟵—————————————————⟶

Make the number with an addition sentence, a subtraction sentence, and a multiplication sentence.

_____ + _____ = _____

_____ − _____ = _____

_____ × _____ = _____

5 multiples of the number _____

3 factors of the number _____

Number of the Day – Fifth Grade

In fifth grade students are working on large numbers. They should be thinking about representing numbers in many ways, understanding the place and value of numbers, adding, subtracting, multiplying, and dividing numbers with a variety of strategies and models, including the traditional ones.

Beginning of the Year

Word form:

Is it prime or composite?

Expanded form:

_____ > _____

_____ < _____

_____ = _____

10 × _____ = _____

100 × _____ = _____

1000 × _____ = _____

Put the number on the number line.

⟵—————————————————⟶

Round the number to the nearest 10. _____
Round the number to the nearest 100. _____
Round the number to the nearest 1000. _____

Make the number with an addition sentence, a subtraction sentence, and a multiplication sentence.

_____ + _____ = _____

_____ − _____ = _____

_____ × _____ = _____

Five multiples of the number _____

Three factors of the number _____

Spell the word:

Is it prime or composite?

Expanded form:

Expanded notation:

_____ > _____
_____ < _____
_____ = _____

10 × _____ = _____

100 × _____ = _____

1000 × _____ = _____

Put the number on the number line.

←——————————————→

Round the number to the nearest 10. _____
Round the number to the nearest 100. _____
Round the number to the nearest 1000. _____

Multiply the number by 17.

Divide the number by 12.

Five multiples of the number _____

Three factors of the number _____

Anchor Chart

> The *Number of the Day* is a routine that we do often. We do it to play around with numbers, work with place value, and practice adding and subtracting.
>
> For Example: The number of the day is 125
>
> Word form: one hundred and twenty-five
>
> Expand it: 100 + 20 + 5
>
> Coins:
>
>
>
> or
>
>
>
>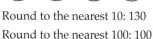
>
> Round to the nearest 10: 130
> Round to the nearest 100: 100

Student Response Sheet

There are many different ways that we have discussed doing *Number of the Day*. Here is another one. Give the students the number of the day and let them pick from a list the things that they want to do.
For example:

> **Things to do with the number of the day:**
> - Make number with addition sentence.
> - Make number with subtraction sentence.
> - Base ten sketch
> - Odd or even
> - Expanded form
> - Word form
> - Plot on a number line
> - 10 more or less
> - 100 more or less
> - Two ways in coins
> - Skip counts
> - Compare

Continued

My Number of the Day Top 4 List

578

1. 600 – 22 = 578
2. This is an even number because it ends in 8 and 8 is even.
3. 100 more would be 678.
4. If I was skip counting by 2, I would say this number. If I was skip counting by 5, I would not say this number.

Bonus: 578 > 399

More Resources

https://hcpss.instructure.com/courses/9414/pages/todays-number

https://www.pinterest.com/drnicki7/number-of-the-day/

Routine #3
Subitizing

The *Subitizing* Routine

(Seeing and knowing small amounts without counting)

Subitizing is a routine that is done throughout the grades. Often subitizing is only done in kindergarten and first grade, but actually it should be done all the way through fifth grade and even in sixth grade. The subjects of subitizing change, but the idea of quick images and being able to perceptually and then conceptually see and discuss numbers is one of the linchpins of number sense. In the primary grades, students are subitizing up to 10 and then eventually up to 100 using hundred grids. In the upper elementary grades, students are subitizing with multiplication and then decimals.

There are two types of subitizing: perceptual subitizing and conceptual subitizing. Perceptual subitizing is when students see it and know it. Conceptual subitizing is when students begin to understand the number. Clements points out that students recognize the number pattern as a composite of parts and as a whole. ... Such actions ... can be stepping stones to constructing more sophisticated procedures with larger numbers. ... This more advanced ability to group and quantify sets quickly in turn supports their development of number sense and arithmetic.

(1999, p. 401)

There is a hierarchy of subitizing. The spatial arrangements influence the difficulty levels. There are 4 levels: first lines, then arrays, then circles and then all scattered. (Clements, 1999, p. 402).

Research Note: Clements has written a great article on subitizing. Clements has also written about the learning trajectory of subitizing through the grade levels. Graham Fletcher has done some great work around subitizing with multiplication. My good friends in Wicomo, Maryland introduced me to subitizing with the hundreds grid for place value, multiplication, and division.

https://vimeo.com/129103233?ref=tw-share
https://gfletchy.com/2015/08/17/not-your-moms-flashcards-conceptual-understanding-of-multiplication/

Also see: http://gse.buffalo.edu/fas/clements/files/subitizing.pdf

Materials and Tools	"I can" statement
Teachers should use both the concrete cards and the virtual sets for subitizing.	**I can** reason about numbers and explain and justify my thinking. I can listen to, understand, and respond to the thinking of others and decide whether or not their reasoning makes sense.

Protocol	Purpose
Overview: The teacher flashes a number card and the students have to state what they saw.	• Reason • Generalize math concepts • Defend their thinking
1. The teacher flashes a number on a card or digitally.	
2. The teacher tells the students to take "private think time" to think about what they saw.	**Questions:**
3. The teacher asks the students, "What did you see?" Notice that this is different than "How many were there?" The first question gets at breaking apart the numbers and analyzing them.	• What do you see? • How did you see it? • Is there another way to see it?
4. After about 30 seconds, the teacher tells the students to "turn and talk to a neighbor."	
5. Everyone comes back together, and students raise their hands and explain their thinking.	

What's the Math?

Subitizing should require students at different levels to explore:

Kindergarten	First Grade	Second Grade
• Addition	• Addition	• Addition

Third Grade	**Fourth Grade**	**Fifth Grade**
• Multiplication	• Multiplication • Decimals	• Multiplication • Decimals

Continued

Classroom Vignette: *Subitizing*

Mrs. Sanders (first grade) flashes this card and asks the students what they saw.

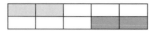

Katie: I saw 4. I saw 2 and 2.

Mr. Tim flashes these cards and asks his third-grade students what they saw.

Carl: I saw 6. I saw 2 × 3 which equals 6. There are 2 groups of 3.

Mr. Hall asks his fifth-grade students what they saw.

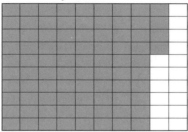

Mary: I saw 84 hundredths. I know this because there is 1 column empty, which is a tenth, and then 6 more. So that means there are 8 tenths and 4 hundredths shaded.

Subitizing – Kindergarten

In kindergarten, students subitize within 10. At the beginning of the year, they begin to subitize to 5 and then to 10.

Beginning of the Year

Dot Card

Dice

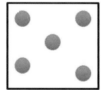

Ten Frame

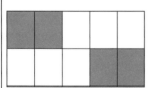

Domino

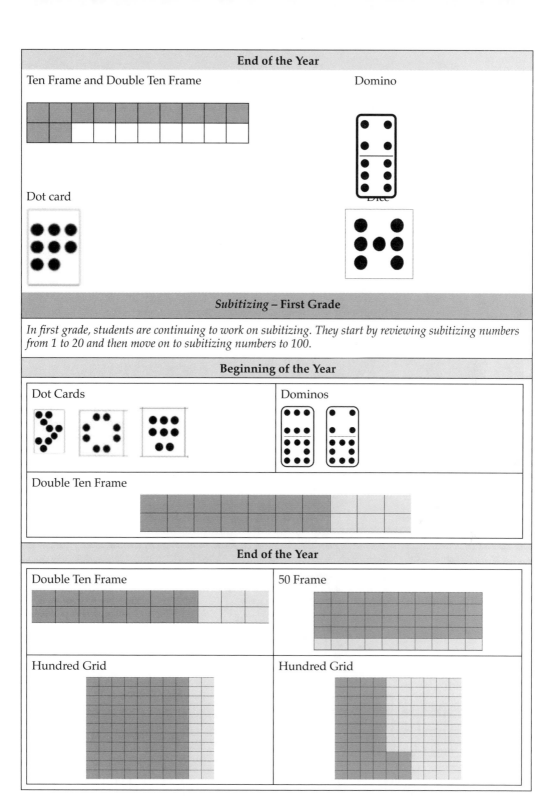

End of the Year

Ten Frame and Double Ten Frame

Domino

Dot card

Dice

Subitizing – First Grade

In first grade, students are continuing to work on subitizing. They start by reviewing subitizing numbers from 1 to 20 and then move on to subitizing numbers to 100.

Beginning of the Year

Dot Cards

Dominos

Double Ten Frame

End of the Year

Double Ten Frame

50 Frame

Hundred Grid

Hundred Grid

Continued

Subitizing – Second Grade

In second grade, students start by reviewing subitizing numbers from 20 to 100 and then move on to subitizing numbers to 1000.

Beginning of the Year

Dot Cards

Dominos

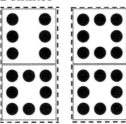

Hundred Grid

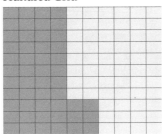

Hundreds Grid

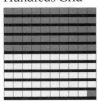

End of the Year

Hundred Grid

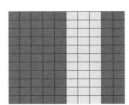

Thousand Grid

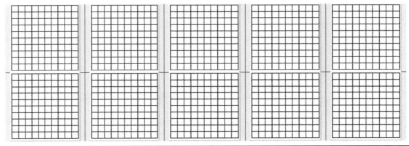

In third grade students should work on hundred and thousand grids. They also start to subitize multiplication cards of equal groups and arrays.

Beginning of the Year

Adapted from https://gfletchy.com/2015/02/10/subitizing-to-foster-multiplicative-thinking/
*Learning Trajectories have 10 levels for subitizing, including subitizing with place value and multiplication (Clements & Sarama, 2004).

Hundred Grid

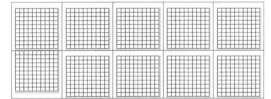

Thousand Grid

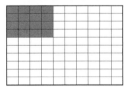

End of the Year

Equal Group Cards

I think it would be helpful to include student responses to some examples showing flexibility of thought. I also love dot patterns that have many in them so that students can break apart into tinier arrays and then add those amounts together. You could also have a rectangular dot pattern with a chunk missing so students could figure out the total and then take away a chunk. This shows flexibility.

Array Cards

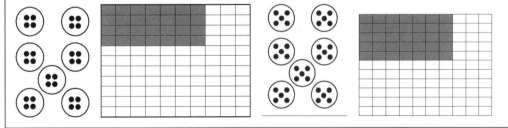

Continued

Continued

In fourth grade students should be working on thousand and ten thousand grids. Students should also be working on using decimal grids.

Beginning of the Year

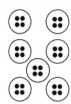 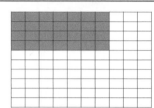

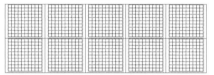

Thousand Grid

End of the Year

Ten Thousand Grid

Subitizing – **Fifth Grade**

In fifth grade students should be working on thousand and ten thousand grids. Students should also be working on using decimal grids.

Beginning of the Year

Hundred Grid (used to teach hundredths as well)

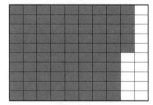

Thousand Grid

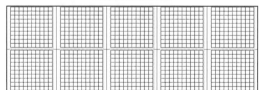

Thousand Grid
Ask students to show you 0.325

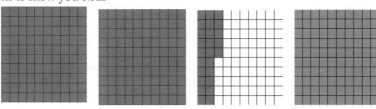

Anchor Chart

Subitizing is a routine where we do "Quick Looks." This helps us to think about addition, subtraction, multiplication, and division.

For Example:
Teacher: What do you see?

Mark: I see 7 tens and 5 ones. I see 75. There are 75 shaded and 25 unshaded. 75 and 25 make 100.

Student Response Sheet

Teacher: Shade in 0.27.

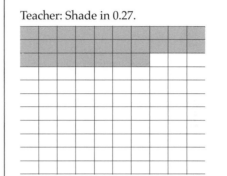

Further Reading

http://gse.buffalo.edu/fas/clements/files/subitizing.pdf

http://teachmath.openschoolnetwork.ca/grade-1/number-sense/subitizing/

https://www.pinterest.com/drnicki7/subitizing/

https://gfletchy.files.wordpress.com/2015/08/multiplication-array-cards1.pdf

www.blainesd.org/users/jdennison/weblog/80583/Decimal_grids.html

https://vimeo.com/131915752

The *Fraction of the Day* Routine

Fraction of the Day builds fraction competence across mathematical topics. During this routine students have to think about numbers in many different ways. The students work on representing the fractions, naming the fractions, and composing and decomposing the fractions as well as doing arithmetic with the fractions.

Materials and Tools	**"I can" statement**
Students should have a variety of tools to think and reason about the numbers being discussed. They should use their toolkits. Students can use manipulatives, drawings, and mental math.	**I can** reason about fractions and explain and justify my thinking. I can listen to, understand, and respond to the thinking of others and decide whether or not their reasoning makes sense.

Protocol	**Purpose:**
Overview: The teacher puts a fraction on the board and the students have to do grade-appropriate activities with that number. The teacher writes a number on the white board, on the interactive board, or on chart paper. 1. The teacher puts up a fraction. 2. The teacher tells the students to take "private think time" to think about the concept. 3. After about 30 seconds, the teacher tells the students to "turn and talk to a neighbor." 4. Everyone comes back together, and students raise their hands and explain their thinking.	• Reason • Generalize math concepts • Defend their thinking **Questions:** • How do you know that? • Are you sure about that? • Can you prove it? • Can you give me an example?

What's the Math?

Fraction of the Day should require students at different levels to explore:

Third Grade	**Fourth Grade**	**Fifth Grade**
• Reviewing halves, thirds, fourths • Understanding fractions as a part of a whole • Plotting fractions on a number line	• Equivalent fractions • Comparing fractions with different numerators and different denominators using symbols >, <, =	• Comparing fractions • Adding and subtracting fractions and mixed numbers with unlike denominators using objects, pictorial models, and properties of operations

- Recognizing and generating equivalent fractions
- Comparing fractions with the same numerator or the same denominator using symbols >, <, =
- Recognizing that the size of the whole matters
- Area, set, and linear models
- Expressing whole numbers as fractions
- Recognizing fractions that are equivalent to whole numbers
- Justifying thinking with visual fraction models
- Reasoning and solving word problems about fractions (comparing and ordering)
- Area and linear models *TEKS

- Representing fractions greater than zero and less than or equal to 1 with strip diagrams and number lines
- Solving partitioning problems among two or more people

- Comparing fractions using common denominators and benchmark fractions
- Area, set, and linear models
- Composing and decomposing fractions with like denominators
- Adding and subtracting fractions and mixed numbers with like denominators
- Multiplying a fraction by a whole number (* not TEKS)
- Justifying thinking with visual fraction models
- Reasoning and solving word problems using addition, subtraction, and multiplication of fractions by whole numbers
- Estimating the reasonableness of calculations with fractions

- Multiplying two fractions
- Multiplying fractions and mixed numbers (* not teks)
- Area, set, and linear models
- Reasoning about and representing division of a fraction by a whole number and a whole number by a unit fraction
- Estimating the reasonableness of calculations with fractions
- (TEKS: *Multiply a fraction and a whole number)

The Models

In the upper elementary grades, students should start doing *Fraction of the Day* at the very beginning of the year. They should begin by reviewing all the fraction standards that came before their current grade level. This is so important because fractions are usually only taught once a year and then soon forgotten about after the test. Research states that students don't like fractions, struggle when working with them, and often forget what they are taught. We need routines that help students to be on friendly terms with fractions. So fraction fluency will be promoted by starting at the beginning of the year with *Fraction of the Day*, doing this at least twice a week, and then making it more complex as new information is taught. It is important to continue using number bonds and having students make visual models and sketches of their thinking. Students should work with both horizontal and vertical number lines as well as marked and unmarked number lines.

Continued

There can be general sheets like this one:

Fraction of the Day	Draw a visual model.	Plot it on a number line.
Write a fraction that is bigger than this fraction. Prove it.	Write a fraction that is smaller than this fraction. Prove it.	Is this fraction closer to 0, ½, or 1?

Or there can be other models as shown in the examples below. These examples are meant to show the variety of things that should be practiced by grade level for this routine.

Fraction of the Day – **Third Grade**

In third grade, students begin to study fractions more intensely. Although students have worked with fractions before in most standards, they start looking at defining fractions, comparing fractions, generating equivalent fractions, and plotting them on a number line. At the beginning of the year, students should immediately start this routine, drawing on all the standards about fractions from prior grades. As the year goes on, the teacher can introduce more and more items and then, during and after the unit on fractions, incorporate the new standards of the grade.

Beginning of the Year

½	
Draw a circle. Partition it into halves. Shade in half of it.	Draw a square. Partition it into fourths. Shade in half.
Draw a circle. Cut it into fourths. Shade in ¼.	Draw a rectangle. Partition it into thirds. Shade in ⅔ of it.

End of the Year

¼	
Word form One-fourth One out of four One-quarter	Visual model
Plot on a number line ¼ ½ ¾	Equivalent fraction ¼ = ²⁄₈

Fraction of the Day – Fourth Grade

In the beginning of fourth grade, students are expanding their understanding of fractions. They continue their work on comparing fractions, plotting fractions on a number line, and generating equivalent fractions. They work on decomposing fractions as well as adding and subtracting fractions and mixed numbers with like denominators. In some states, they even begin multiplying a whole number by a fraction. Start at the beginning of the year, and integrate the new concepts as they are taught.

Beginning of the Year

Prove that $\frac{4}{4}$ is the same as 1 whole.	$\frac{1}{2}$, $\frac{3}{4}$, 1, $\frac{5}{4}$. Plot these on a number line.
Compare $\frac{2}{5}$ and $\frac{3}{5}$ with symbols and visual models.	Generate an equivalent fraction for $\frac{2}{4}$.

End of the Year

Compare $\frac{4}{5}$ and $\frac{3}{4}$.	Multiply 5 by $\frac{1}{2}$ using a visual model.
Add $\frac{1}{4}$ and $\frac{3}{4}$. Model your thinking with a visual model.	Break apart $\frac{5}{6}$ in two different ways.

Fraction of the Day – Fifth Grade

In the beginning of fifth grade, students continue with fraction operations. In most states, students start to add and subtract fractions with unlike denominators as well as to multiply a fraction by a fraction. Students also begin to explore dividing a fraction by a whole number as well as a whole number by a fraction. This routine should start at the beginning of the year, picking up where fourth grade left off and then integrating the new standards as they are taught.

Beginning of the Year

Multiply 5$\frac{1}{2}$ and 2.	Subtract 3$\frac{1}{2}$ from 5$\frac{1}{2}$.
Generate two equivalent fractions for $\frac{4}{7}$.	Break apart $\frac{4}{8}$ two different ways. Use two different number bonds.

Continued

End of the Year	
Add ¼ and ½.	Multiply ⅓ and ½ using a visual model.
Solve: Write a story about 1 divided by ⅓.	Solve: ⅕ ÷ 2.

Anchor Chart

> ***Fraction of the Day*** is a routine that we do to "get great" with fractions! We do it a couple of times a week to review and preview fractions.
>
> For example: ½
>
> Word form: one-half
> Decimal form: 0.50
> Addition sentence: ¼ + ¼ = 2⁄4 = ½
> How much to 1: ½

Student Response Sheet

There are many activities that students can do with Fraction of the Day. Some days you should let students pick from a list.

> ***Fraction of the Day* idea list:**
>
> Plot it on a number line
> Word form
> Decimal form
> Addition sentence
> Subtraction sentence
> How much more to 1
> Compare
> Order

> **My Fraction of the Day ⁴⁄9**
>
> 1. four-ninths
> 2. 2⁄9 + 2⁄9 = 4⁄9
> 3. 1 – 4⁄9 = 5⁄9
> 4. 4⁄9 > 4⁄6
> Bonus: 4⁄9 < ¾

> **More Resources**
> www.dusd.net/cgi/files/2012/12/fraction-number-talks.pdf
> https://www.pinterest.com/drnicki7/fraction-of-the-daydecimal-of-the-day/

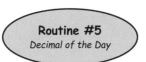

Routine #5
Decimal of the Day

The *Decimal of the Day* Routine
Decimal of the Day builds decimal competence across mathematical topics. During this routine students have to think about numbers in many different ways. The students work on representing the decimals, naming the decimals, composing and decomposing the decimals, as well as doing arithmetic with the decimals.

Materials and Tools	"I can" statement
Students should have a variety of tools to think and reason about the numbers being discussed. They should use their toolkits. Students can use manipulatives, drawings, and mental math.	**I can** reason about decimals and explain and justify my thinking. I can listen to, understand, and respond to the thinking of others and decide whether or not their reasoning makes sense.

Protocol	Purpose:
Overview: The teacher puts a decimal on the board and the students have to do grade-appropriate activities with that number. Students can either do this as an oral routine or write it on their white board or in their thinking notebooks.	• Reason • Generalize math concepts • Defend their thinking
1. The teacher writes a number on the white board, on the interactive board, or on chart paper.	
2. The teacher tells the students to take "private think time" to think about the concept.	**Questions:**
3. After about 30 seconds, the teacher tells the students to "turn and talk to a neighbor."	• How do you know that? • Are you sure about that? • Can you prove it? • Can you give me an example?
4. Everyone comes back together and students raise their hand and explain their thinking.	

What's the Math?
Decimal of the Day should require students at different levels to explore:

Fourth Grade	Fifth Grade
• Understanding decimal notation for fractions • Comparing and ordering decimals using concrete and visual models to the hundredths	• Representing the value of the digit in decimals through the thousandths using expanded notation and numerals • Reading, writing, and comparing decimals to thousandths using base ten numerals, number names, and expanded form

Continued

- Expressing a fraction with denominator 10 as an equivalent fraction with denominator 100
- Adding fractions with respective denominators 10 and 100
- Using decimal notation for fractions with denominators 10 or 100
- Comparing two decimals to hundredths by reasoning about their size
- Recognizing that comparisons are valid only when the two decimals refer to the same whole
- Recording the results of comparisons with the symbols >, =, or <
- Representing fractions and decimals to the tenths and hundredths as distances from zero on a number line
- Justifying thinking about decimals with visual models
- Reasoning about decimals
- Using various models

*TEKS

- Representing decimals, including tenths and hundredths, using concrete and visual models and money
- Adding and subtracting decimals to the hundredths place using the standard algorithm
- Relating decimals to fractions that name tenths and hundredths
- Determining the corresponding decimal to the tenths or hundredths place of a specified point on a number line

- Comparing and ordering two decimals to thousandths based on meanings of the digits in each place and representing comparisons using the symbols >, =, or < to record the results of the comparisons
- Rounding decimals to tenths or hundredths (to any place)
- Adding, subtracting, multiplying, and dividing decimals to hundredths using concrete models or drawings and strategies based on place value, properties of operations, and/or the relationship between addition and subtraction; relating the strategy to a written method and explaining the reasoning used

The Models

In the upper elementary grades, students should start doing *Decimal of the Day* at the very beginning of the year. They should begin by reviewing all the decimal standards that came before their current grade level. This is so important because decimals are usually only taught once a year and then soon forgotten about after the test. Research states that students don't like fractions, struggle when working with them, and often forget what they are taught. We need routines that help students to be on friendly terms with decimals. So fraction fluency will be promoted by starting at the beginning of the year with *Decimals of the Day*, doing this at least twice a week, and then making it more complex as new information is taught. Start at the end of fourth grade and continue on at the beginning of fifth grade. It is important to continue using number bonds and having students do visual models and sketches of their thinking. v should work with both horizontal and vertical number lines as well as marked and unmarked number lines.

There can be general sheets like this one:

Decimal of the Day 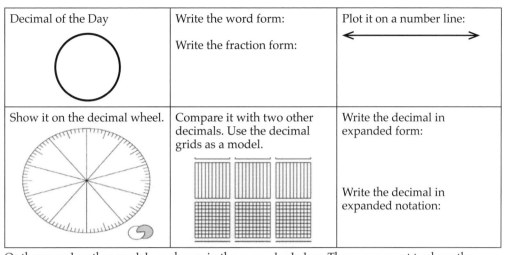	Write the word form: Write the fraction form:	Plot it on a number line: ⟵————————⟶
Show it on the decimal wheel.	Compare it with two other decimals. Use the decimal grids as a model.	Write the decimal in expanded form: Write the decimal in expanded notation:

Or there can be other models as shown in the examples below. These are meant to show the variety of things that should be practiced by grade level for this routine.

Decimal of the Day – Fourth Grade

Students start to work with decimals in fourth grade. During the unit on decimals, start doing Decimal of the Day. In the beginning the focus should be on using concrete models and visual models so that students can define decimals, relate them to fractions, start plotting them on a number line, and compare them with symbols.

Beginning of the Year

Show that ³⁄₁₀ = ³⁰⁄₁₀₀ using the grids.	Compare 0.20 and 0.02 using the decimal wheel model. 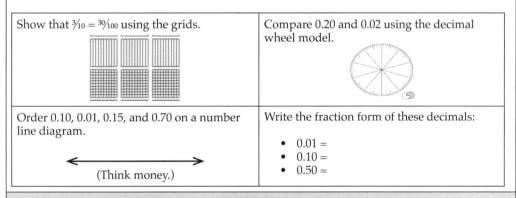
Order 0.10, 0.01, 0.15, and 0.70 on a number line diagram. ⟵————————⟶ (Think money.)	Write the fraction form of these decimals: • 0.01 = • 0.10 = • 0.50 =

End of the Year

Add ³⁄₁₀ and ⁴⁄₁₀₀ using the grid.	Is ⁴⁄₁₀ the same as ⁴⁰⁄₁₀₀? Why or why not? Explain your thinking. 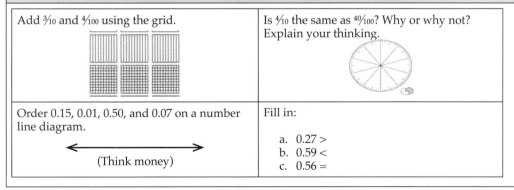
Order 0.15, 0.01, 0.50, and 0.07 on a number line diagram. ⟵————————⟶ (Think money)	Fill in: a. 0.27 > b. 0.59 < c. 0.56 =

Continued

Continued

Decimal of the Day – **Fifth Grade**

Students continue to work on decimals in fifth grade. At the beginning of the year they should pick up where they left off in fourth grade. During the unit on decimals, students learn to add, subtract, multiply, and divide decimals using a variety of strategies and models. They extend their understanding to thousandths. They also learn to round decimals.

Beginning of the Year

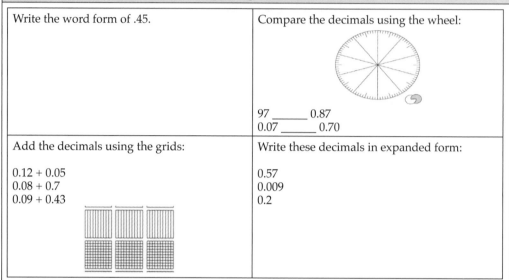

Write the word form of .45.	Compare the decimals using the wheel: 97 _____ 0.87 0.07 _____ 0.70
Add the decimals using the grids: 0.12 + 0.05 0.08 + 0.7 0.09 + 0.43	Write these decimals in expanded form: 0.57 0.009 0.2
Multiply the decimals using the grids: 2 × 0.08 = 3 × 0.10 = 2 × 1.50 =	Round these decimals to the nearest tenth using a number line diagram. Explain your thinking. 0.72 0.98 0.11
Divide the decimal using the wheel. 0.45 ÷ 3	Write these decimals in expanded notation: 0.33 0.75 0.99

Anchor Chart

Decimal of the Day is a routine that we do to "get great" with decimals! We do it a couple of times a week to review and preview decimals.

For example: 0.33
Word form: thirty-three hundredths
Fraction form: $\frac{33}{100}$
Model:

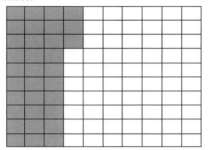

How much to 1: 0.67

Student Response Sheet

Decimal of the Day Idea List:

- Plot it on a number line
- Word form
- Fraction form
- Addition sentence
- Subtraction sentence
- How much more to 1
- Compare
- Order
- Expanded form
- Expanded notation

My Decimal of the Day 0.57

1. $\frac{57}{100}$
2. $\frac{27}{100} + \frac{30}{100} = \frac{57}{100}$
3. $5 \times \frac{1}{10} + 7 \times \frac{1}{100}$
4. $0.57 > 0.34$
Bonus: $0.57 < 0.75$

More Resources

www.dusd.net/cgi/files/2012/12/fraction-number-talks.pdf
https://www.pinterest.com/drnicki7/fraction-of-the-daydecimal-of-the-day/

Routine #6
Number Talks

The *Number Talks* Routine
Number Talks are teacher-led discussions that occur for about 5 to 10 minutes with students discussing different ways to solve problems. The teacher gives the students an expression to think about and solve mentally. Then students share and discuss their strategies.

Materials and Tools	"I can" statement
The only materials for the *Number Talks* routine are the kids' brains.	**I can** describe that pattern. I can extend that pattern.

Continued

Continued

Protocol	Purpose:

Protocol

Overview: The teacher writes a mathematical expression horizontally on the board. The students discuss the problem and state what they think is the answer. The teacher records all answers without any indication of whether they are correct or not. Then the teacher asks the students to defend their thinking. As students defend their thinking, other students remove their thinking from the list of answers, convinced by their classmates of the correct answer.

1. The teacher puts a mathematical expression on the board.
2. The teacher tells the students to take "private think time" to think about the concept. Encourage the students to estimate their answer before solving so they can reason about whether or not their answer will make sense.
3. After about 1 minute, the teacher asks students to show hand signals that indicate different things:

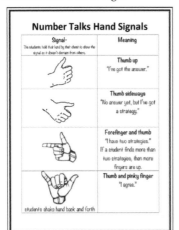

4. The teacher then asks for students to share their answers and their strategies. The students must explain step by step how they arrived at their answers.
5. The teacher records the students' thinking on the white board.

* In some versions, teachers have students use their white boards and share their thinking with a neighbor before they share out loud.

Purpose:

- Think and reason about numbers
- Develop flexibility, efficiency, accuracy, and automaticity with whole numbers, fractions, and decimals

Questions:

- Who wants to defend their thinking?
- What did you do exactly?
- Can you lead us through the steps?
- Tell us why you did that?
- What are some different ways that you might solve this problem?

The Routine

Number Talks is a routine to build strategic competence and procedural fluency. It was first introduced and developed by Kathy Richardson in collaboration with Ruth Parker, and then it was expanded by Sherry Parrish. Most recently, Parker, in collaboration with Cathy Humphreys, wrote a book furthering the discussion (Humphreys & Parker, 2015). *Number Talks* has taken on a life of its own. The basic gist is: The teacher puts up an expression to be solved (appropriate to the grade level). Students have a few minutes to think about strategies, and then they indicate through a variety of signals whether they have a strategy and/or the answer. Then after a few minutes, the teacher goes through and lets everyone talk about his or her thinking. The teacher simply records all the answers, not censoring anyone's thinking. After everyone who wants to gets their answer on the board, the teacher asks, "Who wants to defend their thinking?" The students then begin to share their thought processes. As they do so, everyone notices what is happening, and some students begin to revise their initial thinking and ask the teacher to take down their answers because they now agree with their partners.

Number Talks – Kindergarten

Kindergarten could do Number Talks that focus on composing and decomposing numbers. Later in the year, they would work on addition and subtraction within 10. Number Talks can also be done with ten frames, with dots, or with rekenreks to figure out how many are there and justify thinking.

Beginning of the Year

How can we make 5?	How can we make 5?					Give me ….
0 and 5 1 and 4 2 and 3	4	5	1	2	3	The teacher shows an amount of fingers, and then the students hold up the rest to make the stated total. For example, the teacher holds up 2 fingers and says, "Give me 4." The students then each hold up 2 more fingers so there is a total of 4 between the teacher and each of the students.
	2	0	1	3	4	
	1	3	4	5	2	
	0	2	3	4	1	

End of the Year

How can we make 10?	How can we make 10?					I wish I had …
0 and 10 1 and 9 2 and 8	4	5	1	2	8	**Teacher:** I have 5. I wish I had 10. **Student:** You need 5 more. **Teacher:** I have 1. I wish I had 9. **Student:** You need 8 more.
	2	9	7	6	4	
	1	6	8	5	10	
	8	2	3	0	9	

Continued

Number Talks – First Grade

In first grade, students continue composing and decomposing numbers. Then they start working on basic facts within 10 and 20. They also add a double digit and a single digit and add 10 to a number.

Beginning of the Year

How can we make 12?	How can we make 10?	I wish I had …
0 and 12 1 and 11 2 and 9	<table><tr><td>4</td><td>5</td><td>1</td><td>2</td><td>8</td></tr><tr><td>2</td><td>9</td><td>7</td><td>6</td><td>4</td></tr><tr><td>1</td><td>6</td><td>8</td><td>5</td><td>10</td></tr><tr><td>8</td><td>2</td><td>3</td><td>0</td><td>9</td></tr></table>	**Teacher**: I have 10. I wish I had 20. **Students**: You need 10 more. **Teacher**: I have 1. I wish I had 10. **Students**: You need 9 more.

End of the Year

How could we think about solving this?	What strategies could we use to solve this?	Name a fact that fits this strategy.
5 + 8	3 + 4	DoublesMake TenDoubles Plus 1 Bridge 10 Friends of Ten

Number Talks – Second Grade

In second grade, start with single-digit numbers. Students should be working on adding numbers within 100 and then eventually within 1000.

Beginning of the Year

How can we solve this?	How can we make 10 and 20?	Name a fact that fits this strategy.
9 + 7	<table><tr><td>4</td><td>5</td><td>1</td><td>2</td><td>8</td></tr><tr><td>5</td><td>9</td><td>7</td><td>6</td><td>3</td></tr><tr><td>11</td><td>6</td><td>8</td><td>5</td><td>13</td></tr><tr><td>15</td><td>12</td><td>14</td><td>7</td><td>9</td></tr></table>	Doubles Make Ten Doubles Plus 1 Bridge 10 Friends of Ten

End of the Year

How can we think about solving this?	What strategies could we use to solve this?	Name a fact that fits this strategy:
37 + 55	41 − 29	Number in the Middle Doubles + 1 Doubles + 2 Lucky 8 Add 10

Number Talks – Third Grade

In third grade, start with single-digit numbers. You can move fairly quickly to double-digit numbers. Eventually by the end of the year, you can use larger numbers. Students should be working on adding and subtracting multi-digit numbers. By the end of the year, students should be working on multiplication and division.

Beginning of the Year

How can we solve this?	How can we make 100?				Name a fact that fits this strategy.
$9 + 7$ $9 + 17$ $19 + 7$ $37 + 55$ $41 - 29$	25	35	67	75	Doubles Make Ten Doubles + 1 Bridge 10 Friends of Ten
	65	33	50	38	
	50	62	99	100	
	1	15	0	85	

End of the Year

How can we think about solving these?	What strategies could we use to solve these?	Name a fact that fits this strategy.
5×2 5×4 5×8	7×3 7×6 7×10 7×9	Identity Property Multiplying Doubles Square Numbers Double-Double Facts Double-Double-Double Facts

Number Talks – Fourth Grade

In fourth grade, start with single-digit numbers. Fairly quickly students should move to multi-digit numbers and multiplication and division. By the end of the year, move on to using fractions and decimals (adding tenths and hundredths).

Beginning of the Year

How can we solve this?	How can we make 100?				Name a fact that fits this strategy.
9×10 9×5 9×9	25	35	67	75	Identity Property Multiplying Doubles Square Numbers Double-Double Facts Double-Double-Double Facts
	65	33	50	38	
	50	62	99	100	
	1	15	0	85	

End of the Year

How can we think about solving these?	What strategies could we use to solve these?	Solve these.
2×25 2×50 2×75 2×100 2×150 2×200	7×500 10×500 17×500 17×499	$1600 \div 4$ $523 \div 5$ $321 \div 2$

Continued

Number Talks – Fifth Grade

In fifth grade, start with single-digit numbers. Fairly quickly move to multi-digit numbers and multiplication and division. By the end of the year, move on to fractions and decimals.

Beginning of the Year

How can we solve these?	How can we solve these?	Name a fact that fits this strategy.
$1600 \div 4$ $523 \div 5$ $321 \div 2$	12×15 14×28 328×7	Identity Property Multiplying Doubles Square Numbers Double-Double Facts Double-Double-Double Facts

End of the Year

How can we think about solving these?	What strategies could we use to solve these?	Solve these.
0.25×2 0.25×4 0.25×8 0.25×10	$\frac{1}{5} - \frac{1}{10}$ $\frac{1}{4} - \frac{1}{8}$ $\frac{2}{4} - \frac{1}{2}$	$\frac{3}{10} - \frac{20}{100}$ $\frac{5}{10} - \frac{10}{100}$ $\frac{9}{10} - \frac{70}{100}$

Anchor Chart

Number Talks is a routine that we do to talk about numbers.

We share our thinking. We listen to others. We talk respectfully.

For example: $25 + 19$

We could adjust the numbers and make 25 a 24 and 19 a 20. That would mean $24 + 20 = 44$.

Or we could think $30 + 14$.

Student Response Sheet

$25 + 19$

$24 + 20$

Routine #7
Number Talks (British Style)

The *Number Talks (British Style)* Routine

(adapted from National Centre for Excellence in the Teaching of Mathematics. See: https://www.youtube.com/watch?v=RCCLseBLBSo)

Number Talks **build number competence across mathematical topics. In the traditional *Number Talks* routine, the teacher presents a problem and the students discuss different ways to think about its solution. In the British version, the students actually generate the problem and then discuss how they would solve it. This is a twist on the American version. It is quite cognitively demanding because students have to decide, once they pick their problem, which way they can solve it: in their head; with a model; or with an algorithm.**

Materials and Tools	"I can" statement
Students should have a variety of tools to think and reason about the numbers being discussed. They should use their toolkits. Students can use manipulatives, drawings, and mental math.	**I can** reason about numbers and explain and justify my thinking. I can listen to, understand, and respond to the thinking of others and decide whether or not their reasoning makes sense.

Protocol	Purpose:
Overview: Teachers put up two circles with different numbers in each one. The students pick their numbers and write them in a frame on their white board or thinking notebook.	<ul><li>Reason</li><li>Generalize math concepts</li><li>Defend thinking</li></ul>

Protocol (continued)

1. The teacher puts up the number circles on a white board, interactive board, or chart paper.
2. The teacher tells the students to take "private think time" to think about which numbers they will use.
3. After about 30 seconds, the teacher tells the students to "turn and talk to a neighbor."
4. Everyone comes back together, and students raise their hands and explain their thinking.

I can do it in my head	I can do it with a model	I can do it with an algorithm

Questions:

BEFORE
- What numbers are you going to pick?
- Why?

DURING
- Which numbers did you pick?
- What do you know about those numbers?
- What strategies can you use with those numbers?

AFTER
- What did you do?
- Which models did you all use?
- Which strategies did you use?
- Why did you do that?

What's the Math?

Number Talks (British Version) should require students at different levels to explore:

Kindergarten
- Adding and subtracting

First Grade
- Adding and subtracting

Second Grade
- Adding and subtracting
- Multiplying and dividing

Third Grade
- Adding and subtracting
- Multiplying and dividing

Fourth Grade
- Adding and subtracting
- Multiplying and dividing
- Fractions and decimals

Fifth Grade
- Adding and subtracting
- Multiplying and dividing
- Fractions and decimals

The Models

Students should have access to their toolkits. They should have many tools and templates available to support their thinking.

Continued

Number Talks (British Style) – **Kindergarten**

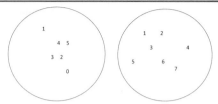

Can you do it in your head?	Can you do it with a model?
5 + 5	3 + 7

Number Talks (British Style) – **First Grade**

In first grade, start with single-digit numbers. Eventually, by the end of the year, put in more numbers in each circle, including two-digit ones.

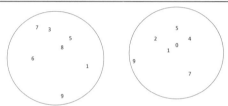

Can you do it in your head?	Can you do it with a model?	Can you do it with numbers?
5 + 1	6 + 4	9 + 7

Number Talks (British Style) – **Second Grade**

In second grade, start with single-digit numbers. Eventually, by the end of the year, put in more numbers and larger numbers in each circle. Students should be working on adding numbers within 100 and then eventually within 1000.

Can you do it in your head?	Can you do it with a model?	Can you do it with an algorithm?
9 + 9 = 18 (doubles fact)		18 + 12 = 20 + 10 = 30 (I added the tens and then the ones.)

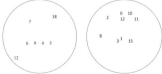

Number Talks (British Style) – Third Grade

In third grade, start with single-digit numbers. You can move fairly quickly to double-digit numbers. Eventually, by the end of the year, put in more numbers and larger numbers in each circle. Students should be working on adding numbers within 100 and then eventually within 10,000.

Can you do it in your head?	Can you do it with a model?	Can you do it with an algorithm?
$15 + 5 = 20$	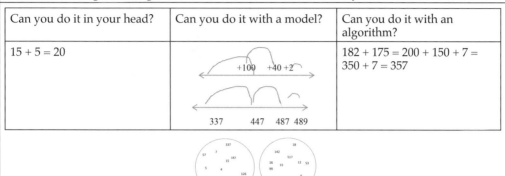	$182 + 175 = 200 + 150 + 7 = 350 + 7 = 357$

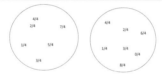

Number Talks (British Style) – Fourth Grade

In fourth grade, start with single-digit numbers. Eventually put in more numbers and larger numbers in each circle. Move on to using fractions and decimals (adding tenths and hundredths) by the end of the year.

Can you do it in your head?	Can you do it with a model?	Can you do it with an algorithm?
$\frac{3}{4} + \frac{2}{4}$	$\frac{5}{4} = \frac{1}{4} + \frac{4}{4}$	$\frac{2}{4} + \frac{3}{4} + \frac{6}{4}$

Number Talks (British Style) – Fifth Grade

In fifth grade, start with single-digit numbers. Eventually put more numbers and larger numbers in each circle. By the end of the year, move on to fractions and decimals.

Can you do it in your head?	Can you do it with a model?	Can you do it with an algorithm?
$0.33 + 0.90$	$0.33 + 0.17$	$0.140 + 0.5 + 0.17$

Continued

Continued

Anchor Chart	Student Response Sheet		
In the *Number Talk (British Style)*, we have two circles and we pick numbers from each of 2 circles. We have to think about, for example, how we are going to add them. We can do it in our heads, we can do it with a model, or we can use an algorithm.  We then discuss our thinking.	**Can you do it in your head?** ¼ + ¾	**Can you do it with a model?** ½ + ¾ = 1 ¼	**Can you do it with an algorithm?** ¾ + ⁵⁄₄ ¼ ⁴⁄₄ ¾ + ¼ = 1 1 + ⁴⁄₄ = 2

Routine #8
Over/Under/Same

The *Over/Under/Same* Routine	
This is a great routine for getting students to actively engage in estimation about different types of numbers. Students are given a number and then asked is it over or under a target number, or the same. If it is over the number, the students make a gesture with their hands over their heads; if it is under, the students make a gesture with their hands towards the ground. If it is the same, students hold their hands straight out to their sides.	
Materials and Tools Students use mental math and estimation skills to solve the problems.	**"I can" statement** **I can** reason about numbers and explain and justify my thinking. I can listen to, understand, and respond to the thinking of others and decide whether or not their reasoning makes sense. I can estimate numbers.
Protocol Overview: The teacher gives students a target number. Then the teacher says a number and students have to decide if it is over, under, or the same as the target number. Students show their vote with hand gestures.	**Purpose** • Reason • Generalize math concepts • Defend thinking
	Questions: • Is this over or under _____? • How do you know that? • Are you sure about that? • Can you prove it? • Can you give me an example?

What's the Math?

Over/Under/Same should require students at different levels to explore:

Kindergarten

- Adding and subtracting

First Grade

- Adding and subtracting
- Doubling
- Halving
- Basic strategies for single-digit and multi-digit computation

Second Grade

- Adding and subtracting
- Doubling
- Halving
- Basic strategies for single-digit and multi-digit computation

Third Grade

- Adding and subtracting
- Multiplying and dividing
- Doubling
- Halving
- Basic strategies for single-digit and multi-digit computation

Fourth Grade

- Adding and subtracting
- Multiplying and dividing
- Doubling
- Halving
- Basic strategies for single-digit and multi-digit computation
- Fractions and decimals

Fifth Grade

- Adding and subtracting
- Multiplying and dividing
- Doubling
- Halving
- Basic strategies for single-digit and multi-digit computation
- Fractions and decimals

Classroom Vignette: *Over/Under/Same*

Mr. Ted: Good morning class. Today for our routine we are going to do *Over/Under/Same*. Remember that we have to think about how big the numbers are and then estimate the answer. So to start, we are going to use the number 50. Are these answers over or under 50? Remember to take your private think time, then turn and talk with a partner, share your thinking, and be sure to say why.

> **Is it over or under 50?**
> A. 100 − 60
> B. 27 + 28
> C. 120 − 60
> D. 48 + 29

Ted: A is over 50 … I mean under 50 because 60 + 40 is 100, so 40 is under 50.

Maite: B is over 50 … I think this because 25 and 25 make 50, so 27 and 28 would be more than 50.

Kelli: B is over 50 … I thought about it like 40 and 15, and I know that is over 50.

Timothy: C is over because it's a half fact and 60 and 60 make 100, so 60 is over 50.

Caitlin: D is over because 48 is almost 50 and 28 is way bigger, so that is going to be over 50.

Mr. Ted: What do you mean that it is "way bigger?"

Caitlin: Like 28 is almost 30, so if you add it to 50, it is going to be over 50.

Mr. Ted: I like the way that you are all justifying your thinking. I can tell that you are not just guessing at answers but really reasoning about the numbers.

Continued

Continued

Over/Under/Same – Kindergarten

(Not applicable at the beginning of the year)

End of the Year

The focus here is on using a number track and thinking about whether the number is greater than or less than. The teacher says a number and the students point to it and decide if it is greater than or less than 10.

5
7
12
15

Over/Under/Same – First Grade	
Beginning of the Year	**End of the Year**
Over or under 10	Over or under 20
5 + 5	7 + 7
7 + 4	7 + 3
9 + 2	17 − 10
4 + 4	15 − 7

Over/Under/Same – Second Grade	
Beginning of the Year	**End of the Year**
Over or under 10 and then 20 Include subtraction	Over or under 50 and then 100 Include subtraction
8 − 6	20 + 20
5 + 5	33 + 9
14 − 8	45 + 10
15 + 9	39 +19

Over/Under/Same – Third Grade	
Beginning of the Year	**End of the Year**
Over or under 50 and then 100 Include subtraction	Over or under different numbers up to 10,000 Include subtraction, multiplication, and division
35 + 8 49 − 10 57 + 57 78 − 9	Over 1000 520 + 488 728 − 199 399 + 399

Over/Under/Same – Fourth Grade	
Beginning of the Year	**End of the Year**
Over or under various numbers through decimals including tenths and hundredths Also include multi-digit numbers +, −, ×, ÷, and decimals appropriate for the beginning of the year. Over 1 whole ¼ + 4/4 ¾ + ¼ ⅓ + ⅓	Over or under various numbers through decimals including tenths and hundredths Also include multi-digit numbers +, −, ×, ÷, and decimals. Over 1 whole 1/10 + 7/10 2/10 + 70/100 4/10 + 5/100

Over/Under/Same – Fifth Grade	
Beginning of the Year	**End of the Year**
Over or under various numbers through decimals including tenths and hundredths Also include multi-digit numbers, +, −, ×, ÷, and decimals, subtraction of fractions.	Over or under various numbers through decimals including tenths and hundredths Also include multi-digit numbers +, −, ×, ÷, and decimals, subtraction with fractions and decimals.
Over 1 whole ⅓ + ¾ ½ + ⅓ ⅘ + ⅙	Over 1 whole 0.58 + 0.42 0.33 + 0.45 0.09 + 0.92
Anchor Chart	**Student Response Sheet**
Over/Under/Same is a routine that we use to think about numbers. We use hand gestures to show if we think that the numbers are over or under a target number. For example: 55 + 27 Over or under 100 **Kelli:** This is under because ball parking it, 60 + 30 is only 90, so this would be under. **Tom:** I agree because you need another 50 to get to 100, and 27 is far from that.	**Over or Under: 100** 27 + 39 This is under because each of these numbers is under 50. 57 + 57 This is over because both of these numbers are over 50. 38 + 99 This is over because 99 is close to 100, and 38 is more than 1 more.

Routine #9
Virtual Dice Roll

The *Virtual Dice Roll* Routine	
Virtual Dice Rolls **are just meant to build flexibility. There are several virtual dice sites on the internet as well as some that are built into different interactive boards. The teacher or the students roll the dice, and then the teacher asks a variety of questions based on the grade level.** www.curriculumbits.com/mathematics/virtual-dice/ (with sound effects – a personal favorite) http://dice.virtuworld.net/ https://www.random.org/dice/?num=2 https://www.freeonlinedice.com/#dice	
Materials and Tools	**"I can" statement**
Students should have a variety of tools to think and reason about the numbers being discussed. They should use their toolkits. Students can use manipulatives, drawings, and mental math.	**I can** reason about numbers and explain and justify my thinking. I can listen to, understand, and respond to the thinking of others and decide whether or not their reasoning makes sense.

Continued

Protocol	Purpose:
Overview: There are at least three different dice rolls to chose from: single dice, double dice, and triple dice. These dice allow for the teacher to ask different questions.	• Reason • Generalize math concepts • Defend thinking
1. The teacher rolls the interactive dice. 2. The teacher tells the students to take "private think time" to think about the concept. 3. After about 30 seconds, the teacher tells the students to "turn and talk to a neighbor." 4. Everyone comes back together, and students raise their hands and explain their thinking.	**Questions:** BEFORE • What can you do if you get stuck? • How can your strategy mat help you? • What should you do when you're not sure? DURING • How do you know that? • Are you sure about that? • Can you prove it? • Can you give me an example? AFTER • What was easy? • What was tricky?

What's the Math?

Virtual Dice Roll should require students at different levels to explore:

Kindergarten
- Adding and subtracting

First Grade
- Adding and subtracting
- Properties of addition

Second Grade
- Even and odd
- Adding and subtracting
- Properties of addition
- Doubling and halving
- Skip counting
- Comparing numbers

Third Grade
- Even and odd
- Doubling and halving
- Adding and subtracting
- Multiplying and dividing
- Properties of addition and multiplication
- Rounding

Fourth Grade
- Multiplying and dividing
- Multiples and factors
- Prime and composite
- Properties of addition and multiplication
- Adding and subtracting

Fifth Grade
- Prime and composite
- Multiples and factors
- Multiplying and dividing
- Decimals
- Properties of addition and multiplication
- Adding and subtracting

Digital Versions

There are so many digital possibilities for this routine. Here are some websites to pull up virtual dice that offer great number generators. I love Curriculum Bits because it has fun music and the sound of the dice rolling. It offers one, two, or three dice, and the possibilities are endless. I like Virtu Roll because you can pick up to several dice to roll. I like Tes because you can focus on specific strategy work. Make sure that the students have their toolkits so they have access to the tools and templates to scaffold their thinking.

Virtu Roll	Curriculum Bits	Tes Dice
http://dice.virtuworld.net/	www.curriculumbits.com/ mathematics/virtual-dice/	www.iboard.co.uk/activity/ Adding-Two-Dice-716

Virtual Dice Roll – **Kindergarten**

In Kindergarten, begin by using the single dice.

Hold up this many fingers.
Hold up this number.
What is 1 less?
What is 1 more?
What is 2 less?
What is 2 more?
How many more to 10?
Find this number and point to it on your number track/number ladder/number line.

Virtual Dice Roll – First Grade, Second Grade

In first and second grade, use up to three dice. In the beginning, use one, then add two and eventually three.

(die showing 6)	Hold up this many fingers. Hold up this number (use your number fan). What is 1 less? What is 1 more? What is 2 less? What is 2 more? How many more to 10? Find it and point to it on your number track/number ladder/number line. Is it odd or even? What is it doubled?
(two dice showing 4 and 5)	Hold up this many fingers. Hold up this number (use your number fan). What is 1 less? What is 1 more? What is 2 less? What is 2 more? How many more to 10? Find it and point to it on your number track/number ladder/number line.
(three dice showing 3, 5, 6)	What is a quick strategy to add these three numbers?

Virtual Dice Roll – Third Grade, Fourth Grade, Fifth Grade

In third, fourth, and fifth grade, use up to three dice. In the beginning use one; then use two and eventually three.

(die showing 6)	Is this number prime or composite? What is this number doubled? Multiply this number by itself. Multiply this number by 0. Multiply this number by 1. Multiply this number by 2. Skip count by this number up to 84.
(two dice showing 4 and 5)	Multiply these two numbers. Name a strategy for multiplying these numbers. Is this an even by an even number or an even by an odd number? What is the product – odd or even?
(three dice showing 4, 5, 6)	What is a quick strategy to add these three numbers? Multiply these numbers. What is a quick strategy for multiplying these numbers?

Anchor Chart

Dice Roll is a routine that we do to think quickly about numbers. We usually use one, two, or three dice.

For example:

We rolled three dice. We have to think about which is the fastest way to group the numbers to add them.

3 + 2 = 5
5 + 5 = 10

Thinking about number combinations helps us to add more efficiently.

Student Response Sheet

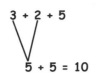

Routine #10
Virtual Cards

The *Virtual Cards* Routine

Virtual Cards are mainly meant to build flexibility, although there are several other skills that can be built with this quick routine. There are a few good virtual card sites on the internet. The teacher or a student deals the cards, and then the teacher asks a variety of questions based on the grade level.

https://www.randomlists.com/draw-cards
http://playingcards.io/ux3q
https://deck-of-cards.js.org/

Materials and Tools	**"I can" statement**
Students should have a variety of tools to think and reason about the numbers being discussed. They should use their toolkits. Students can use manipulatives, drawings, and mental math.	**I can** reason about numbers and explain and justify my thinking. I can listen to, understand, and respond to the thinking of others and decide whether or not their reasoning makes sense.
Protocol	**Purpose:**
Overview: There are different amounts of cards to deal. The teacher deals the cards and then asks different questions. The teacher deals the interactive cards. • The teacher tells the students to take "private think time" to think about the concept.	• Reason • Generalize math concepts • Defend thinking

Continued

- After about 30 seconds, the teacher tells the students to "turn and talk to a neighbor."
- Everyone comes back together, and students raise their hands and explain their thinking.

Questions:

BEFORE

- What can you do if you get stuck?
- How can your strategy mat help you?
- What should you do when you're not sure?

DURING

- How do you know that?
- Are you sure about that?
- Can you prove it?
- Can you give me an example?

AFTER

- What was easy?
- What was tricky?

What's the Math?

Virtual Cards should require students at different levels to explore:

Kindergarten
- Adding and subtracting

First Grade
- Adding and subtracting
- Properties of addition

Second Grade
- Even and odd
- Adding and subtracting
- Properties of addition
- Doubling and halving
- Skip counting
- Comparing numbers

Third Grade
- Even and odd
- Doubling and halving
- Adding and subtracting
- Multiplying and dividing
- Properties of addition and multiplication
- Rounding

Fourth Grade
- Multiplying and dividing
- Multiples and factors
- Prime and composite

Fifth Grade
- Prime and composite
- Multiples and factors
- Multiplying and dividing
- Decimals

Digital Possibilities

There are so many digital possibilities for this routine. These are some fun ones for generating numbers with playing cards.

Playing Cards IO	Random Card Generators
http://playingcards.io/ux3q	https://www.randomlists.com/draw-cards

The Models

Make sure that the students have their toolkits so they have access to the tools and templates to scaffold their thinking. I use a variety of cards for this: virtual, mini, jumbo, giant, and colossal.

Virtual Cards – **Kindergarten**
In Kindergarten, begin by using a single card.
Beginning of the Year

Hold up this many fingers.
Hold up this number.
What is 1 less?
What is 1 more?
What is 2 less?
What is 2 more?
How many more to 10?
How many do you have to take away to have 0 left?
Find this number and point to it on your number track/number ladder/number line.

End of the Year (Include teen numbers)

Show this number on your rekenrek.
Show this number on the double ten frames.
What is 1 less?
What is 1 more?
What is 2 less?
What is 2 more?
What is this number in between?
How many tens and how many ones?

Virtual Cards – **First Grade, Second Grade**
In first and second grade, use up to three cards. In the beginning, use one, then use two and eventually three.

Hold up that many fingers.
Hold up this number (use your number fan).
What is 1 less?
What is 1 more?
What is 2 less?
What is 2 more?
How many more to 10?
How many more to 20?
How many do you need to take away to get 0?
Find this number and point to it on your number track/number ladder/number line.
Is it odd or even?
What is it doubled?

Continued

Continued

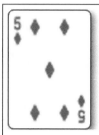 

Add these together.

Write the sum on your white board.

Write the difference between the larger and smaller number on your white board.

Make the largest two-digit number you can.

Make the smallest two-digit number you can.

Draw a number line and plot that number. Write the numbers before and after that number.

Name a strategy to add these two numbers.

What is 1 more?

What is 2 less?

What is 2 more?

How many more to 10?

How many more to 20?

What is a quick strategy to add these three numbers?

Make the largest three-digit number possible. Write it in standard and expanded form.

What is 100 less? 100 more? How many more to 1000?

Make the smallest three-digit number possible? Write it in standard and expanded form.

What is 100 less? 100 more? How many to 1000?

Decompose the number in a three-legged number bond.

Make a two-digit number and a one-digit number, and add them together. What strategy did you use?

Virtual Cards – Third Grade, Fourth Grade, Fifth Grade

In third, fourth, and fifth grades, use up to five cards (depending on the grade and the focus).

Is this number prime or composite?

What is this number doubled?

Multiply this number by itself.

Multiply this number by 0.

Multiply this number by 1.

Multiply this number by 2.

Skip count by this number up to 84.

Divide this number by 1.

Divide this number by itself.

Divide 0 by this number.

	Multiply these two numbers. Name a strategy for multiplying these numbers. Is this an even by an even number or an even by an odd number? What is the product – odd or even?	

What is a quick strategy to add these three numbers?

Multiply these numbers. What is a quick strategy for multiplying these numbers?

Make a two-digit number and a single-digit number. Divide the two-digit number by the single-digit number. Is there a remainder?

Make a two-digit number and divide it by a two-digit number.

Make a three-digit number and divide it by a single-digit number. Estimate the quotient. Model it with an open array.

Make two two-digit numbers. Multiply them. Discuss your strategy. Model it with an open array.

Anchor Chart

 is a routine where we share our thinking. We listen to others. We talk respectively.

For example:

Student 1: The largest number we can make is 652.

Student 2: The smallest number we can make is 256.

Student 3: 652 is even.
Student 4: 700 is the nearest hundred to 652.
Student 5: We need 48 more to get to 700.

Student Response Sheet

652

- **rounds to 700**
- **is even**
- **you need 48 more to get to 700**

The *Do Not Solve* Routine

The *Do Not Solve* routine is another reasoning routine. Students are instructed not to solve the problems, but rather to reason about the numbers and then determine the answers based on their reasoning.

Materials and Tools	"I can" statement
Students should have a variety of tools to think and reason about the numbers being discussed. They should use their toolkits. Students can use manipulatives, drawings, and mental math.	**I can** reason about numbers and explain and justify my thinking. I can listen to, understand, and respond to the thinking of others and decide whether or not their reasoning makes sense.

Protocol	Purpose
Overview: The teacher puts up a few problems and asks some questions. The students have to reason out the answers. 1. The teacher puts a mathematical concept on the board. 2. The teacher tells the students to take "private think time" to think about the concept. 3. After about 30 seconds, the teacher tells the students to "turn and talk to a neighbor." 4. Everyone comes back together, and students raise their hands and explain their thinking.	• Reason out loud • Think about counterexamples • Discuss the example and the counterexamples **Questions:** • What is it? • What do you notice about the numbers?

What's the Math?

This routine is a great routine for Grades 2 through 5. *Do Not Solve* should require students at different levels to explore:

Second Grade
• Adding and subtracting

Third Grade
- Adding and subtracting
- Multiplying and dividing
- Fractions

Fourth Grade
- Adding and subtracting
- Multiplying and dividing
- Fractions
- Decimals

Fifth Grade
- Adding and subtracting
- Multiplying and dividing
- Fractions
- Decimals

Classroom Vignette: **Do Not Solve**

A. 3/4 + 2/2
B. 3/4 + 1/4
C. 1/8 + 1/2
D. 5/4 + 1/8

1. Which problem has a sum that is equal to 1?
2. Which problem has a sum less than 1?
3. Which problem has a sum between 1 and 1 1/2?
4. Which problem is greater than 1 1/2?

Mr. Clark puts this on the board. Then he asks the students to look at the problems and reason about the numbers. After they have had private think time and time to turn and talk to their neighbor about the answers, he asks people to share their thinking.

Sue: B has a sum equal to 1 because 3/4 + 1/4 makes 1 whole.

Mr. Clark: On your white boards, prove what Sue just said.

Some of the students draw a visual representation of this; others take out their pattern block templates; and some use a number line. After having students explain their model to their shoulder buddies, Mr. Clark asks who knows the answer to number 2.

Mia: 1/8 + 1/2 is less than a whole. I know this because it takes 4/8 to make a half. Half and half would make a whole. We only have 1/8. So it has to be less than one whole.

Mr. Clark asks if everyone agrees and who can state what Mia just said in his or her own words.

Tom: I agree. Here is a picture. So it shows half shaded and then 1/8 shaded, so that isn't the whole shaded.

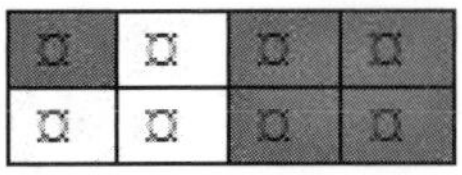

Mr. Clark: Who's got number 3?
Mike: This is tricky but it's not B or C. A is 1 3/4. So it has to be D.

Mr. Clark: OK, so you used a process of elimination. That could work. Who agrees with him?

Taylor: It is D because 5/4 is 1 whole and 1/4, and then we need another 1/4 to get to 1/2. We only have 1/8.

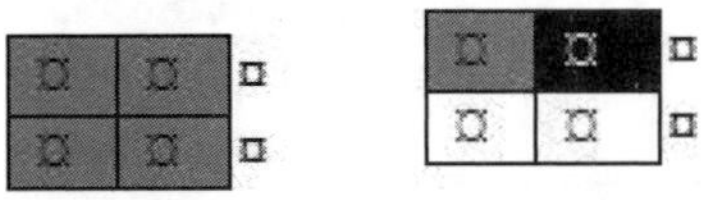

Mr. Clark: So we know that the answer to number 4 is D. Who can tell us why?

Todd: That's easy … because 2/2 is 1 whole and then add 3/4.

Taylor: It is D because 5/4 is 1 whole and 1/4, and then we need another 1/4 to get to 1/2. We only have 1/8.

Continued

Continued

Do Not Solve – Second Grade	
Beginning of the Year	**End of the Year**
A. 2 + 5 B. 39 + 8 C. 80 + 20 D. 50 + 60	A. 12 + 15 B. 99 + 140 C. 70 + 30 D. 58 + 58
A. What sum is less than 10? B. What sum is between 20 and 50? C. What sum is going to make 100? D. What sum is going to be more than 100?	A. What sum is between 100 and 200? B. What sum is less than 50? C. What sum is going to make 100? D. What sum is going to be more than 200?

Do Not Solve – Third Grade	
Beginning of the Year	**End of the Year**
A. 39 + 20 B. 100 + 115 C. 57 + 98 D. 25 + 75	A. 39 + 49 B. 50 + 80 C. 114 + 114 D. 19 + 11 + 20
1. Which problem has a sum that is equal to 100? 2. Which problem has a sum less than 100? 3. Which problem has a sum greater than 200? 4. Which problem has a sum that is between 100 and 200?	1. Which problem has a sum that is equal to 50? 2. Which problem has a sum less than 100? 3. Which problem has a sum greater than 200? 4. Which problem has a sum that is between 100 and 150?

Do Not Solve – Fourth Grade	
Beginning of the Year	**End of the Year**
A. $\frac{1}{3} + \frac{1}{3} + \frac{1}{3}$ B. $\frac{1}{4} + \frac{1}{4}$ C. $\frac{3}{4} + \frac{2}{4}$ D. $\frac{3}{4} + \frac{5}{4}$	A. $\frac{2}{2} + \frac{2}{2}$ B. $\frac{1}{4} + \frac{3}{4} + \frac{1}{4}$ C. $\frac{1}{8} + \frac{1}{8} + \frac{1}{8}$ D. $\frac{2}{3} + \frac{1}{3}$
1. Which problem has a sum that is equal to 1? 2. Which problem has a sum less than 1? 3. Which problem has a sum between 1 and 1 ½? 4. Which problem is greater than 1 ½?	1. Which problem has a sum that is equal to 1? 2. Which problem has a sum less than 1? 3. Which problem has a sum between 1 and 1 ½? 4. Which problem is equal to 2?

Do Not Solve – Fifth Grade	
Beginning of theYear	**End of the Year**
A. ½ + 4/8 B. 12 − ¼ C. ⁵⁄₄ − ²⁄₄ D. ⁶⁄₈ + ⁴⁄₈	A. 6 ÷ ¼ B. 5 ½ × ½ C. ½ × ½ D. 1 ÷ ⅓
1. Which problem has a sum that is equal to 1? 2. Which problem has a difference less than 1? 3. Which problem has a sum between 1 and 1 ½? 4. Which problem has a difference greater than 1 ½?	1. Which problem has a product that is less than ½? 2. Which problem has a quotient that is 3? 3. Which problem has a product between 2 and 3? 4. Which problem has a quotient greater than 20?
Anchor Chart	**Student Response Sheet**

Do Not Solve!

In this routine we are looking at numbers and then reasoning in our heads about the answers. This is partly a process of elimination, but you still have to know why.

Here is an example:

A. ³⁄₆ + ⁴⁄₈   B. 1 − ⅙
C. ¹⁵⁄₃ − ⁵⁄₃   D. ⁶⁄₈ + ⁴⁄₈

   1. Which problem has a sum that is equal to 1?

   2. Which problem has a difference less than 1?

   3. Which problem has a sum between 1 and 1 ½?

   4. Which problem has a difference greater than 2?

Do Not Solve!

Students use their white boards throughout the routines to prove their thinking. Sometimes they record their thinking in a Math Thinking Journal.

³⁄₆ + ⁴⁄₈ = 1 whole

³⁄₆ = ½
⁴⁄₈ = ½
So that makes a whole.

Summary

Number flexes are routines that work specifically on computational fluency. One of these activities should be done every day so that students build their mathematical thinking muscle. One important thing to consider about number flexes is that they should change throughout the year to incorporate new grade-level content. *Number of the Day* is a standard; remember to emphasize the use of various models such as number ladders, lines, tracks, number bonds, and part-part-whole charts.

Be sure to consider both types of *Number Talks* (the American and the British versions) because they offer different types of thinking. The American *Number Talks* really builds flexibility. The British *Number Talks* frames the discussion so that students have to actively think about their thinking. *Subitizing* is an excellent routine that should be extended throughout the grades in upper elementary. It is a visual scaffold to help students talk and reason about numbers. *Fraction of the Day* and *Decimal of the Day* routines allow students to build their conceptual and procedural power with fractions and decimals throughout the year rather than just in a drive-by unit of study. Finally, number flexes like *Virtual Dice Roll* and *Virtual Cards* give students interesting number generators to think conceptually, accurately, flexibly, and efficiently.

Questions for Reflection

1. What routines do you currently use specifically to build fluency?
2. What are three routines from this chapter that you might try immediately?
3. How well do you emphasize representation of the facts with different models?

References

Ball, S., & Fullerton, C. (2013). Daily math investigations: Meaningful math routines. Retrieved December 23, 2016, from https://mindfull.ecwid.com/#!/Free-Downloads/c/15606272/offset=0&sort=normal

Clements, D. (1999). Subitizing: What is it? Why teach it? *Teaching Children Mathematics*, 5(7) 400–405.

Humphreys, C., & Parker, R. (2015). *Making Number Talks matter*. Portland, ME: Stenhouse.

Resnick, L., Lesgold, S., & Bill, V. (1990). From protoquantities to number sense. Paper presented at the Psychology of Mathematics Education Conference (Mexico, July). Retrieved December 20, 2016, from http://files.eric.ed.gov/fulltext/ED335420.pdf

Shumway, J. (2011). *Building number sense through routines*. Portland, ME: Stenhouse.

7

Vocabulary Energizers
Ten Ways to Get Started

Classrooms where students receive sound word instruction are ones where lessons focus their attention on specific words and word-learning strategies, where opportunities to talk about words are many, and where occasions for applying what has been taught with engaging and content-rich texts and with motivating purposes occur with regularity and purpose.

—(Kamil & Hiebert, 2005, p. 10)

Math vocabulary is very important. We have to speak it. We have to make it attainable. We should play games where students get to learn it and use it. After the games, I have the students do reflections. The students should have the math word wall as a reference as well as their own self-authored math dictionary. Teachers should try to do math vocabulary energizers at least once a week as well as having a math workstation where students work with the words.

Oftentimes teachers will tell me that students know the words. We play a quick game of vocabulary tic-tac-toe, and teachers are often surprised at how much the students are challenged by the math vocabulary. Students can point it out but they cannot explain it. Knowing the word means that students can explain, give definitions, give examples, draw illustrations. Graphic organizers are good formats for these (Research Note, below).

RESEARCH NOTE

Graphic organizers help students to unpack the vocabulary word.
www.aea1.k12.ia.us/en/curriculum_instruction_and_assessment/math/english_language_learner_supports/math_vocabulary/

Math vocabulary is notoriously difficult. Researchers have written about the specialized nature of math vocabulary (Gay, 2008; Rubenstein, 2007; Rubenstein & Thompson, 2002). They note that it can be difficult for a variety of reasons, some of which are shown in Figures 7.1 and 7.2.

Figure 7.1 Challenges of Math Words

Math Words Can Be Challenging for Several Reasons							
Everyday words	*Math specific*	*More than one meaning*	*Homonyms*	*More than one way to say it*	*Pairs that people confuse*	*Everyday words used for math*	*Modifiers matter*
Right angle versus right answer	Addend Minuend Quotient	A circle is round, but we round numbers	Table and feet	One-quarter/ one-fourth	Area and perimeter	Diamond for rhombus Corner for vertex	Fraction versus improper fraction Denominator versus common denominator

Figure 7.2 Semantic Features

Messy Semantic Features			
Synonyms	*Homophones*	*Prepositions*	*Passive Structures*
add, plus, combine, sum	sum, some whole, hole pie, pi	divided into, divided by	Ten books were bought

Taking all of this into account, it is absolutely necessary that we do math vocabulary routines on a weekly basis. Students need multiple opportunities to practice the words through writing, games, and talking. "Math vocabulary is inextricably bound to students' conceptual understanding of mathematics" (Dunston & Tyminski, 2013, p. 40). If students don't understand the words, then they won't understand the concepts.

Researchers have outlined three ways to teach students specialized vocabulary (Novak, 1998; Novak & Gowin, 1984):

1. Students need to hear words explained and used in conversation and context three to five times.
2. Make meaning of words with pictures, models, and diagrams.
3. Use graphic organizers to understand the meaning of words.

Some resources are provided below.

Resources					
Math Spelling City	*Virginia Vocabulary Cards*	*Granite Illustrated Math Vocabulary Words (in four languages)*	*Austin Math Vocabulary Graphic Organizers*	*Vocabulary Strategies for the Mathematics Classroom*	*More Great Sites*
https://www. spellingcity. com/math-vocabulary. html	www.doe. virginia.gov/ instruction/ mathematics/ resources/ vocab_cards/ math_vocab_ cards_2.pdf	www.granite schools. org/math-vocabulary/ vocabulary-cards/	http:// mrwaddell. net/blog/ uploadpics/ Made4Math--Reading-in-Math-research_ 116CA/ Building. a.bridge. to.Academic. vocab.in. math.pdf	https:// www. eduplace. com/ state/pdf/ author/ chard_ hmm05.pdf	www. broward.k12. fl.us/student support/ ese/PDF/ MathWord Wall.pdf www.pps. k12.or.us/ curriculum/ math/ vocabulary/3-5MathVocab. pdf

Here are some routines to teach vocabulary:

1. *Alphabet Box*
2. *Frayer Model*
3. *Brainstorm It!*
4. *Word Box*

5. *Charades*
6. *Mystery Word*
7. *Vocabulary Tic-Tac-Toe*
8. *Vocabulary Bingo*
9. *Word of Mouth*
10. *Math Scrabo*
11. *1-Minute Essay*

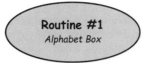

Routine #1
Alphabet Box

A	B	C	D	E
F	G	H	I	J
K	L	M	N	O
P	Q	R	S	T
U	V	W	X	Y
Z				

The teacher gives the students an alphabet box to work on during the unit (see Figure 7.5). Every few days they pull out the alphabet box and fill in new words beginning with the letters that are given.

Routine #2
Frayer Model

½	
Definition A part of a whole	**Picture**
Examples Two out of 4 ½ of the cake	**Non-Examples** The whole cake 2

The Frayer Model (Frayer, Frederick, & Klausemeier, 1969) is shown in Figure 7.6. For other graphic organizers, see Figure 7.4.

Routine #3
Brainstorm IT!

The teacher says a word, and the students have to write words that come to mind when they hear that word. Students record their thinking on their white boards or in thinking notebooks and then share with a neighbor. They have to explain how the word is connected to the starter word. Afterwards, the class comes back together and discusses what they wrote and what it means. For example, if the teachers writes "Fraction," students may write:

- Dividend
- Divisor
- Piece of
- Part of
- Numerator
- Denominator

This is a quick energizer where each small group has a word box. This is a box with four squares. The teacher says the category, and then each of the students have to fill in one of the squares in the word box (see Figure 7.3).

Routine #4
Word Box

Figure 7.3 *Word Box* (Mulgrave-King, 2010 personal communication)

Division	

Division	
Quotient	Dividend
Divisor	Share

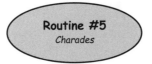

Routine #5
Charades

The class is divided into two teams. One person from each team comes up and picks a card. They have to act out the word on the card. Whichever team guesses the word first wins.

Routine #6
Mystery Word

Version 1: One of the students volunteers to be the person to try and guess the mystery word (they don't get to see the word). The teacher writes the mystery word on the board and shows it to the rest of the class. The class gives clues to the volunteer, who then tries to guess the word.

Version 2: The teacher gives a volunteer a mystery word and they have to get the class to guess what word they have. You can put scaffolded hints on the back of the card.

The students are divided into two teams. One team is the "X"s and the other the "O"s. They pick a number or do rock-paper-scissors to see which team is going to start first. The first team sends someone up. That person is not on the hotspot. They simply have to pick a word. Then the team is asked a series of questions about the word. They might be asked the definition, to come draw an illustration, and/or to give an example. If they can correctly answer the questions (it is a collaborative effort), then their teammate can mark the spot. If not, the other team gets a chance. Sometimes, teams get one free chance to look up the word in a book. (See versions in Figures 7.4-7.6).

Version 1: This version just involves words.

Figure 7.4 *Vocabulary Tic-Tac-Toe* (**Version 1**)

divisor	quotient	fraction
multiple	dividend	factor
product	difference	remainder

add	subtract	~~difference~~
turn around fact	addend	sum
doubles	ten friends	half facts

Possible teacher questions:

1. What does this word mean?
2. Can you use it in a sentence?
3. Who can illustrate this word?

Version 2: This version involves illustrations.

Figure 7.5 *Vocabulary Tic-Tac-Toe* (**Version 2**)

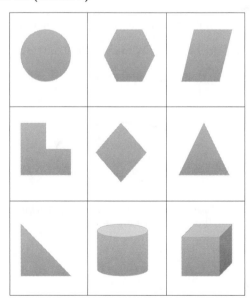

Possible teacher questions:

1. Can you name this shape?
2. Can you tell me three attributes?
3. How is it the same as a _____?
4. How is it different from a _____?

Version 3: This version is a mix of words, illustrations, and/or definitions.

Figure 7.6 *Vocabulary Tic-Tac-Toe* **(Version 3)**

3/4	(circle divided into fifths, shaded)	This is the name for the bottom number of the fraction.
(square divided into eighths, one part shaded)	This is the part that is shared out in a division problem.	30 ÷ **10**
>	<	4 × 5

Possible teacher questions:

1. What is this fraction? Come illustrate it. Name a fraction greater than this. Name a fraction smaller than this.
2. What is this symbol? What does it mean? Who wants to stand up and write a statement using numbers with this symbol?
3. Look at this expression. What is the bold number? What is it called? Tell me a word problem using these numbers.

Routine #8
Vocabulary Bingo

Version 1: The teacher gives the student vocabulary cards and plays bingo by calling out definitions, drawing illustrations, and giving the names (see Figure 7.7).

Figure 7.7 *Vocabulary Bingo*

B	I	N	G	O
fraction	denominator	numerator	multiply	divide
<	divisor		>	dividend
¾	¼	²⁄₄	½	⁴⁄₄
equivalent fraction	6 THIRDS	5 FOURTHS	2 HALVES	4 FOURTHS
equivalent	improper fraction	mixed number	unit fraction	simplify

Sample call-outs:

- B – the symbol that means less than
- I – the number that tells how many groups
- N – a whole number and a fraction
- G – a fraction that is equivalent to ⅜
- 0 – the number being divided

Version 2: The teacher writes a list of vocabulary words and the students populate their pre-made boards. Then bingo continues as usual.

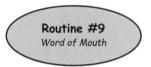

Routine #9
Word of Mouth

Students mingle around the room and then the teacher says a word. Everyone finds a partner and discusses the word for about 2 minutes. The teacher picks a new word and the students mingle with someone new (see Figure 7.7).

Figure 7.7 *Word of Mouth*

Routine #10
Math Scrabbo
(like Scrabble ... kinda)

The teacher draws a Scrabble-type board on a big sheet of chart paper and laminates it. Then once a week the students play as a class. They divide up into teams. The teacher can either give out letters to each team or just let the students figure out math words to make. I start by having the students just submit math words that they can make from the letters on the board. The teacher decides on the amount of points for each square. For example, blue could be double points, purple could be triple points, and red could be a bonus of 10 points (see Figure 7.8).

Figure 7.8 *Math Scrabbo*

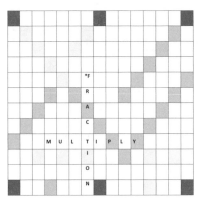

Notes: *Scores for different letters: A–J = 1 point; L–S = 2 points; T–Z = 3 points*

The teacher puts a starter word on the board. Team 1 puts up the word "multiply." So, they got M = 2, U = 3, L = 2, T = 3, I = 1, P = 2 (doubled because it's on a blue square), L = 2, Y = 3 (doubled because it's on a blue square). Total = 19 points.

Bonus Routine
1-Minute Essay

The 1-Minute Essay Routine	
This is a quick writing activity whereby students write about a topic for 1 minute. There is a sense of urgency and fun created by the time element.	
Materials and Tools	**"I can" statement**
Paper and pencil	I **can** write about math.
Protocol	**Purpose:**
Overview: Students write about a topic. 1. The teacher tells the students the topic and tells them to use words, numbers, drawings, and diagrams to write about the specific topic. 2. Students start writing for 1 minute. 3. After a minute, the teacher tells the students to switch papers with someone. 4. That person adds something to their partner's paper. 5. Then they switch back and that person adds some more to their paper.	• Write about mathematics • Explain, discuss, and justify mathematical understanding
	Questions: • What did you write? • What did your partner add? • What else might you write?

What's the Math?

The 1-Minute Essay should require students at different levels to explore:

Kindergarten
- Adding and subtracting

First Grade
- Adding and subtracting
- Properties of addition

Second Grade
- Even and odd
- Adding and subtracting
- Properties of addition
- Doubling

Third Grade
- Even and odd
- Doubling and halving
- Adding and subtracting
- Multiplying and dividing
- Properties of addition and multiplication

Fourth Grade
- Prime and composite
- Even or odd
- Doubling
- Adding and subtracting
- Multiplying and dividing
- Properties of addition and multiplication

Fifth Grade
- Prime and composite
- Even or odd
- Doubling
- Adding and subtracting
- Multiplying and dividing
- Properties of addition and multiplication

Classroom Vignette: *1-Minute Essay*

Mrs. Jones: Today we are going to do a *1-Minute Essay*. OK get ready. I want you to write for 1 minute. Tell me everything you know about fractions. You can use pictures, words, drawings, and diagrams. Go. [*One minute passes.*]

OK now switch with a partner. Your partner has to add something to your paper. You will have 30 seconds to add something to your partner's paper. [*30 seconds pass.*]

Now switch back. Add one more thing to your paper. [*Time passes.*]

OK, now let's talk about what we know.

Kate: I wrote that a fraction is a part of a whole.

Tim: I wrote that ½ is an example. Then my partner wrote that ¾ is bigger than ½.

Luke: I wrote that ²⁄₄ is equivalent to ½.

Maribel: I drew a picture of a circle and then cut it into fourths and then shaded ¾.

Discussion continues with Mrs. Jones taking notes on chart paper.

Fractions

I know that fractions are a part of a whole.
½ is a fraction.
³⁄₆ is an equivalent fraction.

¾ is bigger than ½.
⁵⁄₄ is also bigger than ½.

Notes from our 1-minute essay:

A fraction is part of a whole
¾ is an example
¾ is bigger than ½

Continued

1-Minute Essays – Second Grade
Although you could start 1-minute essays earlier, I really don't do them until second grade.

Beginning of the Year

Write about numbers, addition, and subtraction.

> **Addition**
>
> Addition is when you add. It means to put stuff together. Like 2 + 2 is addition.
>
>

End of the Year

Write about measuring, geometry, and fractions.

> **Polygons**
>
> Polygons are shapes. They have straight sides.
>
> This is a polygon.
>
>
>
> This is not a polygon.
>
>

1-Minute Essays – Third Grade

Beginning of the Year

Write about addition, subtraction, multiplication, and division.

> **Multiplication**
>
> Multiplication is a way to count fast. Here is an example:
> 3 × 2
> We have 3 groups of 2.
>
>

End of the Year

Write about measuring, geometry and fractions.

> **Parallelograms**
>
> Parallelograms are 4-sided figures. They are polygons. They have 2 pairs of parallel sides.

Beginning of the Year

Write about addition, subtraction, multiplication, and division.

The teacher could write feedback on a Post-it – for example, asking what are the math words for tops and bottoms.

Adding Fractions

When you add fractions, you just add the tops, not the bottoms if the bottoms are the same. Like ¾ + ¾ = ⁶⁄₄

End of the Year

Write about measuring, geometry, and fractions.

Lines

There are many different types of line. There are straight lines and curved lines. There are parallel and perpendicular lines.

1-Minute Essays – Fifth Grade

Beginning of the Year

Write about addition, subtraction, multiplication, and division.

Teacher might put up a Post-it note asking what is the confusing part.

Measurement

I know that here in the US we use imperial measurement. We use ounces, pounds, gallons, pints, inches, and feet. In other places in the world, they use the metric system. They use centimeters, meters, kilometers, milliliters, and liters. It can all get confusing.

End of the Year

Write about measuring, geometry, fractions, and decimals.

Decimals

Decimals are a part of a whole. We use decimals every day when we use money. 50 cents is half of a dollar. The decimal is .50. You can put decimals on a number line.

.50

Summary

It is essential that we teach math vocabulary in a planned way. We should not and cannot leave it to chance that the students learn math vocabulary, because math vocabulary *is* math. We speak math. The vocabulary carries the meaning. So we have to find ways to make it meaningful, engaging, and rigorous. It should be done in routines and in workstations and reinforced in whole-group and small-group lessons.

Questions for Reflection

1. What do you currently do to teach math vocabulary?
2. Do your students have their own illustrated math dictionaries that they made themselves?
3. What does your word wall look like? Is it illustrated? Do the students actively use it?

References

Dunston, P., & Tyminski, A. (2013). What's the big deal about vocabulary? *Mathematics Teaching in the Middle School*, 19(1), 38–45.

Frayer, D., Frederick, W.C., & Klausmeier, H.J. (1969). *A schema for testing the level of concept mastery.* Working Paper No. 16. Madison, WI: University of Wisconsin.

Gay, S. (2008). Helping teachers connect vocabulary to conceptual understanding. *The Mathematics Teacher*, 102(3), 218–223.

Kamil, M., & Hiebert, E.H. (2005). The teaching and learning of vocabulary. In E.H. Hiebert & M.H. Kamil (Eds.), *Teaching and learning vocabulary*. Mahway, NJ: Erlbaum, pp. 1–23.

Novak, J.D. (1998). *Learning, creating and using knowledge: Concept maps as facilitative tools in schools and corporations.* Mahway, NJ: Erlbaum.

Novak, J.D., & Gowin, B. (1984). *Learning how to learn.* Cambridge, UK: Cambridge University Press.

Rubenstein, R. (2007). Focused strategies for middle-grades mathematics vocabulary development. *Mathematics Teaching in the Middle School*, 13(4), 200–207.

Rubenstein, R.N., & Thompson, D.R. (2002). Understanding and supporting children's mathematical vocabulary development. *Teaching Children Mathematics*, 9(2), 107–112.

8

Problem Solving as a Daily Math Thinking Routine
Seven Ways to Get Started

For elementary students, the process of writing a word problem is a useful task that serves to develop a deeper understanding of mathematics. Additional benefits of problem writing for students include growth in problem solving and improvement in mathematical attitudes.
—(Whiten, cited in Barlow & Cates, 2007, p. 252)

Problem solving should be done every day. We need to teach students the process/practice of problem solving. There are many things involved in problem solving. It is more than word problems but we will focus on word problems in this chapter. Phil Daro (n.d.) argues we have to go BEYOND ANSWER-GETTING! Answer-getting is not problem solving. They are two completely different things. Answer-getting is where we give students a problem and tell them they have 5 minutes to come up with the answer. Then we go around and share out the answer and quickly go over how each person got it.

Problem solving is different (see Figure 8.1). It involves getting students to visualize and summarize the problem. Students are required to make a plan and then implement their plan. They should solve one way and check another. Then they should double-double-check! They need to make sure the math is correct AND that the answer makes sense. Finally, they should be able to explain their thinking.

All of this requires time. Think of it more as a *Problem of the Week* or at least a *Problem of 2 or 3 days*. There needs to be time to work on each of these steps as students are learning the practice. Day 1 might be simply reading the problem, explaining it, and making a plan. Day 2 might be implementing the plan by solving one way and checking another.

Problem solving should involve reasoning, students communicating their thinking using concrete, pictorial, and digital tools, using precise mathematical language, and unpacking patterns and structures. See chart "Resources for Problem Solving".

Resources for Problem Solving			
Video Problems (Here is a neat way to show word problems in the primary grades)	**Greg Tang's Word Problem Generator** (Scaffolds using the strip diagram through a variety of problems for K–5)	**Thinking Blocks** (Also scaffolds strip diagrams for 2–5)	**Dr. Nicki's Pinterest Word Problem Board**
https://www.pinterest.com/pin/142004194480603086/ https://www.pinterest.com/pin/142004194480603075/	http://gregtangmath.com/wordproblems	www.mathplayground.com/thinkingblocks.html	https://www.pinterest.com/drnicki7/word-problems/

Here are some routines to teach problem solving:

1. *Picture That!*
2. *What's the Problem?*
3. *What's the Question?*
4. *Sort That!*
5. *Two Arguments*
6. *What's the Story?*
7. *Template It!*

Routine #1
Picture That! or Tell Me a Story

The *Picture That!* or *Tell Me a Story* Routine	
This is just a great routine because students get to see, recognize, and discuss math in real life. The pictures are engaging. They are easy to get if you have an interactive board, and even if you don't, just use pictures from magazines. You can show it to the whole class, set up workstations, and even give individuals pictures to talk about.	
Materials and Tools	**"I can" statement**
Use engaging, thought-provoking mathematical pictures.	**I can** see, recognize, and discuss math in real life.
Protocol	**Purpose:**
Overview: The teacher puts a picture on the board and the students have to discuss the math.	• Recognize math all around us • Discuss math all around us • Contextualize the math around us

1. The teacher tells the students to take "private think time" to think about the concept. 2. After about 30 seconds, the teacher tells the students to "turn and talk to a neighbor." 3. Everyone comes back together, and students raise their hands and explain their thinking.	**Questions:** • What do you see happening? • Why do you think that? • Can you tell a story about this?

What's the Math?

Picture That! should require students at different levels to explore:

Kindergarten

• Adding and subtracting

First Grade

• Adding and subtracting
• Properties of addition

Second Grade

• Even and odd
• Adding and subtracting
• Properties of addition
• Doubling and halving

Third Grade

• Even and odd
• Doubling and halving
• Adding and subtracting
• Multiplying and dividing
• Properties of addition and multiplication

Fourth Grade

• Multiplying and dividing
• Multiples and factors
• Prime and composite

Fifth Grade

• Prime and composite
• Multiples and factors
• Multiplying and dividing

Digital Variations for *Picture That!*

There are so many digital possibilities for this routine. Below, I have listed some places to start. I usually find my pictures on Google images. Fawie Geng has put together a great resource list. Public Domain Pictures has a large variety of images. Remember that with any search, you must vet the pictures ahead of time.

Public Domain Pictures	Dr. Nicki's Math Picture Prompts Pinterest Board	Fawie Geng's Blog	Math Photo on Twitter
	https://www.pinterest.com/drnicki7/word-problems/		#mathphoto

Continued

Classroom Vignette: *Picture That!*

Mr. Ralph: Good morning! Today is Picture That! Yaaay! I know you guys love this routine, and you always have such rich thinking around it. Who wants to start?

Markie: It says that 3 apples is about a pound.

Nancy: It says that 1 pound is $1.99.

Kate: So we could say 3 apples are about $2.00. Because what if one apple is really big?

Ted: But it could be less if one apple is really small.

Tammy: I have a multiplication story: Mike bought 3 pounds. The apples cost $2 per pound. How much money did he pay?

Sharon: You can also ask, "How many apples did he get?"

Lucy: He paid $6.

Gina: He got $3 \times 3 = 9$ … he got 9 apples.

Frank: I have a division story: I bought half a pound of apples. I paid $1.

Harry: So how many did you get?

Frank: I got 2 or 3, depending on the size. I only wanted to spend about $1. So I could say that I'm not going to spend more than $1, or I could say I want to spend less than $2.

The students continue discussing what they notice and then they end the routine.

Picture That! – Kindergarten

Beginning of the Year

Possible Questions:

Talk about the number of _____.

How many more _____ are there than _____?

How many fewer _____ are there than _____?

Tell an addition story about the candies.

Tell a subtraction story about the candies.

End of the Year

Possible Questions:

Talk about the number of _____.

How many more _____ are there than _____?

How many fewer _____ are there than _____?

Tell an addition story about the candies.

Tell a subtraction story about the candies.

Beginning of the Year

Possible Questions:

Talk about the number of _____.

How many more _____ are there than _____?

How many fewer _____ are there than _____?

Tell an addition story about the candies.

Tell a subtraction story about the candies.

End of the Year

Possible Questions:

Tell a story about the _____.

Tell an addition story about the _____.

Tell a subtraction story about the _____.

Talk about more and less than with the

_____.

Picture That! – Second Grade

Beginning of the Year

Possible Questions:

Tell a story about the _____.

Tell an addition story about the _____.

Tell a subtraction story about the _____.

Talk about more and less than with the

_____.

What if you were a caterer and you had to plan for a birthday party. How many tables do you need to set? How many cupcakes do you need at each table?

Why is she measuring the arm?

Why do we need to measure clothes?

Tell me a story about this seamstress.

Continued

Continued

End of the Year

Possible Questions:

Tell a story about the _____.
Tell an addition story about the _____.
Tell a subtraction story about the _____.

Picture That! – Third Grade

Beginning of the Year

Possible Questions:

Tell a story about the _____.
Tell an addition story about the _____.
Tell a subtraction story about the _____.
Tell a multiplication story about the _____.
Tell a division story about the candies.

Think about candy stores, bakeries, and flower shops.

End of the Year

Possible Questions:

Talk about the fractions you see.

Do each of the pictures represent fractions? Why, or why not?

Tell me a story about a candy bar fraction.

Picture That! – Fourth Grade

Beginning of the Year

Possible Questions:

Tell me a story about these chocolates?
What could they be making with these chocolates?
How many do they need?
What if they doubled the recipe? What if they tripled it? What if they halved it?

What if you were a florist and you had to make 5 bouquets exactly like this one. How many pink flowers would you need? How many red ones? How many green ones? How many white ones? How do you know?

End of the Year

Possible Questions:

Why would a suitmaker need to measure a suit? Tell me a story about this.

Name a fraction of the candies.

Tell an addition story about a fraction of the _____.

Tell a subtraction story about a fraction of the _____.

Tell a multiplication story about the _____.
Tell a division story about the _____.
Tell a multistep story about the _____.

Picture That! – **Fifth Grade**
Beginning of the Year

Possible Questions:

Tell a story about the _____.
Tell an addition story about a fraction of the _____.

Tell a subtraction story about a fraction of the _____.

Tell a multiplication story about the _____.
Tell a division story about the _____.
Tell a multistep story about the _____.

End of the Year

Possible Questions:

What do these pictures make us think about volume?
What kind of stories can we tell about volume from looking at these pictures?

Continued

Continued

Anchor Chart

Picture That! is a great routine where we look at pictures and tell math stories about them.

For example: We look at this picture of lions.

The teacher says: "There were some lions and then 2 more came. Now there are 7. How many were there in the beginning?"

Somebody tells a subtraction story. There were 7 lions and then 3 left. And then 2 more left. How many are still there? 2 lions are still there.

Student Response Sheet

Although this routine doesn't have an activity sheet for the students to respond on, they will interact on their white boards in class. The students can model their thinking on the interactive board, their individual white boards, or their "thinking notebooks."

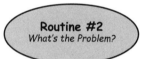

Routine #2
What's the Problem?

In this routine, students are given the answer and they have to think up a word problem that matches that answer. Sometimes the students are given just the answer. Other times students are given the expression or the equation. There is a wonderful article by Barlow and Cates (2007) about how to do this with students, building on the work of Jenner's (2002) "The Answer Is ..." task. They add units to the problems so that students write stories instead of just "number facts" (Barlow & Cates, 2007, p. 253). They give some specific suggestions:

1. **Give clear directions.** They note that students don't necessarily understand what to do at first. I would add that this activity should be done first with the whole class. Lots of modeling and checking for understanding should take place. Then it should be moved to groups where each person has a role (problem writer, illustrator, equation maker, double-checker). Students should also get to work in pairs to do this. Sometimes the students work on it over a period of days and then have a "Gallery Walk" Day where all of the problems are displayed around the room and everyone walks around and puts comments on Post-it notes on the posters (in an organized fashion – for example, have Rotation 1, Rotation 2, etc., and in each rotation, groups stop for 5 minutes and students comment on the poster in front of them). In the last rotation, students end up at their own poster reading the comments and reflecting on their work. Other times, students can take turns coming up and sharing their work in front of the class.
2. **Provide specific units.** They note that adding specific units (such as marbles, dogs, and birds) gets students to contextualize the numbers and also promotes creativity.
3. **Anticipate difficulties.** I think many of these difficulties can be addressed by first doing this activity as a whole-class routine. They do note that you can get students to reflect on their work by asking, "If we took this problem to another class, would a student in that class be able to solve it?" or "What difficulties might someone have if you gave them this problem?" (p. 254).

Prepare to be amazed! I was working in a classroom just the other day, and I was introducing addition and subtraction problems with like denominators to fourth graders. We used fraction bars to scaffold thinking. With just a little bit of modeling, the students were telling amazing two-step stories with fractions that they understood. They were getting quite fancy with the problems, and when reflecting on them, they were impressed with their own selves. One little girl, whose group told a story about a grandmother making a cake and various family members taking pieces, added a twist at the end where one person had taken 3 pieces, then felt rather guilty and put 2 back. As she chuckled and was quite tickled with herself, she said proudly, "I added that twist at the end." It just reminded me that kids will play with numbers when numbers seem friendly. We discussed how the graphic organizer of the fraction bars made the telling of the stories easy.

There are some examples of what that might look like the chart "What's the Problem? (K–5)".

What's the Problem (K—5)					
Kindergarten	**First Grade**	**Second Grade**	**Third Grade**	**Fourth Grade**	**Fifth Grade**
The answer is 5 marbles. What was the question?	The answer is 12 bumblebees. It was an addition problem. What was the question?	The answer is 59 marbles. It was a subtraction problem. What was the question?	Look at this expression: 3×4. Tell me a story about it.	Look at this expression: $\frac{3}{4} - \frac{1}{4}$. Tell me a story about it.	Look at this equation: . $0.50 - 0.27 = 0.23$. Tell me a story about it.

Be sure to read the article by Barlow and Cates (see references at the end of this chapter).

Routine #3
What's the Question?

Another routine involves giving students part of the word problem and then having them decide what the question is (see the chart "What's the Question? (K–5)"). There is research on how this taps into whether or not students are following the structure of the problem; if they are, then they would know what the obvious questions could be.

What's the Question? (K—5)					
Kindergarten	**First Grade**	**Second Grade**	**Third Grade**	**Fourth Grade**	**Fifth Grade**
There were 2 dogs and 2 cats. What's the question?	There were 5 dogs. Some more came. Now there are 10. What's the question?	There were 7 dogs and 5 cats. What's the question?	There were 4 rows of apple trees. There were 5 apple trees in each row. What's the question?	Grandma made a cake. She cut it into fourths. Grandpa ate $\frac{1}{4}$ of it. Sue ate $\frac{1}{4}$ of it. What's the question?	Mike had $1.00. He spent 45 cents on candy, 35 cents on chips, and the rest on something to drink. What's the question?

Continued

Continued

How many animals were there altogether?	How many more came?	How many more dogs than cats were there? How many less cats were there than dogs? How many animals were there altogether?	How many apple trees were there altogether?	How much of the cake is left? How much of the cake did they eat altogether?	How much did he spend on something to drink?

Routine #4
Sort That!

In this routine, the teacher should show or read different types of word problems, and the students have to write the symbol on their white board that shows what type of problem it is.

Sort That! (K—5)			
Kindergarten–1 Addition or subtraction?	**1–5** Are we looking for the bigger part or the smaller part?	**2–5** One-step or two-step?	**3–5** Multiplication or division?
Sue had 5 marbles. She got 2 more. How many does she have now? Teacher asks: *Is this an addition problem or a subtraction problem?*	Maria had 15 rings. Lucy had 2 less than she did. How many more rings did Lucy have? Mike ate ⅗ of his candy bar. Larry ate ⅕ more of his candy bar. How much did Larry eat? Teacher asks: *Are we looking for the bigger part or the smaller part of these problems?*	Luke had 4 toy cars. His brother gave him 5 more. He gave his cousin 1 of them. How many does he have now? Teacher asks: Is this a one-step or a two-step problem?	The bakery had 7 rows of 10 cookies. How many cookies did they have altogether? Teacher asks: *Is this a multiplication or a division problem?*

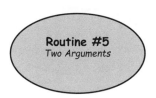

Routine #5
Two Arguments

In this routine, the teacher writes two arguments up on the board and the students read them, discuss them, and then decide which one they agree with.

Two Arguments (Primary; Upper Elementary)	
Primary Example	**Upper Elementary Example**
Kate and Tom read this problem:	Mari and Teddy read this problem:
Luke had some marbles. He got 3 more. Now he has 5 marbles. How many did he have at the beginning?	Doug had 9 marbles. He has 3 times as many as his brother. How many did his brother have?
Tom said the answer is 8. Kate said the answer is 2. Who is correct and why?	Mari said the answer is 27. Teddy said the answer is 3. Who is correct and why?

Routine #6
What's the Story?
(reverse of Model That!)

In this routine, the students are given a model and they have to tell the story that goes with that model. Here's an example:

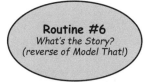

$$5 - 2 = 3$$

Teacher: Everyone look at this model. Look at the equation. I want you to think about a story that would match this equation. For example: Todd had 5 marbles and 2 rolled away. How many does he have left? He has 3 left.

Kylie: I had 5 marbles. I gave my sister 2.

Teacher: Very good. What's the question?

Students struggle with the question a bit.

Teacher: How many marbles does she have left?

Kylie: 3.

There are a variety of templates that students can use. The main idea is that they actually go through the process of visualizing the problem, summarizing the problem, making a plan, solving one way and checking another, and then explaining their thinking. Templates are only a scaffold. At some point they should be faded out and students should internalize the template and the process so that they can just sketch out the template to solve problems.

Template It! – **Primary**	
Decide is it … addition or subtraction + –	Solve it in the ten frame.
Write an equation _____ _____ = _____	Answer:

Template It! – **Upper Elementary**	
Decide if you will use multiplication or division.	Draw a sketch.
Write an equation. _____ _____ = _____	Explain your thinking.

Summary

Problem solving should happen every day. It should be taught as a practice – a way of seeing and doing math. The focus should be on the process of problem solving rather than just getting the answer. This should be done by taking deep dives into problems that are worked on throughout the week rather than solved in 5 minutes or less. There are a variety of routines that can support teaching the process of problem solving. Using picture prompts and routines like *What's the Problem?*, *What's the Question?*, and *What's the Story?* allow for critical thinking with open prompts. Activities such as *Sort That!* and *Two Arguments* allow students to reason about the problems. Templates help students to organize their thinking and work through word problems in an orderly way. Daily Thinking Math Routines help students to get on friendly terms with word problems and to become familiar with the types so that they are not afraid of them, confident that they can solve them, and competent enough to do so.

Questions for Reflection

1. In what ways do you currently do problem solving in your classroom? Is it a daily routine as well as incorporated into math workstation work?
2. What new ideas have you picked up from this chapter?
3. What is one routine that you will try right away, and why did you choose that one?

References

Barlow, A., & Cates, J. (2007). The answer is 20 cookies, what is the question. *Teaching Children Mathematics*, 13(5), 252–255.

Daro, P. (n.d.). Against answer-getting. Retrieved on December 11, 2016, from http://serpmedia.org/daro-talks/

Jenner, D.M. (2002). Stories of "72." In S.E.B. Pirie (Ed.), Problem posing: What can it tell us about students' mathematical understanding? *Proceedings of the Annual Meeting of the North American Chapter of the International Group for the Psychology of Mathematics Education (Athens, Georgia, October 26–29)*. East Lansing, MI: Michigan State University, pp. 947–953.

Part III

Action Planning

9

Action Planning

Routines … play an important role in shaping and directing the intellectual space of the classroom.
—(Ritchhart et al., 2006, p. 1)

Routines are intentional teaching. They address both the immediate and long-term needs of the students. This is a time to think about where they are and where they need to be. Often teachers will say, "Well we are teaching y but my students still don't know x." Routines allow you to review, practice, and extend.

Now that we have discussed all of the strategies, where are you going to start? What do your students need? And based on that, which routines might you incorporate into your practice? How will you reflect on how the routines are going and analyze the success of the routines?

Several protocols have been written about planning a curriculum. I have based the following tools for planning routines on some of these protocols (e.g. Wiggins & McTighe, 2005; Jacobs, 1997).

A Reflection Checklist for Teaching Daily Math Thinking Routines
What opportunities did students have to think and reason in the routine?
What was the purpose of the routine? What conceptual or procedural understanding did you want the students to practice? How did the routines fit into the larger learning goals for the unit and the grade-level expectations? How did the routines build upon one another in order to achieve the instructional outcomes?
What data did you base this routine on?
How well did the students do?

What is one thing that happened during the routine that sticks out for you?
What would you change?

Adapted from Silver, Brunsting, & Walsh (2008)

Daily Math Thinking Routine Planning Guide

What is the purpose of the routine? What is the math? What do students need to know, and what do they need to be able to do?	What questions will you ask to promote mathematical thinking?	What manipulatives and templates will you have available? Will they be concrete or digital?	How will you know that the students are successful? What should they be able to do?	Who is struggling? What are they struggling with exactly? What are the common mis-conceptions and error patterns for this routine?	What will you do next?

Planning for Cognitively Demanding Thinking Mathematical Routines		
Before *Selecting and planning for the daily math routines in a unit of study*	**During** *Supporting students' exploration of the routine*	**After** *Sharing and discussing the routine*
What does the data tell you that the students need to work on? Where are their strengths? Where are their weaknesses?	What will you be listening for during the routine?	When and how will you do a debrief on the routines?
Based on the data, what are your mathematical goals for the routine? What is the focus of the routine that you have selected? Why?	What will you be looking for during the routine?	What are your goals for the discussion about the routine?
What do you want students to know and to be able to do as a result of practicing this routine?	How will you scaffold the routine so that all students have access to the learning?	What questions will you ask to get the students to reflect on their thinking?
In what ways does the routine build on students' prior knowledge? What do they already know about this? What big ideas and enduring understandings do you want students to have in order to participate in this routine?	What questions will you ask to assess students' understanding of the big ideas and enduring understandings? What questions will you ask to assess their conceptual understanding and their use of various procedures? What questions will you ask to encourage students to share their thinking with others?	What specific questions will you ask so that students will get the big ideas and enduring understandings? What specific questions will you ask so that students "walk away with the math in their head"?
What are all the ways to think about the routine? What are the possible error patterns that students might make? What misconceptions might they have?	How will you know that students are thinking about the thinking of others? What questions will you ask that help you to assess students' understanding of their peers' ideas?	What will you see and hear during the routine that lets you know that the students got the big ideas and the enduring understandings?
What tools (and templates) do students need to help them think through the routine?	How will you make sure everyone has access to the task? How will you plan for everyone being fully engaged?	What will you be looking for in the students' recording sheets that lets you know that they "got it."

How wil
through
indepen
small gr

What ev
about stu
Will you
or will th
"thinkin
other rec

Finally, th
room. It is
already ar
make you

Referen

Jacobs, H.
   VA: Ass
Ritchhart,
   of think
   Francis
Silver, H.,
   and incr
Wiggins, C
   sion and